THRIVING AT WORK

What School Doesn't Teach You

International Edition

DENNIS MARK

MICHAEL DAM

Marshall Cavendish
Business

© 2022 Dennis Mark and Michael Dam

Published in 2022 by Marshall Cavendish Business
An imprint of Marshall Cavendish International

All rights reserved

No part of this publication may be reproduced, stored in a retrieval system or transmitted, in any form or by any means, electronic, mechanical, photocopying, recording or otherwise, without the prior permission of the copyright owner. Requests for permission should be addressed to the Publisher, Marshall Cavendish International (Asia) Private Limited, 1 New Industrial Road, Singapore 536196.
Tel: (65) 6213 9300 E-mail: genref@sg.marshallcavendish.com
Website: www.marshallcavendish.com

The publisher makes no representation or warranties with respect to the contents of this book, and specifically disclaims any implied warranties or merchantability or fitness for any particular purpose, and shall in no event be liable for any loss of profit or any other commercial damage, including but not limited to special, incidental, consequential, or other damages.

Other Marshall Cavendish Offices:
Marshall Cavendish Corporation, 800 Westchester Ave, Suite N-641, Rye Brook, NY 10573, USA • Marshall Cavendish International (Thailand) Co Ltd, 253 Asoke, 16th Floor, Sukhumvit 21 Road, Klongtoey Nua, Wattana, Bangkok 10110, Thailand • Marshall Cavendish (Malaysia) Sdn Bhd, Times Subang, Lot 46, Subang Hi-Tech Industrial Park, Batu Tiga, 40000 Shah Alam, Selangor Darul Ehsan, Malaysia

Marshall Cavendish is a registered trademark of Times Publishing Limited

National Library Board, Singapore Cataloguing-in-Publication Data

Name(s): Mark, Dennis. | Dam, Michael, author.
Title: Thriving at work : what school doesn't teach you / Dennis Mark, Michael Dam.
Description: International edition. | Singapore : Marshall Cavendish Business, 2022.
Identifier(s): ISBN 978-981-4974-73-8 (paperback)
Subject(s): LCSH: Vocational guidance. | Career development. | Success in business.
Classification: DDC 650.1--dc23

Printed in Singapore

"Tapping their real-life experiences, Michael and Dennis have put together a great resource especially for young adults joining the workforce. Straightforward and easy to follow, the book maps out every important aspect of work life, giving the reader invaluable advice to navigate the office minefields and arrive at their career goals."
— **Kai Hoe Tan, Chairman, Singapore Red Cross**

"This book succinctly illustrates and depicts the realities of the working world – not only for a new joiner but for an experienced working adult. The practical examples encapsulate the work challenges encountered by all – no matter where you are in your working career. An absolute must-read for all in the working world!"
— **Esther Lim, APAC HR Leader, US Multinational**

"If you want to get a great head-start in your career, this book is for you. The authors show you powerful solutions for handling work challenges and effective ways to fast-track your career. An insightful, practical and interesting read with lots of real work examples. I highly recommend it."
— **Mari Young, Category Management Senior Director, Fortune 100 Company**

"With *Thriving at Work*, you don't have to learn the hard way to succeed at work and fast-track your career. This book shows you how."
— **Raj Das, Senior Director, Seagate Technology**

"This book should have a prominent place on the book shelf of every person entering the workforce. One-of-a-kind book with lots of real work examples, and insightful and valuable suggestions to manage your career successfully."
— **Loretta Li-Sevilla, Senior Director, Fortune 100 Company**

"Wish I'd had something like this when starting out. Concise, well organized and practical insight into work environments. Like having access to a personal career coach."
— **Chris Bennett, former Vice President, NetApp Company**

"This book is an absolute gem! It is a personal bootcamp for invaluable soft skills. Full of actionable insights and real-life scenarios, every future-ready professional should have one!"
— **Kian Chong Lee, Board Director, BNF/Boston Business School**

"Honest, direct and tangible! Invaluable insights and tips to thrive on the most common challenges professionals face at work. This is a must-have career 101 handbook."
— **Shalyn Lee, former Vice President, HP**

"In the many years Michael and I worked together, I was very impressed with his ability to communicate, build consensus and lead in any situation. The insights I learned from Michael have been valuable to my career growth. It's great that Michael is sharing his lifelong career wisdom, learnings and insights through this book. If you can put half of what's in this book to practice, you will do very well in your career."
— **Paul Chou, former Vice President, Foxconn**

Contents

Acknowledgements   9

Introduction   11

Part 1: Starting Out

1. How to Build, Maintain and Grow Your Network   19
2. How to Search for Job Opportunities   26
3. How Companies Hire   33
4. How to Explore Job Options   39
5. How to Write a Compelling Resume   47
6. How to Handle Interviews with Confidence   58
7. How to Start Your Job on the Right Foot   77

Part 2: Communicating

8. How to Communicate Effectively – Verbal and Written   87
9. How to Organize and Develop Presentation Content   98
10. How to Present Persuasively   105
11. How to Communicate and Present to Specific Audiences   113
12. How to Run and Facilitate Meetings   129

Part 3: Collaborating

13. How to Collaborate Successfully — 139
14. How to Earn Trust — 147
15. How to Get People to Listen — 155
16. How to Give and Receive Feedback — 160
17. How to Handle Conflicts and Difficult Situations — 167
18. How to Deal with Difficult Co-workers — 179

Part 4: Negotiating

19. How to Become a Good Negotiator — 191
20. How to Negotiate a Job Offer — 201
21. How to Ask for a Raise — 211
22. How to Say No Smartly — 221
23. How to Stand Out and Promote Yourself — 228

Part 5: Managing Your Manager

24. How to Manage Up — 241
25. How to Work with Different Types of Managers — 248
26. How to Prepare for a Performance Review — 266
27. How to Work with Human Resources (HR) — 279

Part 6: Optimizing Your Success

28. How to Manage Time and Prioritize Effectively	287
29. How to Deal with Changes at Work	297
30. How to Understand and Use Business Idioms	307
31. How to Handle Workplace Politics Smartly	323
32. How to Engage in Small Talk Naturally	338
References	347
About the Authors	349

Acknowledgements

This book is the brainchild of countless hours of discussion with our extended family members, friends, colleagues and students. As Asians working for US multinational companies, we both enjoyed the great learning and growth journey over the decades. We both were fortunate to receive inputs, coaching and exposures in the fast-paced technology business environment that covered most markets across the world. We are grateful for the journey and felt even more privileged to come together to share our experience and learning with our readers, just like those who taught us along the way.

With gratitude:

To Linda for the thorough and excellent initial editing work and the wonderful ideas to keep the content up to date, especially in this fast-changing world.

To Thomas for the great insight and suggestions from the millennial's perspective.

To Orion and Christopher for the tremendous final editing work and for your dedication and labour of love.

To Alice, Esther, Eugene, Thomas for many of the Asian markets' knowledge, youthful insights and encouragement.

To the many colleagues, friends and students for reviewing the book's content and giving us valuable feedback and encouragement.

To the executives for taking the time from your busy schedule to review the book and sharing your valuable insight and wisdom.

To Joey for your creative ideas, loyalty and generosity. You are my inspiration.

To the learning institutions that appreciate the lifelong learning journeys and their supportive effort in expanding the reach of this book content into lessons and learning curriculums.

To our family for your support, unconditional love, sacrifices and heartfelt encouragement. Thank you all from the bottom of our hearts. Thank you for this learning journey. We will get even better learning each and every day! Never stop learning!

Introduction

"Technical" skills + **"Soft" skills** = Work and Career Success

We wrote this book for young people who are beginning to dip their toes in the professional world as well as current professionals. This book provides a proven roadmap for you to achieve immediate success and to fast-track your career. The soft skills discussed in this book will enable you to get a head-start and navigate the many changes and challenges in the workplace and throughout your career. These are the skills not usually taught in school and can otherwise take years to learn.

What This Career Handbook Is About

This book is a comprehensive collection of the best practices and skills to help professionals succeed throughout their career. These career skills were learned and developed over a combined 50 years of professional experience, as well as captured from observing and interviewing successful professionals, from individual contributors to high-level executives.

This book covers different situations in the workplace that employees will likely face and suggests ways to handle them effectively. In addition, it includes important skills required to succeed not only at your job, but also throughout your career.

Why This Book Was Written

Colleges and other tertiary educational institutions, for the most part, focus on teaching students academic and technical skills of their field, and fall short on teaching students the "soft" skills to complement their academic and technical training, such as the ability to work effectively with people to solve difficult business issues.

While mastering academic and technical discipline is fundamental to a student's profession, it's not nearly enough to guarantee them success in their career. According to a survey released by PayScale (PayScale, 2016), the majority of new college graduates in US are not ready for the workplace. Sixty percent of all companies said new graduates lack critical thinking skills, writing proficiency, attention to detail and communication ability. Based on our experience, we believe this is true across the world.

During our years in management, many employees and co-workers frequently asked us for advice on how to handle work issues. We also received lots of questions from employees who came from other countries and who were especially at a disadvantage at work due to cultural differences, not to mention the language barrier.

We believe that much of the success a person achieves in their profession comes from the ability to communicate and work effectively with people to solve different challenges. We call these "soft" skills (whereas accounting skills are "hard" skills). We have seen many people who only have above-average technical competence get promoted repeatedly thanks to their "soft" skills. We learned this the hard way and it took many years to develop the "soft" skills needed to thrive in the professional world. If we had learned and developed more "soft" skills sooner, we truly believe our career growth paths would have been more accelerated.

Who This Book Is Written For

This book is for both college students nearing graduation and for recent professionals who want to join multinational companies (MNCs) or who are working for local/national companies in their country who have business

Introduction 13

with customers and other companies in different countries. Specifically,

- College graduates getting ready to enter the workforce for their first professional job. This book helps these graduates get a head-start in their new career with practical guidance on searching for job opportunities, writing resumes, preparing for interviews, and starting their job on the right foot.

- New employees who recently joined the workforce. This book helps these employees get off on the right foot from day one and deal effectively with potential work challenges and career transitions.

- Professionals who want to be more effective at handling work challenges. This book provides the best tools and practices to help them work effectively with co-workers, manage up successfully and improve their standing in the company.

How This Book Is Organized

This book covers a wide range of topics, with each topic dedicated to a particular skill or situation. The topics are organized into six categories:

1. **Starting out:** Building networks, searching for jobs, writing resumes, handling interviews, and starting your job on the right foot.

2. **Communicating:** Verbal and written, presenting persuasively, and speaking to specific audiences.

3. **Collaborating:** Facilitating meetings, resolving conflicts and challenges, earning people's trust, getting people's attention, and dealing with difficult situations and colleagues at work.

4. **Negotiating:** Negotiating skills, negotiating a job offer, asking for a raise, and saying no smartly.

5. **Managing your manager:** Managing up, working effectively with managers, dealing with difficult managers, working with HR, and preparing for performance reviews.

6. **Optimizing your success:** Managing time and prioritizing, dealing with changes at work, understanding American business culture, and navigating the business environment.

How to Use This Book

This book is designed for you to read any specific topic of interest at any time as well as to be able to refer back to any topic throughout your career.

- This book covers a wide range of relevant topics (chapters). Each topic contains specific and practical solutions, and you can read one or more topics of interest at any time without having to read the whole book.

- Throughout your career, as you encounter different situations, refer back to this book and read the topics applicable to your situation. We have designed this book for you to use as a reference throughout your career.

- If you are/will be working with or want to work for a multinational company in the US or a Western country that has a different business culture, make sure you read the chapters on "How to understand and use business idioms", "How to handle workplace politics smartly", and "How to engage in small talk naturally".

If you have the time, we recommend reading the whole book since many topics complement each other and the book will give you a more comprehensive view over your career cycle.

Happy reading!

Thriving At Work

Starting out
- Develop your network
- Search for job opportunities
- Learn how companies hire
- Explore job options
- Write compelling resume
- Interview with confidence
- Start on the right foot

Communicating
- Communicate effectively
- Develop presentation content
- Present persuasively
- Target specific audiences
- Run meetings

Collaborating
- Collaborate successfully
- Earn others' trust
- Get people to listen
- Give and receive feedback
- Handle conflicts
- Deal with difficult co-workers

Negotiating
- Become a good negotiator
- Negotiate a job offer
- Ask for a raise
- Say no smartly
- Stand out and promote yourself

Managing your manager
- Manage up
- Different types of managers
- Prepare for performance review
- Work with HR

Optimizing your success
- Manage time effectively
- Deal with changes
- Understand business idioms
- Handle workplace politics
- Engage in small talk naturally

PART 1
Starting Out

"People are afraid of the future, of the unknown. If they face up to it and take the dare of the future, they can have some control over their destiny. That's an exciting idea to me, better than waiting with everybody else to see what's going to happen."
— **John H. Glenn, Jr.**

"It's not difficulties that frighten us. Mostly, it's our fear that makes things difficult. Just don't give up easily."
— **Joko Widodo, 7th President of Indonesia**

"Never be afraid to fail. Failure is only a stepping stone to improvement. Never be overconfident, because that will block your improvement."
— **Tony Jaa, Thai martial artist**

How to Network

Networking sources

Past experiences crossed paths
- Classmates
- College alumni
- Co-workers
- Professionals connected to your company

Associations
- Industry organizations
- Industry players/competitors
- Headhunters/recruiting firms
- Friends, family members, neighbours, social groups

Ways to develop

Use social networking tools
- Build profile/personal brand
- Connect for sharing and updates

Stay in touch with co-workers
- Common interest groups

Attend industry events
- Connect with interest groups
- Re-establish contacts

Attend social outings

CHAPTER 1

How to Build, Maintain and Grow Your Network

In today's world, professionals change not only jobs but also careers. In the era of global business and interactions, we are living in a small world. People we went to school with can be our co-workers. People from a company we had dealings with previously are now our peers in the same company. Our competitors from other companies are now our partners. In the fluid world of business, networking is a must. Our network can be instrumental in providing support and a boost to our career. They can be valuable resources and avenues for professional and career opportunities. In this chapter, I'll address a variety of ways to build, maintain and grow your network.

Networking Sources

- **Classmates**. People we went to school with are a great resource. As you and your classmates go different ways after graduating, you will likely find yourselves based in different locations throughout the world. While in school, get to know as many of your classmates as you can and let them get to know you. And keep in touch. Fifteen years after graduating from my MBA programme, a classmate and I met and discussed a business idea which resulted in the creation of a business partnership that's still going strong ten years later. You never know who you may end up working with or getting a great opportunity from.

- **College alumni**. All schools maintain an extensive list of alumni. While fundraising is a major purpose, it's also a way for alumni to stay in touch, share information and provide assistance to each other. Alumni live and work throughout the world and are a good source to identify potential career and job opportunities. An easy way to stay connected is to register in the alumni directory and include your personal and career profile for people to view. Your university's regular networking events such as social get-togethers, anniversaries, recruitment and fundraisers are great opportunities to maintain and grow your contact list.

- **Co-workers**. These include people you're currently working with and those you've worked with in the past. If you have developed a good working relationship with them, gained credibility and earned their trust, they're fantastic resources for finding out and getting potential opportunities. They can be great references and even better, give you endorsements. As with our classmates and school alumni, it's important to maintain contact with them when you or they leave the company. If you can't get together for coffee from time to time, a simple way to keep in touch is sending a hello greeting to let them know you have them in mind. Periodically posting on your social networks is also a good way to stay connected. There have been several times in my career where I was recruited by a former co-worker, and vice versa.

    A valuable venue for co-worker networking is the training sessions within your organization. It's particularly important to reach beyond your usual working peers, across functional teams' boundaries. When I conducted various company in-house trainings, we consciously placed cross-functional teams together on projects. These arrangements were meant to forge relationships across broader organizational teams, especially for remote teams coming together on projects. As a faculty member, I use these occasions to spot potential talents, especially for leadership in multi-functional areas. So, don't treat it as just another training session. Make yourself stand out.

- **Professionals connected to your company.** These include suppliers, partners, service providers or contractors you work with on behalf of your company. A supplier could be a company that provides your company components to build products or packaging materials to ship your products in. Service providers could be consulting companies who provide consultation on different projects in a variety of areas. Your company hires contractors to perform specific tasks. As you work with these partners, follow the same working principle: develop and maintain a good working relationship with them. They are a good resource for future opportunities because they tend to have a lot of visibility of the industry and know many key players. My colleagues have received job offers from these partners as well as recruited them to join our company.

  One other source to keep in mind is your competitors. In today's world, a competitor today could be a partner or peer tomorrow. It's not uncommon for people to switch companies and go to work for a competitor. These people can provide valuable information about job opportunities, insight about the company and in many cases, actively recruit people from their previous company to join them.

  If you are working in sales, marketing or any external-facing position, there would be many opportunities to build close relationships with your customers. These engagements help you develop a deeper understanding in the business professional context but also often help develop close customer relationships at a personal level. I have personally made great connections with many of my customers and business associates, many of whom became my most loyal customers and partners. These contacts are helpful in understanding the various job opportunities across many industries and they could be the first to recommend you for a suitable role in their company or to your competitors.

- **Industry organizations.** If you have industry organizations in your field of work – such as the IEEE for electrical engineers, Association of Finance and Accounting for accounting and finance professionals, or the Marketing Association for marketing professionals – consider joining them. You get useful news and information specific to your field through website postings, newsletters and magazines, as well as exposure to job and career opportunities. Make an effort to attend the periodic events organized by the association; these are excellent networking opportunities.

- **Job recruiters**. Throughout your career, you may receive calls or emails trying to recruit you for one or more job opportunities. Recruiters are hired by their client companies to find qualified candidates. The service they provide includes identifying, recruiting, interviewing and selecting qualified candidates for various positions. They typically get paid by successful hires or by qualified candidates. You will see them at industry seminars, conferences and other networking events, as well as on popular professional sites such as LinkedIn. Introduce yourself and get their contact information. Even if you don't want to leave your company, keep in touch with them as they are a great resource to provide you an up-to-date picture of the market.

- **Friends, family members, neighbours and social groups**. Last but not least, these could be the best ways to find out about new opportunities and to help you find the right job. These people know you well, have a close relationship with you, share common hobbies or values, and would likely be more than willing to help. They probably also have their own network of contacts they can tap into to give you visibility to even more people. When I graduated from college, I gave my sister my resume. Within two weeks, I received a phone interview from Honeywell Inc., a multinational high-tech company. They flew me in for interviews and by the end of the day, I received offers from three different divisions. My sister was a member of a social club and through her friends there, she found out this opportunity from someone working at Honeywell at the time.

Ways to Build, Maintain and Grow Your Network

- **Use your social networking tools**. There are a number of popular social networking and professional sites such as LinkedIn that provide a forum for professionals to communicate and share information. You should join and invite people to join you. Include your personal and professional profile in your account. You can find useful news and information shared by other people as well as job openings through these sites. You can also communicate with a vast number of people about your job interests or career opportunities you want to research.

- **Stay in touch with your co-workers**. As discussed earlier, co-workers are a fantastic resource. Having them join your social networking group is a good start, but don't forget to have face-to-face, direct contact with them if possible. In the age of digital communications, we tend to forget the importance of this. Remember that nothing creates a deeper connection than face-to-face interaction. Try to find time, once every three months or so, to have lunch or coffee. I also know co-workers who have common hobbies that draw them together. For instance, people who like to ride their bike would get together for bike runs on the weekends. The group expands as more people join, and this presents a good way to grow your network.

- **Attend industry seminars and conferences**. These events are typically organized by industry groups or by major consulting firms to have a gathering of professional people in similar fields. In the high-tech industry, big consulting services firms such as IDC or Gartner group typically have at least one major event a year to discuss and share industry news and trends and to network. Of course, their goal is also to offer their consulting services to potential client companies. Since these events tend to draw hundreds or even thousands of professionals from different companies, they present a great opportunity for you to meet with as many people as you want in one place. Over the course of my career, I have met and formed friendships with new people at such events and have also run into co-workers and acquaintances with whom I had lost touch.

- **Attend social outings.** Whether it's through a hobby club, sports club, or some other social organization, get-together events and social outings are good forums to stay connected and get to know people better. They allow more time for us to have longer conversations instead of the usual quick greetings and small talk at a club meeting. Through these kinds of events, I have also seen parents inquire about internship positions or potential jobs for their college children, and more often than not, they meet people who know about openings in their company or know people who are looking to hire college students.

Reverse Mentoring Offers Mutual Benefits

Networking builds up your personal credibility and highlights your work profile and capabilities. Connections made through my network have helped me tap into adjacent opportunities. I have also been able to add value by connecting multiple parties to bring something to fruition. Networking is a force-multiplier, a door-opener, and in certain situations, a tipping point. An example is that of my HR leader Elizabeth, who was actively involved with Singapore universities in mentorship and business faculty classes. She was able to provide critical and relevant information to her MBA students because she was mentored by industry leaders and obtained a lot of industry knowledge from her connections.

There's a recent trend I have benefited greatly from, which young professionals should take advantage of. Reverse mentoring is a value-add in two directions for both senior and younger generations. I have learned a great deal from Millennials, GenZers and *jiulinghou* (post-90s generation), especially in fast-paced Asian economies such as China. It opened my eyes to new cultural norms and market changes. I recruited Thomas – a new-generation HR talent development expert in China – to regularly share his cross-industry learnings, such as the e-commerce market and China talent flow trends. It not only benefited the company employees but also expanded my connections and learnings from the students. As a mentor to younger executives, I firmly believe in the benefits in both directions from reverse mentoring. The younger generations have valuable first-hand experience with new evolving markets. They should seek opportunities to share their knowledge and insights with "older" management teams. And in doing this, they also build up their credibility "bank account" and strengthen their value in the network.

The Asian market's rapid growth and large young consumer segment makes this reverse mentoring ever more important for both the mentor and mentee. The younger workforce – in India and Southeast Asian countries such as Indonesia – makes up a significant market with notable consumer purchasing power and social characteristics. In particular:

- Commerce and society in these markets are fast-changing and driven by youth segment dynamics.

- Young consumers' voice and influence are magnified by their digital-native comfort level.

- For older management teams, the possibility of a generation gap within the organization could pose management challenges. Active learning within the organization is increasingly important to leverage the human capital from different age groups and experience levels. Youths should take advantage of their knowledge and familiarity of the growing market segment they represent. They could be the critical bridge from management to the market.

Wherever you are in the world, your reputation and how well you are connected are critical factors when it comes to business and professional dealings. The relationship-building journey from your networking needs time to be developed, and you should start to network as early as possible in your career.

CHAPTER 2

How to Search for Job Opportunities

In today's business world, you are unlikely to stay with the same company for your entire professional career, even if you want to. Company's loyalty to employees was real at one time, but not so much now. Throughout your career, prepare to change jobs a few times, whether by choice or not. Make it a practice to keep your eyes open for better opportunities, to be proactive and take control of your career. When you want to search for job opportunities, your networking contacts are a great resource and can also be a great reference for you. The best way to get the job you want is through referrals and recommendations from people you know. These people can help you expedite the applying process by connecting you directly to the hiring manager. However, this option may not be available to you all the time. In this chapter, I will cover the different sources and ways to search for job openings.

Job Search Using Your Network Sources

At the point you're looking for a job, hopefully you already have a significant network of contacts you've built and grown over time. Now is the time to tap into this network to help you with your job search. If you have not focused on building your network, start as soon as possible. It's better late than never.

Search for Job Opportunities

Network sources
- Classmates
- College alumni association
- Co-workers
- Professionals connected to the company
- Industry organizations
- Headhunters/recruiting firms
- Friends, family members, neighbours, social groups

Additional sources
- Target companies of interest
  — Search their webpage for job postings
- Professional & job search sites
- Government agency sites
- Other job posting ads, e.g. Classifieds

Additional tips
- Ready resume
- Online resources, e.g. Glassdoor
- Prepared for screening calls

- **Classmates.** This also includes members of school clubs, sport teams or other school organizations you joined and built relationships with. Many of them may be on social media sites such as Facebook and LinkedIn. Contact them using what you think are the most effective ways to reach them: social media, email, phone or if possible, face to face.

- **College or university alumni association.** All schools maintain an extensive list of alumni. Alumni members are encouraged to stay in touch, share information and provide assistance to each other. They present a big exposure to potential job and career opportunities all over the world. If your school's alumni have a website offering a platform for alumni to stay in touch, this would be a convenient way to let people know about your job search. Through the contact list from your college directory, you can reach out to these people as well.

- **Co-workers.** These include people you're currently working with as well as former co-workers whom you have developed good relationships with, earned their trust and gained credibility. They are a fantastic resource for finding and getting job opportunities and can also be great references for you. Your former managers are great contacts to reach out to. They obviously knew you and if they had a good working relationship with you and valued your work, they could be your meal ticket. From the companies you've worked at, you should already have a list of contacts. If you don't, you can put a list together using your phone contact list, email list, social media sites, etc. Contact them and let them know what you are looking for. If they are local, try to meet with them in person.

    During a lunch outing I had with a former student, Samantha, she told me she had recently left her old company to join a financial services company. When I asked her how she got the job, Samantha told me a former colleague, who had joined this new company, recruited and recommended her. Her colleague arranged a lunch meeting for her with the hiring manager. At the end of the lunch, the manager offered her the job on the spot. Although Samantha had a good working relationship with her colleague, she did not know her well. When she left the company, Samantha asked for her contact information and kept in touch periodically. And she was very glad she did. This is not usually how the hiring process works, but it shows the power of networking.

- **Professionals connected to your company.** These include suppliers, service providers and contractors you worked with on behalf of your company, or in some cases, even your company's competitors. You should have a list of the people you had good working relationships with. They are a good resource because they have a lot of visibility of the industry and know many key players. Reach out to them via whatever avenue is most convenient and effective for them.

- **Industry organizations.** There are many professional associations in different industries, such as the IEEE for electrical engineers, the Association of Finance and Accounting for accounting and finance professionals, and the Marketing Association for marketing professionals. If you are a member, you can get useful, relevant information specific to your field through the organization website postings and newsletters. Through the website, you may also be able to post your job inquiries and have access to people in your professional field.

- **Recruiters.** Throughout your career, you will likely receive calls or email messages from recruiters trying to recruit you for job opportunities. You also find them on career and job sites such as LinkedIn. Recruiters want to add to their professional contact list and would be interested in talking to you even if they don't have any opportunity matching your interest and qualifications at the moment. In addition, they are a good source of information since they often have visibility of your industry, key companies and employment outlook.

- **Friends, family members, neighbours and social groups.** They often are the best ways to learn about opportunities and excellent resources to help you find the right job. Many of them have their own networks, so by extension, they can get your word out to many more people.

Job Search Using Additional Sources

- **Companies you're interested in**. Companies post job openings as they become available. You can search on their website for job openings and submit your resume for the job you're interested in. All the openings should have a fairly detailed job description including key responsibilities and requirements. Some may list recruiter contact information but many do not. If you know someone from the company, that person can help find out the recruiter's contact information or even better yet, forward your resume to the hiring manager. Especially in a difficult employment environment, you increase your chances significantly if you can reach out directly to the hiring manager. Many companies hire contractors to handle recruiting and screening, but unfortunately, because of the high turnover rate for recruiters, your resume may fall through the cracks. It's a good idea to follow up periodically to make sure the company still has your resume on file.

- **Professional and job search sites**. There are a number of global sites as well as country or region-specific job search sites. They may have a large number of members, including professional employees, employers and headhunters. Here you can post your profile/resume. Companies also advertise and post their job openings on these sites. They provide great exposure to many job openings as well as employment contacts. From these sites, some of which offer additional features to enhance your job search but may require a premium membership fee, you can customize your search for the specific type of job you're looking for, as well as set up automatic searches to receive reports regularly. LinkedIn is an example of a job search site.

- **Classified ads** in newspapers, magazines and trade publications, including online ads. While these are not as common and popular, they still are a useful source of job opportunities.

Additional Tips

- Hopefully, you have been proactively managing your career on an ongoing basis, including building your network and keeping your resume up to date. If you are new in your professional life and have not built up your network, start one and keep growing it. Don't wait. If you don't have your resume or have not updated it recently, put your focus on creating the best resume possible. After all, your resume is your initial communication vehicle to potential employers. Since they will likely read your resume before deciding to interview you, don't take shortcuts in your resume writing effort. Before you start or at least during your job search, make sure you have a resume ready to go. Refer to the "How to write a compelling resume" chapter for the best way to go about this.

- There are online resources such as Glassdoor.com that provide you useful information in your search for the right job and company. Information you can find includes reviews of salary compensations for specific job titles, benefits, cultures and management teams. Look to see if Glassdoor or similar websites are available in your country.

- Once you apply for a position, you may get a phone call any time. The phone call could be to set up a phone interview or it could be the interview itself. As a result, assume the phone call you get will be a screening interview and be prepared. Your success in the screening interview will get you face-to-face interviews with the hiring manager and other people in the company. You don't want to get caught unprepared for the phone interview because that might be your only one with that company. If you're not prepared, ask to schedule a time soon after so you have time to prepare.

- I saw many cases of students doing internships during their holidays. Internships are very available in Asian markets as many MNCs and local companies are tapping into younger people for ideas and energies. These are great opportunities to understand first-hand the industry as well as how well it fits with your career path. Planting your seed early as an intern also gives you exposure and a head-start for possible long-term employment with the company. I would highly recommend this as an essential pre-career starting point that all should take full advantage of.

- The growing Asian economies provide early career professionals with new potential and options on an ongoing basis. Every opportunity to serve your customers or partners should be a chance to open new doors of knowledge and to be spotted. Your customers and partners are definitely candidates for your career connections.

- The trend in Asia on switching careers across industries should be a factor to consider in broadening your connections. Success in an existing job should not exclude you from learning and exploring other areas that could utilize your current assets. My experience as a volunteer in the Red Cross exposed me to humanitarian needs and skills in saving lives, and gave me a platform to leverage my corporate world experience for a broader purpose to serve.

- You should build your personal brand, a profile that will differentiate you from the rest. This will be useful as you connect to those relevant groups of professional contacts who can endorse you. This would serve as a force multiplier.

CHAPTER 3

How Companies Hire

Many college students and even professionals who have been employed for some time don't really understand how employers conduct and manage the hiring process. Understanding this process helps you better prepare for your job search, interviews and job offer negotiations. This chapter describes a typical hiring process of multinational companies in the United States. While there may be some unique differences for companies outside of US, many of them leverage the hiring process from US companies. It would be beneficial to you to do your research to understand the details of your specific company. Recruiters or Human Resources (HR) staffing managers are good places to get pertinent information. As I spoke to many HR and recruiting professionals, hiring is a challenging task, especially in Asia. With business growth and talent gaps, HR teams are under time pressure to hire strong candidates. By understanding the hiring process, you can make it easier for them to hire you.

How Companies Conduct Staffing and Hiring

- **Staffing decision**. Companies begin working on next year's operating plan a few months prior to the next fiscal year with the goal to have a final approved plan by the start of next fiscal year. Once approved, each department has its specific budget plan showing how many additional positions can be added for the coming year. The additional headcounts include the number of new college graduate as well as experienced hires.

How Companies Hire

Posting job openings

1. Job description and selection criteria
2. Manager submits job positions for posting
3. Screening and interviewing
4. Hiring decision
5. Job offer package
6. Onboarding preparation

Staffing decision

- College hire schedule
- Quarterly operating budget
- Quarterly windows
- Hiring freeze?

Hiring decision
- Narrow to final shortlist
- HR background/reference check

Job offer package
- Inclusive of fixed policies and negotiable terms
- Base salary, sales incentives, stock incentives, sign-on bonus, etc
- Backup offers and backup candidates standing by

Public sector hiring

- Dictated by regulations
- Job postings on organization's website
- Submission requirements: CV with cover letter; job skill test
- Interview and hiring process (one-on-one or panel interviews)

In the US, the new college graduate hiring process is normally completed by May, with offers extended to candidates in February or March. Because of this schedule, companies' college recruiters usually visit colleges and participate in job fair events for graduating students much earlier. The experienced hires can occur throughout the year.

It's important to remember that the annual operating budget is subject to be revised quarterly. The number of hires for each quarter may increase or decrease, depending on the company's business performance and market conditions. An exception to this planning process happens when a manager needs to replace an employee who transitioned to another job or left the company. The appropriate management level must approve this kind of hire. One additional note: the company at any time can decide to freeze all hirings and open positions. Timing also plays an important factor and dictates the manager's hiring process. Due to fiscal calendar constraints of the end of the fiscal quarter or year, managers may be given a deadline to complete their hiring or lose their head count allocations. As a result, managers may shorten the hiring process in order to beat the deadline.

- **Posting job openings**. Once the manager knows how many additional employees to hire, they write a job description for each position. The job description includes job title, main responsibilities and qualification requirements such as college degree, number of years of experience, technical skills, etc. In addition, the job description may also list desirable qualifications. To start the process, an HR staffing recruiter meets with the hiring manager to confirm the position's job level, review criteria for selecting candidates, decide whether to use an external head hunter and how to proceed with the interview process. Then the hiring manager submits the job positions to be posted on the company website and on other external sites as appropriate.

- **Screening and interviewing**. The company staffing recruiter screens the resumes, verifies candidates' qualifications and sends qualified resumes to the hiring manager. The manager or recruiter conducts phone interviews to select candidates for in-person interviews. The manager also puts together an interview team consisting of people from their team and other teams who will be working with the new hire.

Regarding interview methodology, many companies use a behavioural interview method where the interviewer describes certain work scenarios and asks the candidate to respond to the situation. This is an effective method to gauge the candidate's qualities and skills. For example, if the interviewer wants to probe for teamwork ability, they may say: "Give me an example of a time you had a conflict at work with a colleague and describe how you handled it." Or if the interviewer wants to probe for problem-solving skills, they may say: "Give me an example of a complex problem you had to solve and explain how you solved it." In terms of organizing the interview team, some managers are more organized and assign a specific area for each member to probe, such as teamwork, communication, job skills and creativity. Other managers are less structured and may leave it up to the interviewers to decide how they want to conduct the session.

Some companies also have a practice of hiring for a functional area, Supply Chain for example, without focusing on any specific job. They may not have specific jobs defined yet or may want to re-organize the job positions in the organization. After the hiring process is completed, the manager places the employee in a specific job position.

- **Hiring decision**. After all the interviews are completed and feedback collected, the manager narrows the list down to a few finalists and either decides to hire one of them or brings them in for a final interview with high-level executives. Before making the final hiring decision, the manager checks out references and HR conducts background checks on the finalists. During this final stage, the manager stays in touch with the other finalists to update them on the progress and to confirm their availability and interest in joining the company.

- **Job offer package**. Once the manager decides on a candidate, the HR manager and the hiring manager put together an offer package that includes base salary, stock incentives, sign-on cash bonus, etc. Some offer items are firm per company policy while others are negotiable. The HR manager informs the candidate and sends the offer out. The candidate is given a certain number of days to formally accept or reject the offer. This period can be a few days for an experienced hire or as long as two months for college hires due to their college's job accepting policy. During this period, the candidate can ask to clarify unclear items and negotiate the offer. Since time is of the essence, the manager will push the candidate for a decision as soon as possible. The manager likely also has a backup plan in case the offer is rejected. If this happens, the manager will quickly move to make an offer to the second finalist.

- **On-board preparation**. Once the candidate accepts the formal offer, the manager will complete the necessary paperwork and take steps to prepare for the new hire's arrival. This preparation includes procuring IT equipment, setting up the employee in the company HR and IT system, as well as lining up key people for the new hire to meet.

Although companies tend to have a similar hiring framework, they may have differences in specific hiring procedures, depending on the company size and industry. Start-ups and small companies may have simpler hiring process than large employers. For example, instead of a few rounds of interview, it may take one or two, and instead of a team of several interviewers, it may just be a couple of people, including the hiring manager. The budget planning process for smaller companies may also be less formal, and managers have more discretion over when they can hire. Moreover, since smaller companies do not have a fully staffed HR department, they may outsource much of the recruiting and screening tasks to external recruiting firms. When contacted by the company recruiter, ask for information on the hiring process so you can prepare appropriately.

How to Explore Job Options

Approaches to research
- Engage recruiters on possible roles
- Connect with company insiders
- Online job banks and networking platforms, e.g. LinkedIn

Seek out ideal/best-fit jobs
- Questions to gain visibility to explore different options
- To best fit your interests and strengths
- Relevant department or organization in the company

Consider different industry positions
- Available positions best related to field of study
- Understand the match to interests and strengths

Consider different functions within organizations
- Available departments best fit career goals/interests
- Available functions: Sales, Products, Operations, etc
- Geographic territory (international/regional)

CHAPTER 4

How to Explore Job Options

This chapter may be more relevant to new graduating college students as they are about to embark on their career journey. When you start your job search, you may be asking yourself what job you should pursue. While this is an important question, there are other key questions you need to consider as well, such as what department/organization in a company you like to work in. This chapter helps you think through these questions, and provides ways to explore your job options, so you can make the best decision for yourself.

For every college major, there are a number of different job positions where you can utilize your skills. As importantly, there could be a number of organizations within a company that have relevant positions for your college degree. When you explore the different job options and organizations in a company, get as much information and as clear a picture as you can to determine if they fit with your interests and goals.

Refer to the table that follows. For each college major, the table shows: (1) a sample list of possible organizations in a company; and (2) a sample list of job positions in each of these organizations. I'll discuss each of these in detail.

Table 1
Example of matching job positions to organizations in a company

Degree/Major	Organization	Job Position
Electrical Engineering; Computer Science	Engineering Group	Design Engineer
		Test Engineer
		QA/QC Engineer
		BIOS/Firmware Engineer
		Document/Technical Writer
	Manufacturing Operation	Production Engineer
		Process Engineer
		QC Engineer
		Test Engineer
	Technical-Customer Support Organization	Technical Marketing Eng.
		Technical Support Engineer
		Application Engineer
	Field Sales Sales Operation	Solutions Architect
		Application Engineer
		Professional Services Eng.
		Sales Engineer
Math	Finance Dept.	Finance Analyst
		Business Analyst
		Business Planner
	Corporate/Headquarters	Merger & Acquisition Mgr
		Investment Specialist
		Business Strategist
	Engineering Group, Quality Control Dept.	QC Process Specialist
		Product Quality Specialist
		Business/Cost Analyst
Finance; Accounting	Finance Dept. Corporate Finance Dept.	Finance Analyst
		Finance Reporting Manager
		Business Analyst
		Budget Analyst
	Accounting Dept.	Cost Analyst
		Business Analyst
		Accountant
	Field Sales Sales Operation	Finance Analyst
		Finance Reporting Manager
		Business Analyst
		Customer Billing Specialist

How to Explore Job Options

Business	Finance Dept.	Business Analyst
		Programme Manager
		Business Planner
	Marketing Organization	Business Analyst
		Programme Management Specialist
		PR/Communication Specialist
	Field Sales Sales Operation	Sales Support Specialist
		Order Administrator
		Programme Management Specialist
		Salesperson
	Engineering Group Customer Support Operation	Project Manager
		Business Analyst
		Customer Returns & Escalation Manager
Marketing	Marketing Organization	Programme Manager
		Marcom Specialist
		Outbound Marketing Specialist
		Marketing Event Coordinator
	Field Sales Sales Operation	Programme Management
		Promotion/Advertising Specialist
		Event Planning Manager
		Salesperson
	Customer Support Operation	Customer Service Rep
		Event Coordinator
		Programme Manager
		Training Programme Manager
Communications	PR Dept.	Financial Analyst Liaison
		Industry Analyst Liaison
		Marketing Communication Specialist
		Programme Manager
	HR Organization	Training Programme Manager
		Department Liaison
		Employee Development Manager
		Benefit Administrator
	Marketing Organization	Marketing Event Planner
		Programme Manager
		Marcom Specialist
		Business Development Specialist
		Industry Partnership Manager

Note: This table is for illustrative purpose only and not meant to be a complete list. There are online resources that match different careers to college degrees (for example: www.bigfuture.com).

Considering Different Job Positions

As you begin to search for job openings in the market place, you should know all available job positions related to your college degree. You need to understand what the positions entail, the differences between them and which ones best fit your strengths and interests.

- Let's look at an engineering example from the table. For our discussion, let's assume you graduated with a Computer Science bachelor degree (BS degree). Some of the relevant job positions for this major include Software Design Engineer, Test Engineer, Quality Assurance/Quality Control Engineer, Application Engineer and Customer Support Engineer. Each of these positions has specific responsibilities. For example, the responsibilities of a Software Design Engineer include designing an overall solution for a project or a part of a project, clearly defining inputs and outputs, and writing code. On the other hand, a Test Engineer has the responsibilities to test for software bugs and any problems between the different software programmes within the project. The Software Design Engineer position normally offers a higher salary than the Test Engineer position due to the skills required. Depending on your skill level and experience, you may find one of these two Engineering positions a better fit for you.

- Let's look at another example from the table – Finance/Accounting. Similar to Engineering, there are a number of positions applicable to the Finance/Accounting major, such as Finance Analyst, Financial Reporting Manager and Cost Accounting Specialist. These jobs have different responsibilities. One responsibility of a Finance Analyst is performing an ROI (Return on Investment) analysis of a project, whereas a responsibility of a Finance Reporting Manager is gathering key business results and creating a report for company management. The former requires more finance analysis skill while the latter requires the ability to understand business metrics and organize data in a logical manner.

Considering Different Organizations

In addition to the job positions, you should research to determine which organizations in the company are best suited to your career goals and interests.

- With a Computer Science degree, there are several organizations offering job positions relevant for the degree, including Engineering, Customer Support, Sales/Field Operations and Manufacturing Operations. In the Customer Support Organization, you focus on providing technical support to customers, working with customers to design specific solutions, or providing technical training and support to sales people. In addition, you generally interface more frequently with customers and salespeople than if you work in the Engineering organization. If you have an interest in the technical as well as business side and like interacting with customers, you may want to consider the Customer Support Organization.

  On the other hand, if you want to be a Sales Representative in the future, you may apply to work in Sales Operations, where you will have opportunities to work closely with the sales team and have first-hand knowledge of how salespeople work with customers.

- For a Finance/Accounting major, organizations having relevant positions include Finance Department, Corporate Finance Department, Product Operations, Sales Operations and Customer Support Organization. While you may perform similar duties in these organizations, whom you work with is different. In the Finance Department within Product Operations, you interact with engineering teams, whereas you work with sales people if you're in Sales Operations. Working in Sales Operations gives you exposure to the external business world. On the other hand, working in Product Operations gives you a more in-depth view of the internal workings of the company.

  One other factor to consider is which organization may offer opportunities that align with your goal. If you like to gain international experience, working in Sales Operations may present opportunities for you to work in an overseas sales office in the future.

Small and medium-sized companies may have multiple functions combined into one organization or department. For example, Technical Support is within the Engineering department. In addition, employees in smaller companies may perform more than one job function. For example, if you work in the Marketing department, your job duties may include marketing communications, product launches, sales training and public relations. If you work in the Finance department, your job duties may include business analysis, programme management and business reporting. Working in a smaller company offers you the advantage of learning and developing different skills in multiple areas, whereas you tend to develop a more specialized skill in a specific job in a big company.

When you explore the different job options and organizations in a company, get as much information and as clear a picture as you can to determine if they fit with your interests and goals.

How to Research Job Positions and Organizations

If you are in college, meet with as many company recruiters as you can when your school holds career/job fair events. Ask the recruiter about the different positions in the company that match your degree, to describe the different duties from one position to another, and provide you copies of the job description. In addition, talk to the recruiter about the different organizations in the company that have positions where your degree is applicable and to explain to you the differences among these organizations. Many universities also conduct tours to different companies that students may be interested in joining. Take advantage of these opportunities where you can observe first-hand and interact directly with employees and managers. These are great opportunities to build your network of contacts as well.

In addition, contact an HR manager or any manager in the companies of interest for an informational meeting where you can pick their brain. This takes time but be persistent and you may be able to get some managers willing to meet you or at least talk to you over the phone. If you have friends or know people in the company, ask them to refer you to the HR manager or other managers for you to meet. LinkedIn is a good place to locate HR staffing personnel and other recruiters. Explain to them that you are exploring different positions to help you consider the best fit as you start out your career. Also use your network of contacts who work in different jobs and in different organizations.

Although these efforts require a significant amount of time, it's worth the investment. As a new graduate, it's easier to obtain an entry-level position from a list of job openings and in different organizations in a company. Companies are more willing to train new college hires as they will likely start in entry-level positions. On the other hand, if you are an experienced professional in a current job, it's more difficult to move into a different position since the new position will likely require someone with experience.

Write a Compelling Resume

Style
- Maximum 2 pages
- Simple format ready for online submission
- Easy to read and follow
- Bullet-point format
- Come alive with power words
- Attention to detail

Content
- Aim to generate interest for employers
- Create a foundational generic version
- **1. Contact info and job objectives**
- **2. Summary of skills/qualifications**
- **3. Education summary**
- **4. Experience summary**
  - Include both paid and volunteer experience
- **5. Relevant hobbies/technical skills**
  - Enhance your appeal and value-add

Create a LinkedIn profile
- Platform to stay connected
- Leverage resume content
- Endorsements and recommendations
- Keep profile fresh
- Take it as seriously as resume

CHAPTER 5

How to Write a Compelling Resume

A resume enables you to get your foot in the door. While a resume does not get you a job offer by itself, it can get you an interview opportunity that can lead to a job offer. Unless the employer already knows you, a prospective employer will review your resume to determine if they want to interview you. While your ultimate objective is to get a job offer, it's not the goal of a resume. In all my professional years, I very rarely saw or heard of offers being made from just reading a resume, no matter how compelling. The resume's key objective is to generate enough interest for potential employers to want to interview you. You have a much better chance of getting an interview if you produce a compelling resume that matches well with the job's requirements and makes you stand out against other candidates. In this chapter, I'll show you how to write such a resume by focusing on two areas: style and content development. In addition, I'll discuss the type of content to include in your LinkedIn profile.

Creating Resume Style

This is about creating the look and feel of your resume, including how to format, how to organize and how to make it easy to read and follow.

- **Keep a resume to maximum two pages**. If you are a new graduate without much work experience, a one-page resume may be sufficient. Focus on quality instead of quantity. The person reviewing your resume could be an HR (Human Resources) staffing recruiter, outside recruiter, or a hiring manager. Due to the sheer volume of resumes to review, I would typically only spend a few minutes on each resume. I would look to see if you meet the required qualifications and how you stand out against other resumes. If your resume is longer than two pages, I probably would scan through your resume even quicker, which increases the likelihood of missing important information you want me to know. Moreover, a long resume indicates a possible lack of discipline to be succinct and lack of ability to prioritize key information about you. A four-page resume listing everything you have done in your career will likely create a negative impression even before the manager begins reading it.

- **Keep the format simple**. Since you will likely submit your resume online, PDF or text format is appropriate. Some employers use programs to scan for certain keywords on your resume to determine your potential fit. Use normal font size for the body content (10–12 point). There's no need to use fancy fonts or colours.

- **Make the resume easy to read and follow**. Use bullet points instead of long sentences. Try to keep each bullet point to one or two lines. If the manager has a few minutes to read your resume, you don't want them to have to re-read over certain things because they weren't clear on what you meant to say. Moreover, using bullet-point format encourages you to be succinct and to the point.

- **Make your resume come alive**. Use active, "power" words as appropriate. For example, use "I led" instead of "I was involved," "I initiated" instead of "I assisted," and "I delivered the project results ahead of schedule" instead of "I was able to finish…"

- **Check for spelling and grammar errors**. Misspelled words or grammatically incorrect sentences can turn a good resume into a mediocre one and could negatively cloud the reviewer's opinion of you. It also indicates laziness and lack of attention to details. So it's worth it to spend a few minutes running your resume through spell and grammar check.

Developing Resume Content

The objective of a resume is to generate interest for potential employers to want to interview you. To start off, focus on developing a great foundational resume that highlights your skills, experience, education, qualities and accomplishments without focusing on any specific company. In addition, be creative and use any relevant and factual information that will help you stand out and put you in as good a position as possible. Then as you find a specific job you want to apply for, you can tweak this foundational resume for that job. If you did a good job creating the resume, tweaking it to match the requirements should be quick and without a lot of effort needed.

The general structure of a resume includes:

1. Contact information and job objective
2. Summary of skills/qualifications
3. Education summary
4. Experience summary
5. Relevant hobbies/interests/other technical skills

It's not necessary to include a References section. If the employer wants to check for references, they will ask you at that time. The order between Education Summary and Experience Summary can be interchanged. If you have a fair amount of experience, you may want to order your experience before education.

1. **Contact information should be straightforward.** For your contact information, use a phone number that you can be easily reached at. Usually this is your cell phone. Don't list a phone you use infrequently. Since managers are usually busy, they would like to be able to talk to a candidate live on the phone when they call. If they need to leave a message,

you run the risk of playing phone tag since it's a good possibility they will not be available when you call back. Also use an email account you check regularly. If an employer sends you an email message regarding your job interest and doesn't hear from you in a few days, they'll assume you're not interested.

For job objective, reserve a line to fill in the job title/description when you want to apply for a specific job. For example: "Seeking a challenging and interesting Business Analyst position that will enable me to use my skills and grow with the company (Job Requisition# 123REQ)." Remember to include the job requisition number if there is one so you can ensure the resume will reach the right person.

2. **Summary of Skills/Qualifications**. This is the most important section of the resume. This is where you can summarize a few key points you want the managers to remember about you because they're not going to remember everything on your resume. The analogy here is similar to writing a thesis paper where you put your theme and main points at the beginning of the paper. Instead of having the managers try to come up with what to remember about you, why not make it easy for them by stating it upfront. This section should include a short list of 4–5 skills and accomplishments that best match the position's requirements and put you in the best possible light. Here are some example bullet points for graduating college students:

   ▷ Strong technical skills and experience that match very well with the position's requirements

   ▷ Track record of successfully leading different groups of people on multiple school projects

   ▷ Exceptional communication skills developed through communication classes and internship at ABC company

   ▷ University department Dean's List for three consecutive quarters

▷ Demonstrated ability to get up to speed quickly, solve problems and go above and beyond to get things done right and on time

You need to support these skills and qualifications by providing proof in subsequent sections of your resume. If you have difficulty writing this section first, skip it and work on the last three sections. After you have completed those sections, pick out key nuggets and include them in your Summary of Skills/Qualifications section.

3. **Education Summary.** Many graduating students don't make full use of this part of the resume. They simply list their college major and a few classes they completed. As a result, they miss an opportunity to reveal special accomplishments or unique skills they have learned. It's not enough to just list out your major and classes taken. This does not separate you from others. Focus on pointing out and highlighting any excellent results you achieved with your education. Some specific suggestions:

   ▷ Include college major(s), degree, high GPA. If you have a minor degree, list it as well.

   ▷ Include relevant and successfully completed classes as well as results and accomplishments from significant research projects, group projects or other completed papers. Also highlight the skills you developed. For example, learning leadership skills from leading a group project, developing analytical skills from research projects, writing skills from publishing papers, etc.

   If part of your education programme involved working with a real company on a specific project where you/your team delivered tangible benefits to the companies and at the same time, learned and developed concrete skills, you should definitely highlight this experience. This is especially useful in situations where a company requires a certain amount of work experience that you don't have. However, this kind of school experience can serve as a good substitute for the lack of real work experience.

   In a business class I taught, we had a business plan group project.

Students formed in teams of four and their objective was to create a business startup that serves an unmet need in the community. They developed a complete business plan with detailed marketing strategy, operational plan, financial analysis and forecast. Upon completion of the project, each team gave a presentation on their business plan. For a member/leader of the team, this would be a great experience to include in their resume – highlighting skills they developed, including leadership, communication, collaboration, analytical and presentation skills. The hiring manager would view this positively.

- Include key awards and accomplishments during your educational years such as Honour Roll, Valedictorian, Dean's List, top 10% of class, scholarships, etc.

4. **Experience Summary.** I want to emphasize two important points here. First, focus on highlighting your positive results and accomplishments on each of your jobs. Many people only provide a list of job responsibilities and activities they performed. While it makes sense to describe the job, it's not enough and is only a small part of what you should include. You want to make yourself stand out as much as possible. Just listing your job responsibilities does nothing to highlight you. Pointing out good results and accomplishments will separate you from others. Secondly, think about your paying as well as non-paying jobs and volunteer work experience. Work experience is not limited to paid positions only. The experience and skills you gained in your volunteer work are as meaningful and valuable, and in many cases, create a better impression on hiring managers than a paid position.

If you have a long work history, put more focus on recent employment experience (within the last five years). If you limit your resume to two pages, you will not have enough space to cover every job in detail. Here is how to develop the content for the Experience Summary section:

- For each position, list the job title, company's name, location and employment duration.

- ▷ Describe briefly your job and key responsibilities. Keep this to one or two lines.

- ▷ List successful results and key accomplishments. Think about how your results contributed to your team or your company's success. Excellent results include finishing a project ahead of schedule or below budget, helping sales to exceed target, saving company cost, increasing customer satisfaction, and improving quality of product and services. It's best if you can show quantitative results. For example, finishing a key project two months ahead of schedule or reducing the defective products by 20% is a tangible result. When I was a product manager working on a new computer product, we completed the project three months ahead of schedule. This allowed the company to launch the product in a peak-buying season and as a result, the company gained an advantage in the market. You bet I included this in my resume. One more point: you need be able to support your claims and explain them in detail if you're asked about them in the interview.

- ▷ Think about examples that demonstrate your value and standing in the company, such as bonus awards, excellent job review/ranking, praise from managers, company recognition, customer/partner appreciation, employee of the month/year award, significant salary raises and stock grants. Don't forget to include anything that makes you look good and separate you from the crowd. This is not the time to be bashful.

- ▷ Another way to show your skills and qualities is highlighting the times you were a leader or played a leading role in motivating people and driving the team to get the job done. This shows you were a skilled, dedicated leader and not just an average employee. Companies don't want to hire average employees.

5. **Relevant hobbies/interests/technical skills.** Use this section to highlight yourself in other areas you have not covered in the resume. Many people

give this section little attention, putting the same hobbies most people put on their resume, which doesn't convey anything unique about them. Here's what you should do:

- Include hobbies or interests that enhance your appeal to the position or provide even more support for the qualities you highlighted. For example, if you are a long-distance runner and have participated in long-distance races, including this hobby demonstrates your self-motivation, dedication and discipline. If you play a musical instrument, including this hobby shows you have creativity. If you participated in competitive events in sports, technology or arts, including this shows your passion, competitiveness and motivation to succeed.

- If you hold professional certificates, even ones not related to your area, including them demonstrates your range of interests and curiosity. If you belong to the IEEE association or have a professional accounting certificate, highlight it. Although I was a product manager for a high-tech company, I also had a real estate licence. I included this in my resume to highlight my people skills, negotiation skills and communication skills – all important qualities for my product management job.

- Include organizations you belong to and hold a key position in, such as Treasurer, Finance Analyst or Marketing Specialist. All this goes to show your ability or at least, your motivation to develop and improve key skills required in the workplace.

- Any other technical skills that highlight you even more, such as expertise in certain technology areas – web design, for example – or deep knowledge about specific and unique accounting audit processes.

Creating Your LinkedIn Profile

LinkedIn is a popular online networking site for professionals. It's a platform where they can stay connected, share information, stay current in their field, research for job opportunities, and advertise themselves. The good news is you can leverage your resume's content for your LinkedIn profile. With LinkedIn, you have an opportunity to personalize your resume and tell more of a story about you. Below are a few things to keep in mind when creating your profile.

- You can expand on your resume's specific content. While I advocate keeping your resume content succinct, you can use your profile space here to add more colour to your bullet points. If you mentioned a great accomplishment in your resume, you can tell a story behind that result. For example, during your internship, you delivered a proposal that impressed company management so much they decided to implement it. On your profile, you can elaborate on what made the proposal compelling and go into more detail about your role and contributions.

- With your LinkedIn profile, you don't need to be as narrowly focused on your professional skills as you are in your resume. You should include other skills and areas of interest and expertise to demonstrate your versatility, curiosity and aspirations.

- Another excellent LinkedIn feature you can use is posting endorsements and recommendations. A powerful way to promote yourself is to have other people endorse you. Solicit your co-workers, managers, professors and others to write you a recommendation on LinkedIn or endorse your specific skills or expertise. It's also a great way to support your claims. For instance, if you claim that you have excellent leadership skills and ability to work with people to get things done, having your manager or colleague's testimony is powerful proof.

- Sharing photos, posting videos or articles is an effective way to stay connected with people as well as highlighting your unique skill or expertise.

You can keep your profile fresh by posting professional or personal updates as often as you like. Through LinkedIn, you can greatly expand your network of contacts. It suggests people you have either a direct or indirect connection with to link to your network. Through LinkedIn, I was able to stay connected with people whom I would have otherwise lost touch with years ago.

- Take your profile as seriously as you take your resume. Be thoughtful and careful about what you include in your description. Since anyone can look at your profile, you don't want to post anything that could affect your image negatively or show you in a bad light. This advice applies to your LinkedIn account as well as all your other social media platforms. Employers may check your social media postings, and anything that raises a red flag can potentially hurt your employment chances.

Additional Tips

- Don't include a cover letter unless you are asked to provide one. This is not a common practice. Most managers only have time to read the resume to determine your fit for the position.

- Don't include references on resume. This is not needed. If you get far enough into the hiring process, the employer will ask for references at that time. So use the extra space on your resume to promote yourself.

- Don't use slang, jargon or acronyms that are not easy to understand, unless the acronym is common and widely understood (such as IEEE). If you need to, spell out the acronyms. People whose native language is not English may not understand slang easily.

- Don't include personal information that may negatively affect your chances of getting an interview, particularly if you don't know who will be reviewing your resume and whether that person has any biases. You need to use your judgment here; there is no right or wrong answer. For example, a student asked me whether he should include in the resume his membership in a gun association. Since neither he nor I knew if the potential hiring manager had any strong opposition to people owning guns, I advised him to use his judgment and to think whether this detail was relevant and helpful to the position and whether it was worth taking the risk.

- Don't lie. While you definitely should make yourself look as good as possible, be sure that every fact or claim is accurate and can be supported. In today's world, your records can be easily verified. You probably have heard of famous people losing their jobs because they lied on their resume. On a consulting service project with a high-tech company, the prospective employer did a background check on me before I started the job. When I received the report, it provided a detailed record of the last ten years of my life.

- The use of Artificial Intelligence (AI) scans is a potential approach companies may use for initial sorting and matching. Your resume should focus on relevant key words for AI scanning. Read the job description carefully and leverage your LinkedIn and other social profiles to understand the job position's keywords and to provide an expanded view of your brand.

- Have a look at some good examples of resumes as www.careeratwork.net.

CHAPTER 6

How to Handle Interviews with Confidence

What is a successful job interview? You may think a successful interview is one that results in a job offer. While that is the desired result, you can have an excellent interview without getting a job offer. That may sound contradictory and illogical, but let me explain. The fact of the matter is you don't have much control over the hiring decision. You don't know how many other people also interviewed for the job or what factors the hiring manager considered in making the decision. You may not receive a job offer even though you felt you did well in the interview. For instance, I have seen one case where there were two qualified candidates, each with different strengths. The manager ended up choosing one person over the other due to experience level. Or in another case where there were three equally qualified candidates, one female and two male candidates, the hiring manager, wanting to have a more diverse team, decided to offer the job to the female candidate.

However, do not despair. In my mind, a successful interview is one where you were prepared, gave your best effort answering questions, engaged the interviewer fully and were satisfied with the information you learned about the company. Your goal for the interview is to do so well you make it easy for the manager to want to hire you. Managers have to juggle many balls at work. When they need to hire a new employee for their team, they have to squeeze the time into their schedule. It takes a lot of time to conduct the hiring process, including writing the job description, completing the required

Interview with Confidence

Before interview

- Know the target: Company, job details, interviewers
- Prepare list of potential questions and your answers:
  - Job skills
  - Problem-solving skills
  - Teamwork
  - Communication skills
  - Dedication/commitment
- Prepare questions to ask the interviewers
  — *To learn more about the fit with your career goals*

During interview

- Make good first impression: Punctuality, attire
- Speak clearly
- Maintain eye contact
- Show energy/enthusiasm
- Buy time to respond if needed
- Ask leading questions to highlight yourself
- Ask for clarifications
- Turn negative questions to your strengths
- Get contact information

Don't

- Don't ask about salary/benefits during interview
- Don't talk bad about previous company/manager
- Don't take anyone with you for the interview

paperwork, posting the job opening, reviewing resumes, interviewing candidates and negotiating the job offer.

Let's take an example. A manager has five candidates going through the in-person interviews and it takes a total of three hours to spend on each candidate. That takes almost two workdays, not including the time the manager has spent reviewing other resumes or the amount of time the interview team spends interviewing. If the manager is really impressed with you and satisfied that you are an excellent fit, they have a great incentive to hire you quickly because that would save a lot of time. It's in your best interest to do your best to make it as easy as possible for the manager to make the hiring decision.

However, even if you did not get the job but did well in the interview and left a good impression, the manager will remember you and would likely recommend you to other managers who have openings. I saw this many times in my career. When I was looking to hire a forecasting specialist, I had two qualified candidates but could only hire one. Even though I did not hire Ted, I kept his resume. When I learned two weeks later that a colleague was looking to hire a demand planner – a different position but with similar skillset requirements – I recommended Ted. After interviewing Ted, the manager offered him the job. This example illustrates the importance of being thoroughly prepared and giving your best effort to impress the hiring manager and interviewers. If you achieve that, be satisfied with your effort, regardless of the outcome.

In this chapter, I will cover two areas: what to do before your interview and how to conduct yourself at the interview. This chapter is especially helpful if you will be interviewing with a multinational company that has employees in other countries with a different culture from that of your country.

Before the Interview

How you prepare for an interview is extremely important as it determines how well you will perform at the interview.

- **Know the company**. Inevitably one of the interviewers will ask why you are interested in working for this company. If you are stumped by this question, you just hurt your chances of getting a job offer. After all, why should I hire you if you cannot tell me why you are interested in joining my company? Another key reason to know about the company is for you to determine whether this is a company you want to join. Company information is available publicly. The company website provides most of the relevant information – its products, services, reputation, culture, etc. Other online websites such as Indeed.com or Glassdoor.com also give good insight about the company's culture, reviews from employees, etc. Let's say you find out company ABC is known for offering innovative products, has been growing faster than its competitors and is rated one of the top places to work. When asked, you can tell the interviewer you are impressed with the company's innovative products, its reputation as a great place to work, its leadership in the industry, and you would like to be a part of this growing company. Take a little time to research and learn about the company. It'll be worth your time investment.

- **Know the job details**. Knowing as much about the position as possible will help you prepare for the interview, both in the potential questions you may get as well as the information you want to find out. Before the interview, you should have a copy of the job description describing the main responsibilities, people you will be working with, your role in the overall organization and the job requirements. Usually the job description is listed on the company's website. If you don't have a job description, ask the company representative to email you a copy. Sometimes you can find out useful information by asking the representative for any specific qualities or requirements the hiring manager is especially keen on. Be sure to read the job description carefully to help you anticipate questions about the position and formulate your answers.

- **Know the interviewers**. This is not a must but will help you feel more at ease at the interview. Many companies have a team of people to interview you. These tend to be people you will be working with. Ask for the interview schedule if you did not receive one. It should show each interviewer's name and their title. This reveals their job level status and the function they work in. Today, many professionals are on social media sites, such as LinkedIn, where you can get relevant information on them. Knowing something about the interviewers helps you think about what questions you want to ask them. For example, if a person has been with the company for several years in a few different positions, you can ask this person about the company's support in developing employees and providing different opportunities. At the very least, when you meet with the interviewers face to face, your knowledge about them will put you more at ease and help you establish a rapport with them.

- **Prepare a list of potential questions and your answers**. Different companies may have differences in what they want to find out about you. However, I find that there are some common categories companies want to focus on:

  1. Job skills

  2. Problem-solving skills and creativity

  3. Teamwork – how effective you are working with other people

  4. Communication skills – your ability to listen and understand people's viewpoints as well as express your thoughts clearly and compellingly

  5. Dedication/commitment – your willingness to take the extra step, to go above and beyond to get the job done

Many companies use a behavioural approach when they interview you. Simply put, instead of asking you if you have the ability to do something, such as: "Are you good at presenting?" the interviewer gives you a specific situation and asks you to respond. This type of open-ended question enables the interviewer to glean greater insight about you because it requires you to think on your feet, consider things thoroughly and give well-thought-out answers. For example: "Give me an example of a situation where you had to present to a large group of unhappy customers and how you managed it." Regardless of how the interviewer asks questions, preparing for the interview as a behavioural interview will help you do your best.

I will describe the five categories above in more detail. For each category, think of a few questions and your own answers to them. Also, for each category, think of a couple of specific examples to strengthen your answers and highlight your qualifications. Why examples? Your examples add "meat to the bones" of your answers, personalize you and make you unique. Before we dive deeper into these areas, take an example of two answers to the question: "Are you a good communicator?"

- Answer 1: "I consider myself a good communicator with good verbal and writing skills. I've always been able to express myself clearly and persuasively."

- Answer 2: "I consider myself an excellent communicator with strong verbal and writing skills. For example, during my previous job at XYZ, I led a major product launch where I developed the marketing materials, provided training to sales people and presented to many customers. I received excellent feedback on my communication skills."

The second answer is by far a better one. The first answer is so general anybody can give the same answer. It does not distinguish you from other candidates. Answer 2 demonstrates your ability with a specific example.

Now let's look at the categories in more detail.

1. **Job skills.** This is simply to find out if you have the technical skills to do the job. If you are applying for a position in the accounting department, you must have good accounting and finance knowledge. The job description I mentioned earlier should list specific job responsibilities and tasks you will be doing as well as the job's requirements. This is a fundamental category. If you cannot demonstrate you have the knowledge and technical skills to do the job, you won't get the job offer regardless of how well you do in the other categories. The questions here are specific to your field. If you are a software engineer, you may be asked to write a short program using a specific programming language. If you are a finance

analyst, you may be asked about cost/benefit analysis. If you apply for a job as a marketing analyst, you may be asked about conducting customer surveys or return-on-investment methodology. Make sure to study the job description because it will give you a good idea on how to prepare and brush up on your technical skills.

2. **Problem-solving skills.** Practically any job will involve business problems and require the ability to solve them. Problems may range from customer issues to sales and quality issues. Demonstrating your ability to solve problems will help you stand out among the candidates. While most people can follow instructions, people who take the initiative to solve problems are viewed as high performers and valuable assets to the company.

    The question you get could be a general question such as: "How do you go about solving a problem?" or you could be given a specific problem situation and asked to solve it. For example: "You are working in the customer support department and the customer's level of satisfaction has been declining for the past two quarters. What would you do to improve customer satisfaction?" Many fall into the trap of jumping to solutions. That is a wrong approach. Since you have not worked at the company and don't have much insight, the interviewer doesn't expect you to give specific solutions. Whether it's a generic question or a specific one like this example, the interviewer is looking to understand your approach to problem-solving, your thought process on how you would go about arriving at the answer. A smart approach to solving problem is: (1) understanding the problem; (2) finding out root causes of the problem; (3) brainstorming and identifying possible solutions; (4) weighing the pros/cons and benefits/costs of potential solutions; and (5) deciding the best solution.

    For the "customer satisfaction" example above, this is how I would answer the question: "First, I will go about finding out the root causes of the problem by analyzing customer data, customer feedback reports and by talking to customers and salespeople if possible. Once I identify the root causes, I will engage with the appropriate experts inside and outside the company to brainstorm specific ideas to improve customer satisfaction. Then I would analyze the pros/cons and cost/benefit of these ideas to determine the best one for the company and then make the appropriate recommendation." And if you have time, give an example from your previous experience where you solved a problem successfully. This will strengthen your answer even more.

3. **Teamwork.** This is to find out how effective you are at working with people, or more specifically, how you handle difficult situations working with others. For the vast majority of the time at work, you will be working with other people on certain projects. The ability to work well with people to get things done is highly valued, and companies examine this quality closely in deciding which candidate to hire. Questions on teamwork may be phrased like this: "You are a leader working on a project where one of your team members is not meeting his deadline and putting the team's project at risk. How would you handle this situation with this individual?" With this kind of question, avoid jumping to the answer. When I used this question in interviews, I heard candidates say they would try to get the person off the team or fired. While removing the person from the team may ultimately be the answer, it's more important to try to understand why, and then come up with the appropriate plan. After all, it's difficult to address this situation with the team member if you don't you know why he was not meeting his commitment.

Early in my career I faced a similar situation with Joy, a team member. Fortunately, a more seasoned colleague advised me to go talk to her to find out why. Joy told me she had some recent family medical issues that required her to leave work unexpectedly and early sometimes. As a result, she missed a few team meetings and fell behind on her work. Once I heard this, I offered to help take on some of her tasks and she accepted. She was very appreciative and felt bad she hadn't come to me sooner. She was embarrassed about her situation and didn't want to reveal it.

The moral of the story here is that there could be a number of reasons for this situation and it's prudent to find out before taking action. If asked this question, this is how I would answer: "First of all, I would let him know the team depends on him meeting his commitment in order for the project to stay on track. Then I would tell him I'd like to know why so I could find ways to help. Once I know the reasons, he and I can brainstorm potential solutions. If we reach a dead end, I'll escalate to the manager for help and, at the same time, let him know I'm taking this action to ensure that the project stays on track." My answer shows that I am a team player who goes out of my way to work with people to resolve issues and get things done. At the same time, I understand the team goal and, if I need to, I would escalate to make sure the project stays on schedule. While the team member may not like my escalation, he would respect me for being straight with him. This also enables me to build trust with him for any future project we may work on together.

4. **Communication skills.** This is to probe your ability to listen and express your views clearly and persuasively. Regardless of what the job is, you will likely be working with other people, people from your team, from other functions in the company as well as outside the company. The ability to communicate effectively is critical to your success and that of the company. You will be tested for this skill in the interview. I covered this important skill in detail in the "How to communicate effectively" chapter. Think of a couple of examples from your experience where you used your communication skills successfully to persuade a colleague or manager to go with your view, or where you gave a strong presentation to a new audience. The interviewers will judge your ability in this area by watching to see how you come across and listening to your answers. A lot of this is about your style – do you come across confident, persuasive and engaging? Here are some questions you may get:

   ▷ Your manager gives you an additional project and you feel that your plate is already full. How do you handle this situation and how do you say no?

   ▷ How do you rate your communication skills? Which part of your communication skills needs to be improved the most?

   ▷ Describe a situation where you had to give an important presentation to a new audience and how you handled it.

How to Handle Interviews with Confidence 67

> ▷ The company creates a new exciting project that many people, you included, want to lead. I am in charge of selecting a project manager for this new project. Convince me you are the best person to lead this project.

5. **Dedication/commitment**. We want to know about your work ethics and your commitment to get the job done. Think of a time when you took the extra steps and went above and beyond the call of duty to help out co-workers to ensure the team project was completed successfully and on time. Also think of an example where you identified a need that was not being addressed and took the initiative to work on it. This shows you have the company's best interest in mind and you are a team player willing to do what it takes to help the team succeed. Possible questions you may get include:

> ▷ Give me an example when the project you were working on with other people was at risk of missing an important deadline, and describe what you did to get the project back on track and completed on schedule.

> ▷ Give me an example where you show initiative to take on a task important to the company even though it was outside your job scope.

> ▷ You have a situation where your manager asks you to work the next weekend in order to meet a project deadline but you already had other personal plans. Describe how you would handle it.

- **Prepare a list of questions you want to ask the interviewers.** Think of the interview as a conversation. Although most of the time you will be answering questions, you will have time to ask questions. It's an opportunity to find out information you want to know about the company, about the job, about people you will be working with. This helps you determine whether this is the right company and the right job for you. Since time is limited, be selective about which questions you want to ask. Here are some potential questions:

▷ What would be my specific duties in the first 90 days? (This is a specific question for the hiring manager.)

▷ What are the key success factors in this job?

▷ What are the key challenges in this job?

▷ What are the key characteristics of successful people at this company?

▷ What experience and growth opportunities will I be able to gain from this job?

▷ What do you like about the company and what are the challenges you see for the company in future?

▷ What are the next steps in the hiring process? (This is a specific question for the hiring manager.)

At the Interview

You have done your homework in preparing for the interview. Now you are at the interview with the opportunity to show how qualified you are and why the company should hire you. To accomplish this, you need to know how to conduct yourself. The key word here is "how". A lot of it is about optics – your personality and the way you carry yourself. In all likelihood, the interviewers don't know you and they're meeting you for the first time. Therefore, the impression they form of you will be what they remember. Following these guidelines below will help you perform your best and help you come across as confident, energetic and engaging.

- **Speak clearly**. If you have a soft voice, this is an area you need to pay attention to. If the interviewer has to strain to hear you or have to constantly ask you to repeat, it doesn't make for a good conversation and it brings into question your ability to communicate. Also, when we are nervous, we tend to speak faster than usual. If you need to improve in this area, practise and focus on speaking clearly and loudly enough for the person sitting across the table from you to hear comfortably.

- **Maintain eye contact**. It's a good way to establish rapport and to show you are engaged in the conversation. Imagine what impression you would create if you were looking at your feet while answering questions. You give the impression of being disengaged, timid and not confident.

- **Show energy and enthusiasm**. When I have other people interview my candidates, their initial feedback on the candidate oftentimes is about their energy level – whether the candidate had good energy, showed enthusiasm and was excited to be there. If you maintain eye contact and engage in the conversation, your energy will show. You don't have to jump up and down to show your enthusiasm.

  On one occasion when I was interviewing a candidate, Kelly, for a position on my team over lunch, I asked her when she would like to start. I expected a typical answer of two weeks after offer acceptance. Instead, she answered: "How about after lunch?" I knew Kelly was joking and it made me laugh, but her answer showed her energy and excitement about joining my company.

- **Buy time when you need to**. When you get a question you're not sure how to answer, don't get rattled or feel you have to give an answer immediately. You can buy some time to think about it and come back to answer later in the interview. You can buy time by saying: "That's a good question. Let me give it some thought and get back to you in a little bit if that's okay?" Then while you're answering other questions or talking about other topics, you can think about it in the back of your mind and when ready, re-engage the interviewer on the question.

- **Ask for clarification**. If you get a question you're not quite clear on, don't hesitate to ask for clarification. It's important that you understand the question clearly so you can answer appropriately. The interviewer would be happy to elaborate on the question and this may also give you some clues on what the interviewer is looking for. You can say something like: "I just want to make sure I understand your question, would you mind repeating it for me?" or "I want to make sure I understand, you're asking ABC. Is my understanding correct?" After giving your answer, you can also ask a follow-up question to determine if you were on the right track, such as: "Did I address your question?" or "Is there anything else you would like me to cover?"

- **Turn negative/tough questions to your strengths**. You may get questions such as: "Tell me about your biggest weakness" or "Tell me a major mistake you made." The weakness question is intended to understand if you are objective in your assessment of yourself and what you are doing to address it. Don't answer: "I have no weaknesses." You come across as arrogant and not having self-awareness. The way to answer this question is to give a weakness trait that shows your desire and effort to mitigate it, and at the same time, can be seen as having upsides. One such trait is impatience. If you are a "go-getter" type of person who drives to get things done right and as soon as possible, you tend to have less patience with other people. However, you recognize that other people may work at a different pace and you are consciously working to give them more space and assistance to get their work done. Moreover, impatience also reflects positively on your motivation, dedication and commitment to complete the job. The mistake question is intended to determine what you learned from your mistake and what you have done differently going forward. Think of a work mistake you made that you learned from and worked to rectify.

- **Get contact information**. Thank the interviewers and ask for their email address at the end of interview. This helps in case you have a question you want to ask but didn't have a chance during the interview. You may run out of time before you get a chance to ask your question. This also is a good way to build your network of contacts.

Additional Tips

- Show up five minutes early. Don't be late. Remember what I said earlier about making a good impression. Also bring a copy of your resume and a pen to take notes.

- Dress business professional unless you are told otherwise. If you're not sure, ask your contact if the company has a preferred dress code.

- Turn your phone off or put it on silent mode. You want to eliminate any potential distraction during your interview.

- Take notes as needed. This helps you to ask follow-up questions and may give you additional clues on what the interviewer is looking for from their questions.

- Don't ask about salary, vacation days or benefits during the interview. When you get a job offer, you will know what the offer includes and you will have an opportunity to negotiate the terms of the offer. You have limited time in the interview so ask questions that are most relevant and helpful to you. In addition, you want to avoid giving the impression that you care most about the money and benefits.

- Never talk bad about your current/previous company or your manager, whether they deserve it or not. It may create a suspicion in the interviewer's mind about your professionalism.

- Don't get rattled by the question. Think about the category of the question being asked and refer to your mental list of answers and examples. Also remember that you can always buy time.

- If you have an interviewer who is not disciplined and rambles on instead of interviewing you, don't be confused or think you don't need to say much. If the interviewer finishes the interview without knowing much about your qualifications, it's a lost opportunity. Find opportunities to ask questions that will help you talk about your qualifications. You can accomplish this by asking, for example, about the qualities that will enable you to be successful. By listening to the interviewer's answer, you can then highlight your own qualities with relevant examples. Or you can ask for the challenges they see with this position and prepare to respond appropriately.

- Be aware of posting things on social media sites. Don't post things that may reflect negatively on you. I have seen examples of people not getting a job offer because of comments or things they posted on their social media page. On one occasion, I interviewed a candidate for a management position on my manager's team. She was very qualified and seemed a good fit for the company. As part of the background check, my manager learned of insulting remarks on her Facebook page about a previous manager. This raised a red flag to my manager and made him reconsider his decision.

- Attend the interview alone and don't take anyone with you to the reception area or worse, to the interview room. You may find this suggestion unnecessary and amusing, but it has happened. You want to come across as independent and a self-starter who doesn't need hand-holding.

- Last but most important, practise your interview and role-playing with a friend or someone you're comfortable with. This will give you the confidence when you're at the real interview.

Tips for Phone and Video Interviews

In addition to the discussion above, there are a few specific things to keep in mind when doing your interview over the phone or video call.

- Have the information you want with you to refer to, such as your examples and answers. However, do not read from them. It's easy to notice if someone is reading instead of talking. Have the materials there as references, but talk normally on the phone.

- Your voice is the main instrument to show your energy and engagement level. It's even more important to make sure the interviewer can hear and understand you clearly. So be sure to speak clearly and loudly enough. Don't mumble or whisper. Think of the interview as two-way conversation. Engage the interviewer by asking clarifying questions, asking about the job, and giving examples in your answers.

- If English is not your native language, make sure to speak clearly and don't mumble. If your accent is a bit heavy, you may need to speak slower. Pause from time to time to confirm that the interviewers understand what you said by asking them if they have any questions or want you to explain something in more detail.

- Some companies use a different interview format to screen candidates. For example, instead of interviewing over the phone or video, the interview is conducted online without a live interviewer. You may be videotaped for this session. Through an online website, you are given a series of questions, one at a time, to answer verbally. After reviewing your recorded interview, the company representative or the hiring manager will decide whether to invite you in for an in-person interview. With this interview format, you need to be even more thorough in your preparation since you cannot ask for clarification or buy time to think about the answers. Even though it may seem awkward talking to a computer screen, you need to make sure you stay engaged as if you were talking to a live person. Smile, stay relaxed and keep your eyes on the screen as you answer the questions. If you're looking down or away, the reviewer would see your head instead of your face.

- Video-conferencing interviews are getting more popular. It's time-efficient for the hiring companies. Preparing your appearance and readiness over the computer screen is important. Pay attention to your video camera angle, background and lighting. For multinational and international companies, keep in mind the time difference in your scheduled interview.

As an interviewer, I am particularly impressed with candidates who come in prepared and ready for a meaningful discussion. Asking questions is key in showing your strengths, your interest level and to end the interview session on a high note.

Since there is typically a pool of candidates, we have to pick the best candidates. Aim to be unique and different while being true to yourself so you can stand out. There is no advantage if you are seen as average in the pool of candidates. I often suggest to people I mentor to think about what personal brand and related attributes they want to establish.

Potential Interview Questions

1. You are given a business problem. Our sales this quarter were below target. What steps would you take to increase sales?

2. What accomplishments are you most proud of?

3. What are your biggest strengths? Biggest weaknesses?

4. Tell me about a major mistake you made.

5. How do you resolve a conflict with a co-worker at work?

6. If you're working on a team and the project's going to be late because a member of the team is not meeting his commitment, what would you do?

7. Your manager gives you an additional project and your plate is already full. You can't take on any more responsibility without jeopardizing your work. How would you handle this situation?

8. What did you like and dislike about your last job? And why?

9. What classes did you like/dislike in school? And why?

10. What drives you? What motivates you? How do we help you do your best work?

11. Where do you see yourself three years from now?

12. Describe a difficult challenge you faced and how you handled it.

13. Describe a situation where you had to give an important presentation to a new group of audience and how you handled it.

14. The company has created a new exciting and popular project. I am in charge of selecting a project manager for this new project. Convince me you are the best person to lead this project.

15. Why are you interested in joining this company?

16. If you had a chance for a do-over, what would that be and why?

17. Tell me a time when you were under a lot of pressure to meet a tight deadline and how you handled it.

18. What did you like and dislike about your last manager?

19. Tell me a time you had to multi-task and how you prioritized and handled the tasks.

How to Start on the Right Foot

BEFORE DAY 1

1. Get ready for Day 1
   - Get assigned a buddy
   - Connect early for IT access needs
2. Read up on corporate info, plans
3. Settle living arrangements (if relocating)

STARTING YOUR JOB

4. Create company ecosystem map
5. Meet your buddy and get oriented
6. Get connected to IT system
7. Understand from your manager
8. Get introduced to key work counterparts
   - Understand how to work with them
   - One-on-ones to build rapport
9. Company product/service training
   - Great platform to connect with others in the company too
10. Attend team and company meetings
    - Shadow your manager to observe
    - Great insiders' view
11. Familiarise with work tools/systems
12. Start off with regular hours
    - Staying a little late could help
    - Starting late/leaving early gives bad impression
13. Familiarise with corporate "look and feel"
    - Presentation format
    - Content and style guidelines

CHAPTER 7

How to Start Your Job on the Right Foot

The initial weeks when you start your job provide you a good opportunity to take advantage of the "honeymoon" period to learn the lay of the land, to get up to speed and make a good first impression. Given the pace of work these days, new employees have less time to learn the ropes and are expected to contribute quickly. Employees who prove to be quick learners and contributors will make a great impression, gain credibility and confidence with co-workers and management. You need to have a plan to hit the deck running on the first day and this chapter will show you how. Your company may have some differences from the information presented in this chapter, but the bulk of information from this chapter should be useful to you.

What to Do Before You Start Your First Day

Before your start date, there are a number of tasks you can do to put yourself in a position to be productive from day one on your job.

- Work with your new manager to make sure all your IT equipment and services will be in working order and ready for you to use on the first day. Submit all your IT needs soon after you accept the offer to give the IT department time to order equipment and set up. A few days before you start your job, follow up to make sure things are on track and in case of any issues, you have time to resolve them before your first day. Don't just trust that everything will be there in working order the day you start. Your manager may forget to follow up due to his busy schedule and he would appreciate a reminder from you. Moreover, ask your manager for a buddy – someone with a good reputation at work and is valued by the manager. This person is a valuable resource for you to learn the ropes from. Ask the manager to set up a one-on-one meeting with your buddy on your first day.

- Obtain approval and permission to access company services you need for your job. Your manager can help you with this and get the approvals needed. Double-check with your manager and don't assume it will be taken care of. For example, meetings conducted over video or audio conference are quite common. If you schedule these meetings, you need to have the system access code to use the equipment, or if you will need to access and use company sensitive data, you need to receive permission and the passcode since accessibility is restricted to certain employees. It's frustrating and a waste of time when you start your job and have to wait a few days to be able to access the data.

- Familiarize yourself with company materials. Ask for company materials relevant to your job that you can read before you start. This may be your manager's annual team plan, status reports on current activities or projects, product or project plans, last quarter's CEO presentation, etc. Reading these ahead of time will give you a feel for the current state of the company business and insight about your job. Your manager should be aware of company policy on confidential materials to determine which documents you can have access to.

- Get settled in if you are relocating. When moving to a new town or city, you will need to take care of your living arrangements and other personal tasks. Try completing them before you start your job so you don't have to spend time and energy trying to settle in and do work at the same time. These tasks can consume a lot of time and if you have to take time out of work to finish, that will slow you down at work. When you start, you want to focus your energy and time to get up to speed as quickly as possible.

What to Do When You Start Your Job

Use your first couple of weeks to get a good feel for the lay of the land as it relates to your job. Understand the ecosystem in the company – how things get done, how people work and communicate, important processes, key people you will be working with, decision-makers and influencers, and how decisions are made. In addition, spend time obtaining knowledge and insight on company products and services. Having a good understanding of the company's ecosystem is paramount to your job's success.

Think of this ecosystem as the Global Positioning System (GPS) of a new city you just moved to. This smart system shows you the different routes to get from place A to place B, with all the variables that can affect which route you're going to take, including speed limits, traffic flows and road closures. Moreover, these variables can change at any moment, depending on the time of day, weather conditions and traffic flow changes. The smart GPS helps you determine the best route to take and navigate through these unpredictable obstacles. Without knowledge of your company's ecosystem, it would be similar to driving without a GPS in trying to get to your destination and not having a clue how to get there.

- Create the ecosystem map. With help from your buddy and manager, start putting together an ecosystem map pertinent to you and your job. This is a chart of important people whom you will be working with, key influencers, decision-makers and potential executives who could be your champions. This group includes people in your organization as well as other functions. Make notes of their title, organization, job responsibilities, keys to working with them, and if possible, their reputation in the company. Then get to know them because your success depends on how effectively you work with them and help them be successful in their job. A second key part of the ecosystem is to capture how things are done in the company – decision-making processes, communication methods, operational processes, project management, teamwork dynamics and unwritten rules. Your buddy and manager are great resources for this.

- Meet with your buddy and spend a good amount of time with this person on the first day. Ask them to share with you how things get done, how people work and communicate, key people you will be working with, how decisions are made, and who the influencers, decision-makers and potential advocates are. Use the information to help complete your ecosystem map. Find out the best ways to do things at work, major issues and "elephants in the room" you should be aware of. In addition, get your buddy's thoughts on your manager – the best ways to work with your manager, his hot buttons and his strengths and weaknesses. Also ask your buddy to show you how to access and use the company IT system, and take you on a tour of all the facilities so you can be familiar with the buildings and the people working in them.

- Use your computer and IT systems to go through the login process to make sure the systems are in working order and you have access to the services you need. If you run into any issues, call the helpdesk. You should also get into the company's internal website and familiarize yourself with the company's services, including Human Resources, market research and IT support. In addition, through the company internal website, you can learn about other organizations and their role in the company.

- Meet with your manager. Find out his or her expectations, how best to work together, hot buttons, how your manager wants to be updated, and the key challenges and priorities. Also ask the manager similar questions as what you asked your buddy, especially the important co-workers and managers you need to be on the good side of, as well as people who can be your advocates. If time permits, discuss with your manager about your annual plan. Otherwise, schedule a meeting for this. Typically, every company requires the manager to have a yearly plan for each employee. This plan is critical to your performance review and it includes the objectives, expected results and timelines.

- If you are working remotely and will not have regular face-to-face interactions with your manager, make sure you and your manager work out a way to stay connected and keep you in the loop. The most common feedback I hear is that remote employees feel disconnected from the rest of the company, don't know what's going on and don't receive real-time information. Since you and your manager will not be able to touch base frequently, commit to having regular one-on-one meetings. Moreover, discuss how to keep you in the loop. Some managers are not on the ball when it comes to sharing information, especially sending a message out to their team. It's not top of mind and they tend to share information verbally and often, informally. This doesn't work for you. I would suggest using a portion of your weekly one-on-one meetings for your manager to update you. In addition, find out if your manager uses or would consider using a trusted onsite employee to help disseminate information to the rest of the team, especially remote employees.

- Schedule one-on-one meetings with the key people you will be working with, including the project lead, team members and other managers. Try to meet with them in the first two weeks. Your goal is to get to know them, find out their needs, expectations, priorities, issues and concerns, and how you can best work with them. If possible, meet with them over lunch where they'll have more time to talk with you. Finally, since it's not feasible to meet everyone, send out a greeting email to introduce yourself. If you work with other people in remote locations such as another country, set up a phone meeting where you can introduce yourself.

- If your company offers product and/or service training classes, take them as soon as you can. Other types of classes may also be available, including meeting facilitation, public speaking, project management and time management. This is the time to take advantage of these classes. You get the knowledge you need and gain the confidence to do your job. In addition, attend the company orientation and meetings set up for new employees with company executives. This is an opportunity to hear directly their thoughts and ask them questions.

- Attend team and other company meetings to get a feel for how the company works, key issues, challenges and decision-making process. The people you work with will let you know what meetings you should attend. Ask your buddy and manager for suggestions on meetings that you can tag along to observe even though you're not required to be there. In addition, find out about customer visits and briefing events where customers meet and talk with company representatives about a variety of topics. Contact the company speakers for approval to come and observe. Even if your job doesn't require you to interact with customers directly, this is a good way to learn about company information being shared with customers, their issues and needs, and observe how the company representatives interact with them.

- If there are data mining and analytics programs you need for your job, learn and practise using them during this time. Moreover, if there are external services available to the company from industry service firms, request access to these services if they are relevant to your job. These services include industry reports, research projects and consultation.

- Keep your regular work hours when you start your job, or better yet, stay a little later at work. Since you probably have a lot to learn, it's a good idea to use the extra time to get up to speed. Coming in late or leaving early leaves a bad impression.

- Familiarize yourself with the company "look and feel" guidelines for creating media and other materials. For example, when you create presentation slides for a meeting with company suppliers, you need to use the company's content and style guidelines. It helps you present a consistent company image and saves you the headache of hearing from the company's brand police.

For those who like a head-start, some of the above can be done offline before your first day. From outside resources in the public domain, you can get some understanding of the company's strategy and direction. While it may seem foreign, it will form the foundations for you to connect the dots when you are in the system. That will give you an accelerated head-start, especially if you are amongst a large group of new employees. You need to breakout from the pack as early as you can.

You should not expect to stay only in one department or function for your entire career and expect regular job progression and promotions. In some companies I was involved with, cross-team experience is a promotion criterion and hence, job rotations and career developments are required. So take full advantage of the initial period to understand the breath of the company. Familiarity with the broader company culture helps lay a strong and wide foundation for your career. HR is a great resource for you to reach out to in these areas. Refer to the "How to work with Human Resources" chapter for more details.

From my personal experience, my move into marketing function was one of the best things that happened for my career. Despite the early reluctance, it was like a fish taking to water. I wish I had pursued that change much earlier. So, my advice is to start early in your career to keep an open eye, be curious and to explore interesting, even out-of-the-box opportunities.

PART 2
Communicating

"Half the world is composed of people who have something to say and can't, and the other half who have nothing to say and keep on saying it."
— **Robert Frost**

"If you said it, it's not necessarily an opportunity,
If you didn't say it, it's definitely a lost opportunity."
— **The Answers of AliRen, Alibaba Group**

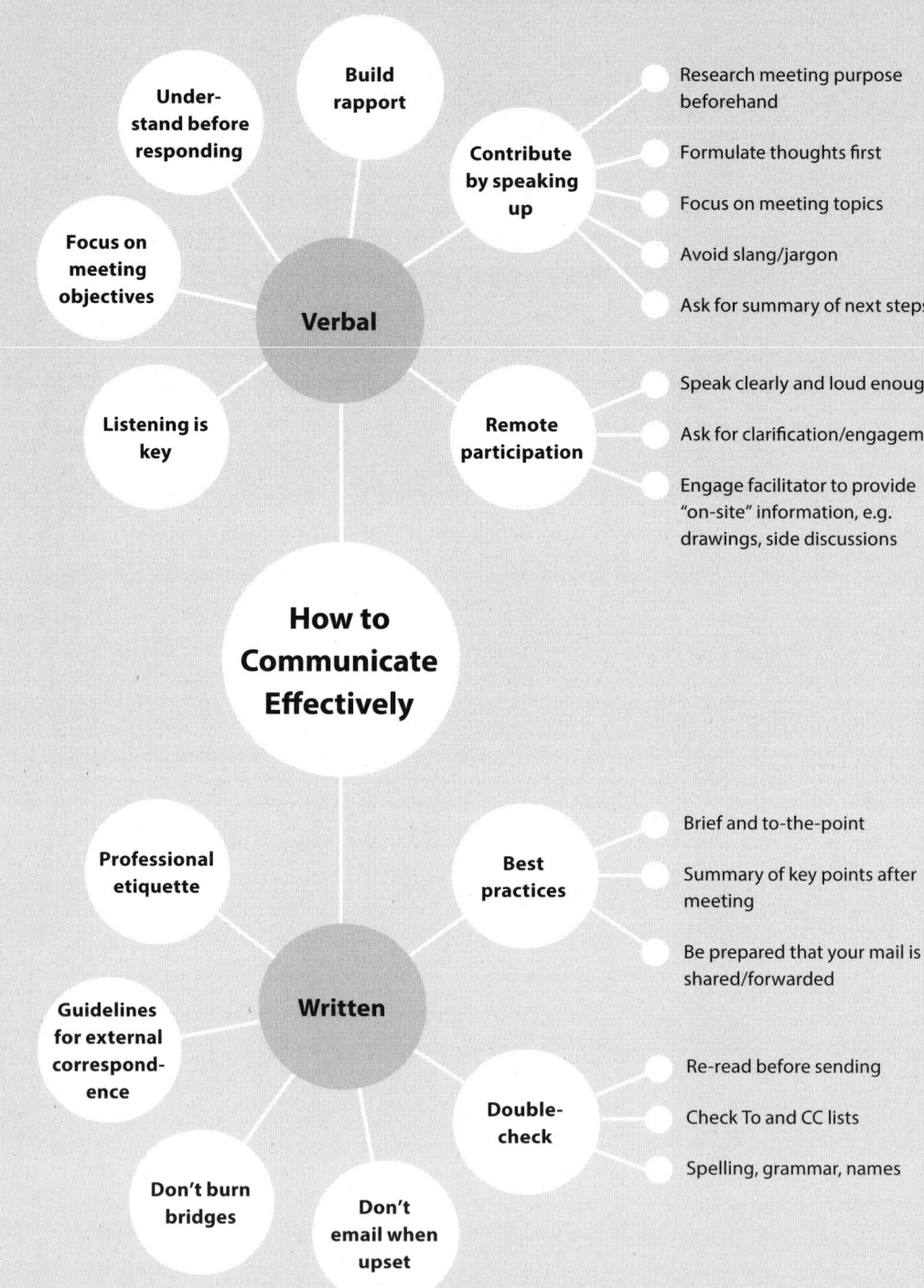

CHAPTER 8

How to Communicate Effectively – Verbal and Written

If I had to pick one skill that separates a star performer from an average employee, it would be communication. Communication is the ability to convey information to other people effectively and efficiently. It is how you articulate your views and opinions clearly and persuasively, either verbally or written. From my experience, it is the number one factor that determines how successful you will be in your job. It is as important to understand as it is to be understood. Far too often in Asia, I notice Asians not being vocal about expressing their thoughts and accepting too easily pushbacks and one-way communication. To go beyond average to outstanding, especially in the context of international benchmarks, you must learn and practise the art of communicating.

Why It Is Important to Be a Good Communicator

When I was a Senior Director at a Fortune 100 company, I had an opportunity to promote one employee on my team. I had two talented candidates who had been delivering excellent results, Robert and Timothy. As part of the process, I solicited input from people who had worked with each of them. Their feedback was consistent that both were dedicated team members who worked hard, met their commitments and delivered excellent results. However, I received very different feedback in the area of communication. For Robert, his peers said he needed to improve his communication skills. Often, he wasn't clear in expressing his points and they had to ask him to repeat or elaborate. Due to this weakness, the team couldn't work very efficiently at times since they had to spend more time clearing up any confusion. In addition, two company executives commented that, when doing a presentation, Robert came across a bit timid and unsure of his recommendations. Timothy, on the other hand, received rave feedback for his communication skills. He expressed his views clearly and persuasively, and asked for and welcomed feedback from other people. Executives commended him for his presentation skills and his ability to get his point across and handle questions. Based on the feedback I received, I decided to recommend Timothy for the promotion. He deserved it and my recommendation was easily approved. If I had recommended Robert, I would have gotten strong pushback from my boss and company executives who favoured Timothy more. I committed to get Robert the necessary resources to help him work on improving his communication skills.

Being a good communicator also enables you to be more productive and efficient. Time is precious and having more time to do your work is a big plus. Moreover, if you are recognized for your communication skills, you will get more opportunities to present to company executives, to represent your company at industry events and customer meetings. Taking advantage of these opportunities is a natural way to promote yourself, gain visibility and enhance your standing in the company.

In today's work environment, both verbal and written communication methods are common. In this chapter, I will cover the best approach and practices for both. While a successful professional must have both strong speaking and writing skills, I would rank verbal communication above written skills. The main reason being that the business world focuses on visible optics – how we look, how we appear, how we carry ourselves, how we speak, how we respond, etc. However, I want to emphasize that mastering both verbal and written communication skills is the best way to achieve success and advance your career. An important criterion of being a good communicator is to have a keen sense of the business culture in the company you work for. This is especially important if you work for a multinational company in the US or a Western country. Make sure you read "How to understand and use business idioms" chapter to familiarize yourself with Western business culture.

Verbal Communication

I believe verbal communication is a more difficult skill to master than written. In speaking, we often have to think on our feet with little time to formulate and articulate our thoughts. Once the words leave our mouths, they are gone and we cannot really take them back. In this section, I'll focus on the skills and techniques to help you gain confidence in speaking up and getting your point across. We'll focus on group settings – team meetings, project meetings, meetings with management, customers and partners. By mastering communication skills in group meetings, you will easily be able to handle other settings, such as one-on-one meetings. Asians tend to be more introverted and are relatively less vocal compared to the West. The education system and social norms in many Asian countries further push students to value teams and not individuals. Particularly if you are interested a career with multinational companies, you need to stand out from the pack to avoid under-selling yourself against international competition.

Verbal Communication Techniques and Best Practices

- Listening is a key part of communication. Excellent communicators I know and have observed over the years are good listeners. Chloe, a friend of mine who is a great listener, told me of a dinner meeting with a client. Through the entire dinner, she spent most of her time listening and maybe ten percent of the time talking. When they said goodbye after the dinner, her client thanked her for an enjoyable evening and commended her for being a great conversationalist, even though for most of the dinner, she just sat back and listened. Most people like to talk about themselves. By listening, we understand their views and that will help us respond more appropriately. In addition, if you are new to a meeting, asking questions and listening to the responses are good ways to build rapport. Oftentimes, we may be listening but not really hearing what the other person is saying.

- Know objectives of the meeting. This helps you ask the right questions and keep everyone in the meeting focused on the right business issue when a discussion goes off track. Sometimes we don't spend enough time making sure the objective is clear with everyone on the team. When problems arise during a project, as they inevitably will, the best way to get the project back on track is to reset and get everyone to focus on the objective the team is trying to achieve.

- Seek to understand before you respond. Use your listening skills here. When you don't understand what someone is saying, ask them to clarify. Something like: "Could you elaborate for me? I just want to make sure I understand your points," or "What I heard you say is XYZ. Is my understanding accurate?" When you want to respond, having a full understanding of their comment will help you respond appropriately. I would be a rich man if I got a dollar for every time I heard someone giving a response to another person, only to have that person say "That's not what I meant."

- Build rapport. Asking for clarification and rephrasing others' comments are also good ways to connect with your co-workers because they show you are interested and engaged in the conversation. This also helps other people feel comfortable engaging with you and giving you feedback on your work. If you're new to the team and are hesitant to ask "dumb" questions, you can preface your question with: "I'm new to this. Sorry if this is redundant, but I was wondering if you could elaborate on that point for me." Also, acknowledge and add to other people's comments. For example: "That's a good point, John. I also would like to add to that…" Again, this shows your interest, engagement and willingness to share feedback and add value to the discussion.

- Contribute by speaking up. Find out the purpose of the meeting beforehand and ask questions relating to the topic. This helps you formulate your thoughts ahead of time so you can contribute to the meeting meaningfully. Having well-thought-out comments gives you the confidence to speak up and helps you gain credibility. One more point – it's important for you to speak up in meetings. If you don't, people tend not to notice your presence. If you don't think you have any valid points to add, ask someone to clarify their points. At least this allows people to see you, hear you and helps you to feel more comfortable speaking up later. Make a habit of speaking in any meeting at least twice, especially when you are in a meeting with your boss or company executives. Since you may not get this kind of opportunity often, it's your chance to be recognized, get visibility and make a good impression with the management team. You may not want to take the risk of looking bad; however, preparing and thinking beforehand on how you want to contribute to the meeting will give you more confidence speaking up in these situations.

    When I taught business leadership classes to college students, I invited one of the country's youngest mayors to speak to my class. Rob was a 28-year-old public official serving a second term. Since he wasn't much older than the students, they could relate to him. When he started his political career, speaking was not natural to him and he had to learn to master his communication skills. One advice he gave to the students was to speak up in meetings in order to be noticed. He said: "You must speak up when you're in a meeting with other people. If you don't, nobody knows who you are."

- Focus your comments on the meeting topic. Avoid making your comments personal. Express your disagreement in a professional manner and base your comments on the topic at hand. By focusing on co-workers' actions and not who they are, they will more likely have productive discussions with you. For example: "I believe your analysis needs more supporting data" as opposed to: "You are clueless." This is a bit extreme but you get my point. Acknowledge their comments before expressing your viewpoints. For example: "I understand and appreciate your perspective, but I see the issue a bit differently. Here's why…" Avoid saying: "That is the most stupid thing I've ever heard."

Don't take people's criticism personally. Ask for examples. Even when someone gets personal with you and makes condescending remarks, resist the temptation to lash back. Put the spotlight back on that person by making them focus on the topic and the facts. For instance, if Debbie says: "Your analysis is horrible," you could reply with: "Debbie, can you give me specific details on the part of my analysis you think is bad." This forces Debbie to be specific. If she was putting you down for her own enjoyment, she looks bad in front of others and probably will not repeat that behaviour next time. You put her on notice that she will not be able to get away with such behaviour. If she gives you the specifics, you can thank her and follow up by asking for suggestions on how to improve your analysis.

If the discussion is getting heated and straying away from the meeting's purpose, propose to take the issue offline and discuss later. For example: "Let's not take more time in this meeting. How about we take it offline and talk afterward?"

- Avoid using slang and jargon when communicating with people from different backgrounds whose native language is not yours because it could be confusing to them and can come across as disrespectful.

- Speak clearly and loudly enough, especially if you have a soft voice. This is particularly important in a phone conference or in a meeting with people from different countries with different native languages. It's helpful to ask follow-up questions to make sure everyone understood your comment, such as: "Any question?", "Is that clear?" or "Anything you would like me to clarify?"

- At the end of the meeting, ask for a summary of the meeting's outcomes and next steps. In addition, if you did not run the meeting, ask the meeting facilitator to send out a summary email to everyone after the meeting. This helps ensure everyone is on the same page, and if there was any confusion or miscommunication, this provides a chance to resolve the issue right away.

- Staying actively engaged in meetings is more challenging if you're working remotely and calling in to a meeting. You're not really able to read people's reactions in the room, and if there are side discussions, you probably can't hear them. Moreover, because you're not physically present, people tend to not notice you. To avoid feeling disconnected from the meeting, make sure you speak up at least a couple of times. Ask people to repeat or clarify their comments to make sure you fully understand. Sometimes people are looking at a picture or a graph specifically related to their discussion and you're lost because you can't see what they're talking about. They don't mean to exclude you. They just aren't cognizant of you because you're not physically there. Don't hesitate to interject and ask them to describe it or email it to you; if you wait, the discussion will pass you by and it's too late to revisit later. Better yet, make a point of asking the meeting facilitator to send you the materials to be discussed prior to the meeting.

The next best alternative to attending the meeting in person is via video-conferencing. When you receive the meeting schedule, ask the facilitator to set up video-conferencing if possible. The meeting will be more productive and easier for you and other people from remote locations to participate.

Self-awareness is important in this increasingly international competitive landscape. In the global talent context, Asians are brought up and trained in very polite environments. Working within international multinational companies with a mix of cultural backgrounds, Asians need to calibrate this politeness. I would suggest to *not* wait:

- For your turn to speak
- For questions to be directed at you
- Others to finish all possible points

Staying quiet will be perceived as a lack of ideas or lack of interest. Both do not look good in building a positive personal brand. I have also noticed that in many countries across Asia, education systems are stressing more life skills such as presentation and communication skills. Since English is typically not the native language, Asians could still be at a disadvantage. However, there are specific strengths Asians could leverage to enhance their presenting and communicating skills, such as:

- Using a graphical approach in communicating. To effectively tell a story or convey an idea, use a drawing to complement your speaking. Pre-drawn graphs projected or freehand on whiteboard helps take away the sole attention and pressure on the speaker and their verbal communication. For example, I once observed that a China team's use of a pre-structured storyline along with the graphs helped ease the delivery of content by having the audience focus their attention on the projected storyboard and not the speaker's language ability.

- Injecting your conviction and passion into your delivery. Preparing your state of mind is a key factor to overcome any potential language barrier. Don't be intimidated by the English language just because it's not your native language. It's a tool for communicating and we don't have to be an English expert to be able to express our views clearly. Your content and ideas are at least as equally important. Practise delivering your content clearly and with conviction is key. I remember when I started up the China marketing team, most of them were not familiar with English as a daily business tool. But two of my team members, Rollin and Stella, were particularly passionate about their business ideas and China market insights. So even with their imperfect English, they were persuasive through their willingness to share their views supported by well-thought-out content and conviction. Today, they are well respected for their business knowledge internationally and they converse fluently in both Mandarin and English.

Written Communication

I believe written communication is easier to master than verbal because we have time to think about what to write, review what we wrote and make changes as we wish before sending out. However, you should not have any doubt about the importance of writing skills. Capturing relevant notes from a meeting is critical to ensure everyone is on the same page. All contracts and agreements are written documents. Even the presentations you deliver include written content. Every strategy plan, product plan or marketing plan is a written document. In addition, people we interact with outside our company or co-workers in other countries may prefer to communicate in writing. In this section, I will discuss useful techniques for written communication.

Written communication includes emails, texts, tweets, memos, slides, marketing materials, social media content, etc. A common method of communication in the workplace today is email, especially when discussing business topics. However, given how busy work is, no one has enough time to read through all the emails and memos they receive daily. When we send out a message, we need to be aware of this and make smart use of the recipient's time.

Best Practices and Techniques for Writing

- Professional etiquette I discussed for verbal communication earlier in this chapter applies here as well. You should focus on the topic at hand and not get personal. Avoid being sarcastic, condescending or insulting to the person you are addressing. Even if you send out a critical message, focus on the action that person did and not on their character. Absolutely avoid calling people names. While it may make you feel better temporarily, it can and often will come back to hurt you.

- If you are writing a message when you're upset, do not send it immediately when finished. Wait until you're calmer. Take a short break and then go back to read your message over to see if you want to make any changes. Chances are you will want to modify your original message before you hit the "Send" button.

- Keep your message brief and to the point. People are busy and have short attention spans; each day they probably have to sort through and read hundreds of email messages, not to mention reports and memos. You need to get their attention quickly, so state the objective and key points of your message up front. If the message addresses a complex topic, explain briefly and let them know you will set up a meeting to discuss. You lose their attention with a lengthy message.

- After an important meeting, summarize the key points, decisions, next steps to send to the meeting attendees and other appropriate people. This will offer them a chance to bring up and clarify any unclear issue right away. The written message serves as proof of the decision or agreement, and to prevent unnecessary revisiting of the decision. This helps everyone to be more efficient with their time.

- Re-read your message to make sure you're satisfied with the content. Without fail, whenever I re-read a message, I inevitably find a way to make it more succinct or discover that I had forgotten to include some key information that would strengthen my message.

- Similarly, double-check for spelling and grammar errors. Having spelling errors or grammatically incorrect sentences is sloppy. If you have spent a lot of effort writing a strong message, don't risk weakening it with some careless errors.

- Double-check the "To" distribution list to make sure the recipients are the people you want to send your message to. I have made the mistake of copying and pasting a list of email addresses I thought I wanted to send to. However, after sending the message, I discovered, to my embarrassment, there were people on the list I didn't want to read the message. This can create an embarrassing situation – or worse, ill will – especially if your message is not a pleasant one.

- Don't burn bridges or insult people in your message. Getting even may bring you short-term satisfaction but usually has long-term consequences, especially with people you need to continue to work with. Even if you take it back, it makes little difference since the damage has already been done. Keep in mind your emails can have a long life. Even if you delete your messages later, copies of your messages are stored and may be shared without your knowledge.

- When writing to external parties, follow the company's policy and guidelines. Every company has procedures, policies and format for written documents to external parties. Make sure you are familiar with and follow them. There could be legal or ethical issues if you don't adhere to the guidelines. If your message has potential legal implications, have legal personnel review your message first.

CHAPTER 9

How to Organize and Develop Presentation Content

How well you create and organize your slides plays an important role in your presentation success. The structure, flow and organization of your content are a reflection of your thought process. If the content flow is difficult to follow and the structure is confusing, you will be hard pressed to keep the audience engaged. In this chapter, I'll discuss strategies to organize your presentation slides and to make them compelling. This can be a difficult task as attention span is limited with the many distractions from mobile phones. As a result, we must present the information with focus, a clear story line and key takeaways.

How to Organize Your Presentation

Since slides are commonly used visual materials in presentations, we'll use slides as the presentation format in this chapter. However, there are other formats, such as video, visual props, or just verbal presentation. Regardless of the format you use, the fundamentals for organizing your presentation are the same.

Develop Presentation Content

Basics
- Know your audience
- Determine your goal
- Be clear on topic
- Organise into 3 parts:
  - Introduction
  - Main body
  - Conclusion

Design compelling presentations
- Right amount of content
- Prioritize important content
- Put supporting data in backup slides
- 1 key message + 5 bulletpoints per slide
- Use animation to reveal bulletpoints one at a time
- Graphics for impact
- Graphs instead of numbers
- Reinforce with summary to close
- Create flow first; craft words later

Common mistakes
- Unreadable or confusing graphics
- Over-animated slides
- Spelling/numerical errors

- **Know your audience**. You absolutely should know whom you will be presenting to – your co-workers/peers, company executives, and other workers from different departments or external parties. This will help you tailor your content as well as your style for the target audience. For example, if you present to customers, the look and feel of your slides must be professional and adhere to company standards, and the presentation content tends to gear toward more selling and persuading.

- **Determine the goal of your presentation**. Knowing the goal of your presentation helps you focus on developing the right content and helps you stay on topic during your presentation. Is your purpose to share information, persuade, educate or seek approval? If your presentation is a proposal to management and your goal is to get their approval, your slides will be about why the proposal is good for company business, what the expected results will be and what you need from the executives. On the other hand, if your purpose is to inform, your slides will simply contain the information you want to share, relevant explanation and data you believe your audience wants to know. If your goal is to persuade a customer to be interested in your company's products, your slides will focus on highlighting the benefits of the products and how they will solve the customer's problems better than the competitors. This customer will be front and centre of your slides and your presentation.

- **Be clear on the topic**. This seems basic, but don't assume the audience has knowledge of the topic before they sit down to hear your presentation. If you present new product technology, make sure this is clear at the beginning of the presentation. This helps you keep the presentation on track. When the audience discusses something else or asks questions not related to the presentation, you can draw them back to your topic. For example: "That's a good question. Since it's about a different topic, I don't want to take time away from today's presentation. But I'll happy to discuss that after the meeting. Would that work for you?"

- **Organize the presentation into three parts: introduction, body, and conclusion.** Remember the presentation adage: "Tell them what you're about to tell them. Then tell them. And when done, tell them what you just told them." This is similar to how you would structure writing an essay. In the introduction, you tell the audience your goal for the meeting, the topic you present, set expectations and give any request or expectation you have for the audience. The body is the meat of your presentation. This is where you provide details, explain, expand and support your points. And the conclusion is your chance to summarize the key points you would like the audience to remember.

How to Make Your Slides Compelling

Your slides should be easy for the audience to follow, yet intriguing enough for them to want to listen to you. These steps will show you how.

- **Plan for the right amount of content**. Plan to fit your presentation content within the amount of time allocated to you. Plan for an average of four minutes per slide to account for audience questions. For example, if the presentation is for one hour, plan to have no more than 15 slides. People tend to have too many slides for the allotted time. What usually happens is the presenter spends a lot of time on the first few slides and either rushes through the rest or cuts the presentation short because they ran out of time. The audience ends up missing a significant portion of the presentation, and the presenter misses a chance to summarize the key messages for the audience to remember. That is not a successful presentation, and it happens more often than not.

- **Prioritize your content**. If you have a lot of content to cover, prioritize the most important content and put the rest in backup slides that people can review on their own after the meeting. Also put most of the supporting data in backup slides. This will help you manage and pace your presentation better. I would start with an executive summary, a single page capturing the key ideas, recommendations or decisions needed. Depending on the flow, it could be positioned as a closing summary. You should not be surprised that in some cases, five minutes could be the only time you have left to cover your content and this page serves that purpose perfectly. Time management is not a best practice in Asia and overrun meetings are common situations you need to be aware of and accommodate.

- **Keep it simple**. Ideally, you should have one key message and no more than five bullet points for each slide. The slide should get the audience's attention and allow you to expand your point. Using examples to illustrate your points is an effective technique. However, some companies, such as consulting firms, use the practice of putting all the details on the slides. Their reason for this practice is to ensure the audience does not misunderstand or forget any information. This practice is ineffective due to the sheer amount of information that saturates a slide. If you have a lot of information to give to the audience, prioritize and put the secondary or supporting information in backup slides, and let the audience know the details are available for them to refer to.

- **Save the wordsmith for later**. When writing the content for your slides, don't spend too much time trying to phrase perfectly. You want to keep your creative juices flowing and put your thoughts on the slides. Afterward, you can read the slides over and decide what to include, delete or put in backup slides. Then you can polish your words to get your points across clearly. Since there is limited space on the slide, be succinct and focus on using only appropriate words to convey your points. Don't write sentences as they take up too much space and may confuse the audience. Bullet points are the most effective.

- **Use animation**. If you have several bullet points on your slide and you want to go over each point at a time, animation is an excellent way to manage this. You can reveal the bullet points one at a time, which gets the audience to focus on the one you're talking about and not get ahead of your presentation.

- **"A picture paints a thousand words."** Displaying graphic icons or pictures on your slides is a powerful way to illustrate your message. Graphics can also help make your slides livelier and more dynamic. Slides that only have words can be dull and look uninteresting. However, use your judgment to balance the use of graphics, because too much can distract the audience from the message you want to convey. The use of font colours, size and format can help highlight and emphasize your key messages. However, excessive use of formatting dilutes your message and even distracts the audience from paying attention to your presentation.

- **Show graphs instead of numbers**. If you have a lot of numbers in your presentation, create graphs instead of showing tables. Tables put too much burden on the audience to read and draw their own conclusions. Trend lines, pie charts or bar graphs make it much easier for the audience to understand your message. For example, having a line graph with a trend line showing increasing sales for the past few quarters is far more preferable to a table full of sales figures. It's better to help the audience see your point than requiring them to try to figure it out and risk having them form the wrong conclusion. Too many numbers also run the risk of audience fatigue or unintended discussions in different directions. Avoid numbers that could counter or complicate your story line. Less is more.

- **Include agenda and takeaways**. The first slide should clearly show the purpose of the meeting and the topics you plan to cover. The last slide should have a summary of the key takeaways and if appropriate, a list of the next steps.

- **Run spelling/grammar checks.** More often than not, I've had spelling or grammar errors when creating slides. Taking a few minutes to double-check will save you from potential embarrassment. The errors may also detract from the quality of your slides and make them look sloppy. Since you have invested a lot of time in making your slides as clean as possible, spending a few extra minutes running a spell and grammar check is easy and worthwhile.

Common Mistakes in Creating Slides

- **Unreadable or confusing graphics.** The audience will spend too much time trying to make sense of your graphics and determine what you are trying to say instead of paying attention to what you are actually saying.

- **Over-animated slides.** Too much animation is distracting. Also avoid using sound effects in a professional meeting environment unless there is a good reason for it. Make a mental note to test your animated slides before you actually present to make sure they work the way you want them to. Avoid dancing or lots of movement animations.

- **Failure to proofread.** As suggested earlier, use spelling/grammar check to correct errors. In addition, make the font size large enough so the audience can read easily, especially for people in the back of the room. Don't try to squeeze in more text on the slides by reducing the font size. If people cannot read your slides, you will lose their attention. Moreover, if you use coloured text or a background, make sure the text is easily readable.

CHAPTER 10

How to Present Persuasively

Presentation skills are an integral component of your overall communication. Regardless of your field of work, you will likely have to present many times in your career. Whether you feel comfortable or not, giving presentations and speaking publicly provide you a great opportunity to shine and get noticed by your co-workers and management. Whenever the opportunity presents itself, take full advantage and make the best of it. Your goal is to make a great impression on these people. The impression you make, or the perception the executives have of you, is based on your presentation performance, good or bad. While this may not seem fair because this could be one of just a few times they see your work, their impression plays an important role in your next performance review and standing in the company.

Moreover, speaking in public is important in a number of activities, including conducting meetings, training sales people, interviewing with the press, meeting with customers, negotiating with company suppliers and representing your company in industry conferences. As a result, being perceived as a good communicator/presenter will open doors to opportunities and serve you well in your career. If you have aspirations to be a high-level executive or run a company someday, keep in mind that most, if not all, executives or people in powerful positions have excellent communication skills, especially public speaking.

Some people are natural speakers. Presenting and public speaking seem to come easy to them while others struggle. From observing many

Present Persuasively

- **Confidence is key**
  - Build on content expertise

- **Begin and end well**
  - Start with focus ideas
  - End with summary

- **Speak loud and clear**

- **Maintain poise and momentum**
  - Hold off questions/interruptions
  - "Parking lots"
  - Respond when ready

- **Engage audience**
  - Maintain eye contact
  - Ask questions to gain participation
  - Acknowledge good questions
  - For remote audiences, check frequently for signs; pause to re-engage

- **Improve readiness and skills**
  - Practice to build confidence
  - Get feedback for improvement
  - Join presentation training

- **Common mistakes**
  - Lack of professionalism
  - Distracting gestures/words
  - Reading slides to audience
  - Misunderstanding purpose of presentation

outstanding speakers, I firmly believe that this skill can be learned and anyone can be a good speaker, regardless of their personality. I cited Mayor Rob in Chapter 8, one of the youngest mayors in the US, who came to speak to my students about his career path and public service. Before Rob became a seasoned politician, he was not great at public speaking. He was a bit shy and tended to be quiet in meetings. Through a lot of work and coaching, he gradually improved his communication skills and became an accomplished speaker. If you see him delivering a speech today, you would think he was a born natural.

Even if you don't think you're a good or natural speaker, embrace the challenge and train yourself to improve. This chapter will show you the techniques and best practices to deliver a great presentation. The goal here is to have confidence in yourself so that when an opportunity arises, you will be excited to volunteer instead of waiting to see if you will be asked to do it while secretly hoping you won't have to. As you continue to improve your public speaking skill, you will feel free to explore future job opportunities without feeling limited by a lack of confidence in your presentation skills.

Regardless of your audience – whether it is co-workers, company executives, internal partners or external parties – there is a set of best practices you can follow to deliver a successful presentation.

How to Conduct Your Presentation

Equipped with a well-organized and compelling content package, now the time comes for you to present. It is natural to have butterflies in your stomach. The key to handling nervousness is confidence. You must believe you are the content expert and you know more about the topic than anyone in the audience. They should not have more knowledge about the topic than you. Otherwise, you wouldn't be presenting. This belief will give you confidence and also motivate you to prepare the content thoroughly and to practise your presentation until you feel fully prepared. Another confidence booster is to develop a passion for the topic. Subject matter expertise combined with passion for the topic would come across as authentic communication instead of a "canned" presentation. If you are prepared, your confidence will enable you to deliver an outstanding presentation. Below are the best practices you can use.

- Start the presentation by telling the audience what you will cover, then proceed to tell them, and then wrap up by telling them what you just told them. Wrapping up allows you to summarize the main ideas you want the audience to remember.

- Maintain eye contact with the audience and engage them. This can be accomplished by asking questions to get the audience to participate. Start the presentation with a lighthearted joke to break the ice or a quiz question about your presentation to have the audience take a stab at the answer. During the presentation, when you finish making a key point or before moving on to the next point, ask: "Is this clear? Do you have any questions?" This offers the audience opportunities to comment. If you have a colleague in the audience, a good technique is to have them ask a question that will allow you to elaborate. Many people don't want to be the first one to ask a question but once somebody does, they tend to follow. Moreover, don't just read from the slide. Use the slide as a guide for you to expand on and give examples. If you spend most of your talk looking at the slides, you disengage from the audience and create an impression that you may not know your material well.

- Speak clearly and loudly enough for everyone to hear. Make it a practice to ask the audience before you start if they can hear you. When speaking publicly, speak louder than normal so people can hear clearly without having to strain. In addition, when we are a little nervous, we tend to speak faster than usual. Be aware of this and slow your pace down a bit. A good technique to maintain your voice and speaking pace is breathing. We sometimes forget to breathe under the excitement or pressure, and that can negatively affect our ability to control our voice.

- Maintain your poise and don't let questions rattle you. If you're not clear on the question, ask the questioner to repeat: "I just want to make sure I understand your question, can you repeat it for me?" If you don't know

How to Present Persuasively 109

the answer to a question, no need to panic. You can say: "I don't have the information off the top of my head. I'll find out after this meeting and get back to you." If you're not ready to give your opinion on a question, buy time by saying: "Good question. I'd like to give it some thought and get back to you." This allows you time to think in the back of your mind while maintaining your composure. When you're ready to answer, you can then get back to that person.

- Remember to acknowledge the audience's good questions or comments. For example, you could say: "That's an excellent question", before proceeding to answer. This connects you to the audience and motivates them to participate.

- Put unrelated issues in the "parking lot". If and when other topics come up during your presentation, resist diving into them, even if your audience wants to, because these issues will distract from the purpose of your meeting and take up valuable time from your presentation. A good technique to handle this without offending your audience is to "park" the issue – capture them on the whiteboard for offline discussion. Your audience is satisfied the issues are noted and will be addressed later, and you are happy to continue with your presentation.

- Wrap up the meeting by summarizing the key points. If there are action items, summarize them with the names of the people responsible for those action items. If the objective of the meeting is to get approval, confirm if you have the approval. If the management team is not ready to make a decision, ask for a timeline you can expect to hear from them or the next step.

- Remember to practise giving the presentation in front of the mirror. Or record yourself on video. Speak as if you're presenting in real time. It may be a bit awkward at first to see yourself, but you can get useful feedback on what you need to improve. You can also practise in front of your friends or family members, who can give you direct feedback. Don't rush into the meeting without rehearsing your presentation. You worked hard to create your slides and develop compelling content, so don't leave it to chance on the most important step – delivering your presentation. Even practising just once is beneficial. Some people prefer framing their presentation as a "story" for practice and having a conversation with their friends instead of actually presenting to them. I find that rehearsing my presentation as if it were real works better for me. Use whatever technique works best for you and remember: you are the expert. Be confident.

- Get feedback on your presentation performance from your manager or co-workers who are good presenters and were present at the meeting. Consult with people who will give you objective feedback. Ask what they liked and didn't like about the presentation, what else they would have liked to see and where you can improve.

- If your company offers presentation classes where you can be recorded on video, take advantage of the opportunity. Given your busy schedule, it can be inconvenient to take time out from work, but make this a priority and it will provide a long-lasting benefit to you.

- If you are presenting to a remote audience over the phone, there are a couple of additional points to remember. If you cannot see the audience's reaction, you have to use your verbal skills to gauge the audience's response and feedback. You need to pause more during your presentation to check for their understanding and solicit questions to avoid misunderstandings. If your manager is in the audience, ask your manager to be your eyes and to help getting the audience to engage. Moreover, the manager can help reset the meeting and pull people back to the topic of the presentation if they get off on a tangent. Before wrapping up the meeting, confirm the key takeaways, next steps and address any disconnects that may arise. If there are open issues, make sure you assign owners for these action items and deadlines to resolve.

- Prepare and have a response plan for some common disruptions:

  ▷ Presentation time suddenly cut short due to schedule changes. Very common with customers or company executives. See the next chapter, "How to communicate and present to specific audiences".

▷ Before your meeting starts, emotions can spill over from the previous session. Be alert to this and if you sense it, wait for everyone to calm down and reset before you begin.

▷ Leading questions from the audience that aim to get you off track or off balance. Park the questions and pull them back to your main topic.

Common Presentation Mistakes

- Lack of professionalism. Failure to dress professionally or appropriately. If you are presenting to customers, don't come in jeans and t-shirt unless that is what the customers are comfortable with. When in doubt, dress businesslike to show respect. This goes without saying, but you must avoid exhibiting unprofessional demeanour such as appearing intoxicated, making off-colour jokes, being sarcastic or condescending to the audience. These are not only unacceptable but can get you in serious trouble.

- Distracting gestures or movements. Gesturing during a presentation is a good thing, but dancing, or repetitive, distracting gestures and movements detract from your message. Again, recognizing your audience and remembering the purpose of your presentation will help you act appropriately.

- Distracting filler words such as "and", "um", "ah" and "basically". Everyone uses these sometimes and it is fine to use them from time to time, but try to limit the frequency. When it's repetitive, it becomes a distraction.

- Reading to your audience. If you put everything you have to say on your slides and just read to your audience, you might as well just email them the slides and they can read them on their own time. Moreover, try not to use notes or note cards because they encourage reading and discourage eye contact with your audience.

- Misunderstanding of the purpose of your presentation between you and the decision-makers. Make sure everyone is on the same page on the topic and objective of the meeting before you deliver your presentation. This happens more frequently than you think. To prevent this, send an email confirming the purpose of your meeting to the audience prior to your presentation date so any confusion of the meeting objective can be cleared up immediately.

CHAPTER 11

How to Communicate and Present to Specific Audiences

Before proceeding with this chapter, read the chapters on "How to organize and develop presentation content" and "How to present persuasively" first if you have not, since that content complements the material here. While the techniques described in those chapters are relevant to all audiences, specific audiences also have their own unique characteristics, which you should be aware of and tailor your presentation to. This chapter covers various audiences you may encounter, their differences and how best to address them.

Communicating and Presenting to Executives

I have had many opportunities to present to company executives as well as observing first-hand how they conduct themselves in meetings. I also have heard well-known Chief Executive Officers (CEOs) of multinational companies talk about their expectations when attending presentations. Here's a summary of what I learned.

- **Limited available time**. Company executives normally have a tight schedule. Usually you have a short amount of time (30–60 minutes) to meet with them, depending on the topic and objective of the meeting. They are unlikely to extend your meeting time because they typically have other meetings scheduled already. As a result, you must prepare your content to be able to finish your meeting within the allotted time while also achieving your meeting goal, especially if it's a meeting where you need a decision from them.

- **Possible interruptions and meeting time reduced**. It's not unusual for your meeting to be shortened due to the executive team getting interrupted by other matters or if they decided to extend the meeting prior to yours. This can be a real-time decision you need to make just before your meeting begins or worse, during your meeting. Therefore, you need to be prepared to handle these unexpected situations and still be able to accomplish your goal.

- **Impatience**. Patience is not their strong suit, given the demands on their time and attention. They don't tolerate unclear meetings where they don't know the meeting's purpose or what is expected of them. They tend to lose their patience if the meeting gets sidetracked or if they're not getting answers to their questions. The irony is that sometimes the executives can get the meeting off track by their own discussion with each other. While they like to see a well run, disciplined meeting from you, they sometimes are not disciplined and need to be guided back to the topic at hand. You need to be aware of this and prepared accordingly.

Here are the keys to preparing your content and conducting presentations.

- **Organize your content to be able to adapt on the fly**. Since you likely will have more material to cover than the time allowed, prioritize the content that the executives care most about. Also, allocate time for questions and discussions from the executives. Keep in mind the rule of thumb of having one slide for every four minutes of meeting time. If it's a 60-minute meeting, have no more than 15 slides. Put other more detailed slides in backup in case you need to refer to them. In addition, organize your presentation slides into modules so if you need to, you can prioritize

How to Communicate and Present to Specific Audiences

Executives
Impatient
May cut meetings short

→ Organize content to be adaptable on the fly
→ Keep content succinct, clear and at executive level
→ Be clear on meeting's objective
→ Confirm amount of time available
→ Balance between executive discussion and meeting goals
→ Get a champion ready to support

Customers
Like to be heard
Big investment of time

→ Be clear on meeting's objective
→ Know who you are meeting with
→ Balance between company advocate and being honest
→ Be careful with confidential information
→ Be careful about making commitments
→ Maintain professionalism with upset customers

Third parties
Similar to customers

→ Contract agreement and negotiation
→ Read Chapter 19 on being a good negotiator
→ Legal review of contract

International audiences
Differences in language, business culture, etc

→ Be aware and sensitive of differences
→ Speak at the audience's pace
→ Work with a translator
→ Avoid jargon, slang, acronyms
→ Make use of visual aids
→ One-on-one follow-on meetings

and use the most important modules first and leave other details for the executives to review later at their convenience.

- **Keep your content succinct, clear and at the right level.** How well you do this determines how likely you and the executive team can stay on track and finish the meeting as you hope. Adhering to having one slide for every four minutes will help you accomplish your meeting goal. However, this doesn't mean you should cram as much detail as possible into every slide. We have a desire to show how extensive our work is and are afraid we may leave out something important that executives care about. Avoid the urge to do this.

    You should have one key message for each slide you want your executives to remember. Many executives are data-driven and the more data you show, the more likely they will drill down and not able to see the forest from the trees. If this happens, your meeting is at risk of getting derailed. Moreover, you don't want your analysis to be questioned since it is your job to make sure it's thorough and to deliver the key conclusions you want the executive to keep in mind. If they question your analysis, it brings your credibility into question and will cloud your overall meeting goal.

    There is one story in particular I would like to share with you that still brings a smile to my face whenever I think about it. As a manager leading a team of marketing professionals in my company's server business unit, I normally reviewed my team's presentations before they presented to the management team. Before one important business review meeting with our General Manager and Marketing Vice-President, I reviewed the presentation slides from my employee, Elaine. Elaine had done an extensive and thorough analysis, but put a great deal of detail on already crowded slides. I suggested to Elaine to "dumb it down" and simplify her slides so the executives could understand. Well, during her presentation, our GM, a brilliant executive who had a tendency to drill down on numbers, started asking detailed questions and getting into a rat hole with Elaine. After getting a few questions too many, she stopped her presentation and said to him: "Well, I had all the details on the original slides to show you, but my manager told me to keep it really simple because otherwise you won't get it." I felt like hiding under the desk. Fortunately, I had a good enough relationship with the GM and he laughed it off because he recognized his data-driven tendencies. He understood that we wanted to highlight the key points for him and the Marketing VP to make decisions instead of using their valuable time to talk about the numbers.

- **Be clear on your meeting's objective.** When you start your meeting, this is the first thing you should cover. You need to state clearly the purpose of the meeting and more importantly, what you want from them. Do you need them to make decisions on your proposal? Do you need them to provide their input and guidance on your project? Or are you there to only give them updates and share information? This will prepare their mindset for the meeting since they probably have not seen your presentation materials.

- **Confirm the amount of time you have.** Confirm this at the beginning of the meeting even if you had been told earlier how much time you have. If you learn you have less time now, adjust in real time to make sure your meeting agenda fits into the time constraint. And even if you have confirmed the time at the start of meeting, your time could still be cut short by unexpected events. However, if you had organized your content as we discussed above, you are prepared to handle these unexpected interruptions.

- **Balance between executive discussions and achieving your meeting goals.** In your meeting, the executive team may become animated and get into lengthy discussions with each other. While it's important for them to talk and think through the information to help them make decisions, you need to determine whether the discussion focuses on the meeting topic or on another unrelated topic. I have seen numerous meetings where the discussion evolved from the original topic to something completely different. Also keep in mind some executives may not be disciplined about staying on topic. Moreover, be aware of the politics at play because some of the executives may be trying to score points with the CEO.

If you see the discussion getting off track, look for an appropriate time to interject and remind the executive team to get back on topic. A good time could be when an executive finishes their thoughts. You can be polite but firm by saying: "Sorry to interrupt, but we only have 20 minutes left in this meeting and we have quite a bit of material to cover. Can I continue?" Or if they seem to be in the middle of some serious discussion, you can suggest: "Sorry to interrupt, but we only have 20 minutes left in this meeting and we have quite a bit of material to cover with you and I would like to continue, or would you like me to schedule another time?" Chances are they will ask you to continue. You may need to do this a couple of times throughout your presentation to keep the meeting on track. This is also a good way to show your leadership ability.

- **Have a champion to support you**. This can be your manager who is high enough on the management chain relative to the executives, or this can be one of the executives you and/or your manager have a good relationship with. With this executive, try to have a little bit of time beforehand to give her an update, your recommendation and most important, to ask for her support. She can play a pivotal role in providing you support and "air cover" during the meeting. Because of her status and credibility, she can help placate other executives who may have concerns about your recommendation. If you have an important decision-making meeting, try your best to meet with the key stakeholders prior to meeting to get their buy-in or at least to understand what issues they may have. This will help your meeting go smoother and minimize surprises.

There will be times when you're attending a meeting but not presenting, and in these cases, you don't need to be as prepared as the presenter. However, since it's not often you get a chance to be in a meeting with key executives, you should view the meeting as an opportunity for you to participate intelligently, contribute to the discussion and gain visibility. In order to do this, yes, you need to spend a little time to prepare.

- Know the purpose of the meeting. This provides you some ideas for your participation. If the meeting is to make a decision, you can play a role in making sure there is closure – a decision is made or clear next steps are understood. In certain meetings, especially difficult ones, people are reluctant to make decisions and the presenter or meeting facilitator is hesitant to push the executives for an answer. If you see this situation, you can speak up to remind everyone of the objective of the meeting and the importance of reaching closure. People will respect you for your assertiveness. No one wants to come out of a meeting confused or unclear about the outcomes or next steps.

- Know your role in the meeting. If you are responsible for the content of a particular agenda item, prepare to provide insights even if you're not presenting, or to answer potential questions from the executives. If you don't have the agenda, ask the presenter/meeting facilitator so you can anticipate potential areas where you can speak up and add value to the meeting.

- Be ready to provide support to the presenter or other team members. This is a natural way to gain credibility and visibility at the same time. Presenting under the spotlight can be stressful and rattle anyone, especially when facing tough questions. This is where you can help. If the presenter seems unsure about the answer or doesn't seem to have the information to a question and you do, you should volunteer and give your answer. The presenter will appreciate your help and the executives will be impressed with your knowledge and teamwork. You do need to keep in mind the balance between stepping in to help out and showing up the presenter. If you repeatedly chime in, you come across as overbearing, especially since you're not the focus of the meeting.

- Asking questions to get the presenter to elaborate on certain points is another way to provide support. Oftentimes in the heat of presenting, the presenter or meeting leader may forget to elaborate on certain important points. By asking them to elaborate, you help them slow down and stress the key points. Something as simple as saying "To the point you just mentioned, can you elaborate and provide more detail?" would serve as a trigger for the presenter to expand their point. Throughout my career I have used this technique many times with my peers and my team members and they very much appreciated my gesture. Many of them have asked me to play this role for them when they had important presentations.

- Speak up once or twice even if you have no visible role in the meeting. Obviously you should make comments relevant to the meeting. Many times we don't speak up because we're afraid to ask stupid questions or say something silly. However, asking for clarification is a good and safe technique to use. For example, if an executive makes a comment that's unclear to you, you should ask the executive to elaborate. For example, "Can you elaborate on that point a little more? I just want to make sure I understand" is a perfectly acceptable response. Some people in the meeting are likely to have the same question but were afraid to ask and would appreciate that you did.

Communicating and Presenting to Customers

If you have a chance to meet and interact with customers, take advantage of the opportunity. You can gain great insight about the customer's business and their challenges. You can read reports about customers but nothing hits home quite like meeting them in person and talking to them directly.

- **Customers like to be heard**. Customers frequently have business challenges they need to address in order to improve their company's performance. When they meet you, they like to talk to you about their challenges and look to you as a source of information that potentially can help them. Moreover, if customers have some issues with your company's service and products, they will definitely want to let you know.

- **Big investment of time**. Whether they come to visit at your company's site or vice-versa, it's a significant investment of their time and resources, and as result, they have specific objectives and expectations in meeting you. You probably also have specific needs you want to get from them. Therefore, it's important to understand their objectives and balance those with yours to make sure both parties get what each wants from the meeting.

- **You are your company.** When you meet the customer, they see you as representing your company. They don't see you as an engineer in the engineering department or customer support representative or product manager. They don't look at you as only having specific responsibilities for your job. When I visited and presented to customers, they didn't see me as a Product Management Director responsible for hardware products. They saw me as my company's representative and would feel free to discuss anything relating to their business with my company. When you meet them and if they have a request or demand, they will ask you and expect you to follow through.

Here are the keys to preparing your content and conducting presentations:

- **Be clear about the objective of your meeting with the customer.** As with meeting with executives, find out the customer's objectives for the meeting, their issues, topics they want to discuss, etc. The customer Sales Representative (SR) or Account Manager (AM) is a great resource to find out. Most SRs or AMs will contact you to let you know ahead of time about the meeting details. They have a vested interest in keeping their customer happy and making sure they get what they come for.

    If you don't hear from the sales team, get in touch with them prior to the meeting to get all the information you need so you can properly prepare. As importantly, when you meet with the customer, confirm the agenda and topics with them. Ask questions to find out what is top of mind, what issues they are facing, what they want to discuss and what their expectations are. Between the time of your meeting with the sales team and your meeting with the customer, they could have met with other competitors and learned new information they want to discuss with you.

- **Know whom you are meeting with.** Different companies may have different representatives meeting you, including technical people (IT managers, system administrators, CIO) and business people (purchasing managers, business line managers, CEO). Knowing whom you will meet and what they have in mind helps you determine if you need to invite other experts from your company to cover topics that you don't have the expertise on. In the course of briefing with the sales team, you can also learn if there is someone from the customer company who is a champion for your company – someone you can count on to support you in the meeting.

- **Balance between being the company advocate and projecting honesty.** While customers understand you are there to advocate and promote your company, they do not expect you to be just a talking mouthpiece for your company. You will earn respect and credibility if you are objective about the strengths and weaknesses of your company's products or services while promoting your company at the same time. They don't expect your company's products or services to be perfect but they do want to know about any product issues and how your company is addressing them. In particular, if they hear from one of your competitors pointing out the weaknesses of your product or services, they would definitely want to validate the credibility of the competitor's claims.

    A common place where customers want objectivity is in comparing your company versus your competitors. Customers realize every company wants to differentiate themselves from others, but what they look for is whether the comparisons are credible and can be validated. As a result, you will earn the customer's trust and gain credibility by balancing between being an advocate for your company and being objective in your assessment of potential solutions to solve their problems. However, before you give your opinion, make sure you listen and ask a lot of questions so you have a clear understanding of what they heard as well as their own perception. I have seen instances where my company's presenter turned the customer off and lost their interest by being in complete selling mode regardless of what the customer was saying.

- **Be cautious with confidential information.** Customers are interested to hear about your company's future strategy and product roadmap so they can plan accordingly. Since much of your company's future plan is confidential, exercise caution. Customers typically sign a non-disclosure agreement (NDA). However, even with an NDA, proceed with caution. If the customer is a loyal customer and has a good track record with your company, it may be fine to share confidential information with the confidence they would not divulge it to your competitors. My rule of thumb, especially with customers I'm not sure about, is to assume that whatever information I share, confidential or not, will get into the hands of my competitors.

- **Be careful about making commitments**. Oftentimes customers will take advantage of the opportunity to ask for certain commitments – for example, commitment for a date to fix a problem, to deliver a replacement product, to provide a new software upgrade, to provide longer support to discontinued products, or to give special pricing. Unless it is within your power and you are sure it's the right thing to do and you can deliver on your promise, do not commit. Although you may feel a lot of pressure to agree to the request, especially if you have an unhappy customer, resist the urge. It's worse if you cannot deliver and, trust me, the customer will hold you to it. Instead, commit that you will take the request back to the company to have the right person work on the request and get back to them. You must follow through on this commitment.

- **Maintain your professionalism when facing an upset customer**. Sometimes you may get blindsided by an unhappy customer with issues you were not aware of. On one of my customer visits, I wanted to discuss with the customer about our future printer technology. Prior to the meeting, I had a briefing with the account Sales Representative and no issues or concerns came up. When a co-worker and I arrived at the customer site to meet them in a conference room, they proceeded to lay into us about the problems they had and their dissatisfaction with our company. We sensed their frustration and anger as the volume of their voices got louder. We were caught completely by surprise and worse, the SR was nowhere to be found and he never warned us about the customer issues.

We were clueless because their issues were related to the computer business unit and not our printer business unit. However, we realized that we represented our company, not just the business unit we worked in. There was only one thing we could do. We sat down and listened patiently. We did not even attempt to mention the reason for our visit. We asked questions to make sure we captured their problem accurately. When they finished venting and giving us a list of things they wanted answers on, my colleague calmly thanked them for their feedback. Then he explained that we were not aware of the issues beforehand, and although we were not directly involved in these issues, we would make sure that the appropriate people would get back to them. We committed to them that we would personally let them know who their contact would be.

After the customers calmed down, I asked them if I could take a little bit of their time to show them a new printer technology and get their feedback to help us design the right product. They agreed, listened attentively and actively gave us feedback. They ended up talking with us for another hour. The moral of the story here is that when we meet customers, we are our company's spokespersons, we listen to their needs and concerns, and we take ownership to follow through with them.

Communicating and Presenting to Third Parties

Third parties include suppliers who provide your company with materials to produce your products, contractors who perform services for you such as programming or creating marketing plans, partners who team up with your company to provide solutions, or distribution partners who market and sell your company's products.

- While this relationship is different than that between your company and customers, the discussion points on customers are applicable here as well – confidentiality, understanding the other side's perspective, the need to listen, etc.

- One area I want to emphasize is regarding contract agreement and negotiation. Usually it takes many meetings to negotiate an agreement on how the two companies will work together and what to commit to. Refer to the "How to be a good negotiator" chapter for details. Don't rush or get pushed into an agreement. Take your time to understand the other party's issues and needs as well as explore all possible options in order to arrive at a win-win agreement. Moreover, don't commit to an agreement unless you have full authority on the final contract and you're confident about the terms and conditions. Review the terms with your manager and other experts in the company to ensure you have covered all the bases. Finally, have the legal department review the contract. This review process can be lengthy but it's better to take this step to avoid any legal issues or liability in the future.

Communicating and Presenting to International Audiences

This applies to company employees and customers, as well as partners in other countries who have different native languages, customs and business cultures. The points we've discussed in this chapter apply to these audiences too. In addition, I'll focus on the unique characteristics of these audiences and how to present to them.

- **Be aware and sensitive to their differences**. These include differences in language, business culture and customs. The more you understand the unique differences and how to work effectively with them, the more successful you will be. For example, if English is not your native language, you have an accent and you are presenting to a group of American people, remember to speak louder than your normal speaking voice and speak slower to make sure that they can understand what you're saying clearly. Culturally, people in other countries may not be as direct as Americans. For example, Japanese customers are polite and tend to listen and not ask a lot of questions in public. Moreover, they're not comfortable saying no, even if they cannot commit to your request. Silence does not mean yes. It's prudent to confirm in writing all agreements before proceeding.

- **Speaking at a pace that works for your audience**. As suggested above, speak a little bit slower and louder to make sure your audience can follow you. This is true especially if you are a fast speaker or have a soft voice. After every key point, pause and ask for understanding and anything the audience wants you to repeat or elaborate. This will ensure that the audience understands what you say. Don't assume the audience understands. Americans are more straightforward and will ask you to explain or repeat if they don't understand, but Asian people are subtler and don't want to interrupt you. So remember to double-check.

- **Learn to work with a translator**. In your speaking engagements, you may have a translator to interpret for the audience. This can be a bit awkward since it doesn't promote a smooth presentation. However, you should plan your presentation to accommodate the translator if there will be one. Meet with the translator prior to your talk to brief her on your topic and give her a quick overview of your presentation. Also work with her on how to coordinate the presentation, including where you should pause for the translation. Some translators prefer short sentences or one message at time while others can handle multiple points at a time. Syncing up and coordinating with the translator will make your presentation delivery more seamless to the audience.

- **Ask for clarification/explanation if you hear jargon, slang or acronyms that you don't recognize**. This can happen while you're presenting to an international audience (from the US, for example). People may be so used to the way they speak normally at work with their colleagues and even though they are aware that you are from a different country, they may talk to you or ask you questions in the same way they speak to their colleagues. So they speak American English business jargon or use acronyms that you're not familiar with. The way to handle this is to not get flustered or look intimidated, but to politely and clearly let them know that you don't understand and ask then to explain. For example, a common English phrase we use in the US is "I'm between a rock and a hard place", which means that I'm in a tough situation where neither of my choices or decisions is ideal and both have undesirable impacts. Don't be shy – ask for explanation. Refer to the "How to understand and use business idioms" chapter for more details.

- **Use of graphics or visual aids**. This is a good way to make your presentation easier to understand and get your point across. For example, when my team presented to a Chinese audience about our new computer, we would have the actual computer in the room. We opened the computer casing to show the key sections and components inside. The team used the computer as a visual aid to demonstrate their key points and it was also an effective technique to get the audience engaged. While your customers may not feel comfortable asking questions in the room, they can inspect the product first-hand and get many of their questions answered.

- **Offer one-on-one meetings after the presentation.** Because the audience may not feel comfortable asking questions publicly, they may welcome a chance to speak to you one-on-one. This is very common in Asia and almost a must have. If possible, time and space should be set aside for these follow-on interactions. Remember to allocate time after your presentation and invite them to talk with you and discuss any questions they may have.

Communicating and Presenting to a Large Audience

With a larger audience size, presentations must have an even more focused and clear story line. As a volunteer for the Red Cross training academy, I often present and teach humanitarian subjects. To connect with the audience and highlight the relevance of the context, I have often used the Korean drama, "Descendants of the Sun". In all cases, it immediately connected with the audience as the majority of Asians can relate to the story lines and characters. In addition, during the presentation, scan the audience for supporters that you can call on to share their insights. It serves as reinforcement of ideas for the audience.

Communicating and Presenting Spontaneously

With more and more companies having a flat organization structure, employees are more likely to engage top management in hallway conversations or water-cooler chats. Such situations could take the place of some formal meetings. With so much information overloading the executives, it's essential to have the ability to engage in productive and brief conversations (3–5 minutes). While this activity may not be natural to all of us, I would recommend that you practise conversing in this kind of situation as it is increasingly an important skillset professionally as well as socially.

Three characteristics of such spontaneous situations:

- Listen and recognize the broader conversation setting so you can align your topic to it. Whether it's a business meeting or trade conference, you should seize the opportunity and prepare potential topical content for exchanging ideas thoughtfully and engaging in relevant dialogues.

- Be flexible to the meeting format. The key objective is to convey your main theme, ideas, and passion to the target audience in a succinct way.

- Be able to summarize. To convey a lot of information in a few minutes, being able to summarize is a key skill to practise. Structure the dialogue by summarizing the top ideas, then the follow-on actions for impact and benefits, as well as briefly covering important background information.

CHAPTER 12

How to Run and Facilitate Meetings

One of the most precious commodities we have is time. We value time. We usually feel we don't have enough time to get things done. This is especially true at work. We are rushing against deadlines and wishing we had more time to do a more thorough job. One of the most time-consuming activities at work is attending meetings. There are many types of meeting: company meetings, staff meetings, project team meetings, one-on-one meetings with your manager or co-workers, meetings with customers and external parties, meetings to address unexpected crises or urgent issues, impromptu meetings, etc.

The majority of meetings are run inefficiently. They take longer than needed, and oftentimes, little gets accomplished, or worse yet, confusion arises and as a result, another meeting has to be called to revisit the issue. This wastes time and frustrates people who could have used the time more productively. One main reason for inefficiently run meetings is the lack of know-how from the meeting facilitator.

You will have opportunities to run meetings in your career. Knowing how to do so effectively will save you and your co-workers valuable time and foster a positive working environment. In this chapter, I will cover the best ways to run an effective meeting and achieve the meeting's goals.

Successful Meetings

Pre-meeting: Structure it right

- Clear objective
- Only invite those who matter
- Agenda planning
- Reasonable time slots

Managing the meeting

- Start on time
- Reiterate meeting objective
- Drive closure on topics
- Time management – start/end each agenda item on time
- Manage the flow, encourage participation
- Don't be sidetracked by irrelevant discussions
- End meeting on time
- Summarise outcomes
- Document key agreements
- Create follow-up actions

Post-meeting: Follow up tight

- Follow-up meetings
- Progress to next checkpoint meeting
- Continuation to close unfinished topics
- Offline meetings for spin-off discussions
- Track action item completions

How to Prepare for the Meeting

- **Understand the meeting's goal clearly.** Is it an informational meeting where people share knowledge, a meeting to review project status and progress, a meeting to discuss and solve a problem, or a meeting to reach a decision? This helps you determine the right people to attend the meeting, set the agenda, determine the length of the meeting and ensure people are prepared.

- **Determine the meeting's attendees.** For the meeting to be effective and productive, only people who are needed should attend. Very often, a meeting has too many people, including some who don't add any value. If these people like to talk, they can dominate the meeting and run the risk of ending it without accomplishing what you wanted. When you put the list of attendees together, ask yourself what each of their roles are, what value they add, and what the impact would be without their participation. This is especially important for working meetings where the team needs to make decisions, solve a problem or review project progress. When you schedule a meeting and send out the agenda, include a note to let meeting participants know to check with you if they would like to invite anyone else. You are the meeting facilitator and you have the final say on the attendees.

- **Have a clear agenda.** When you schedule the meeting and send out the invites, include a short but clear message stating:

    ▷ Purpose of the meeting. For example: "Purpose of meeting is to finalize the project proposal to be sent to CEO Executive staff for approval" or "Purpose of the meeting is to finalize the XYZ project schedule."

    ▷ Agenda items. List out the items you plan to cover with the team during the meeting. List the name of each person responsible for covering a specific item. Allocate the amount of time for each item so the item's owner knows how to prepare. For example, if the meeting is to finalize the project schedule, your agenda could be as follows:

- Product requirements – John S (15 minutes)
- Design requirements – Betty J (15 minutes)
- Quality plan – Manish T (15 minutes)
- Manufacturing plan – Tom R (15 minutes)

▷ Ask anyone who has suggestions on the agenda to contact you before the meeting. Also ask the item owners to let you know if they will not be ready so you can revise the agenda accordingly.

▷ Include the meeting location in your invite if possible. If you have people who will be attending on the phone or via video-conferencing, make sure the meeting room has the IT equipment you need. Many meetings start late due to people scrambling to find out where the meeting is or missing the IT equipment needed for the meeting.

How to Manage the Meeting

- Start on time. It is common to be late to events or meetings. However, in conducting business, especially with American colleagues, customers or partners and others in the Western world, punctuality is not only important, but is a judgment on a person's credibility. We are creatures of habit. If you set a hard start time and stick to it, eventually people will get the message and be at the meeting on time. You may want to allocate five minutes at the beginning of the meeting to allow people leaving from a previous meeting to get to your meeting. But do not let five minutes become ten. Remember, you probably won't have the luxury to make up for lost time.

- Start the meeting by reiterating the purpose of the meeting and reviewing the agenda to make sure everyone is on the same page. If someone wants to modify the meeting or add to the meeting, you need to make a judgment call on whether their request is appropriate for the meeting and can be accommodated within the meeting's time. Normally, I would recommend no. That person should have added it to the agenda prior to the meeting. If the request is important enough to the meeting's objectives and the person is ready to cover the new item, you may add it to the agenda. Otherwise, ask that person to work offline with you.

- Monitor the progress of the agenda to make sure each item has the allocated time. If the discussion on a particular item is taking longer, you can check with the team to see if the remaining agenda items would take less time and allow this person to continue. Or you can ask them to wrap up and continue offline after the meeting. If someone asks a question that's not relevant to the topic, remind that person of the topic being discussed and ask to discuss it after the meeting. For example: "Sorry Pat, we are tight on time and we're discussing topic ABC. Can you discuss that offline after the meeting?"

- Confirm the outcome of each major agenda item. For the example above, when a team member finishes his product requirement discussion and agrees to a timeline, capture the results and confirm with him.

- If a conflict or debate occurs, let the discussion happen within the time allowed. However, make sure people don't talk over each other and each person is heard. If everyone is talking at the same time, you can interject firmly to remind people that one person should speak at a time. Make sure the discussion is focusing on the work issue and not personal. If someone is getting emotional and attacking someone personally, you need to intervene immediately and emphasize the need to focus on the issue. Cut off that discussion and continue with the meeting's topic. You need to take control of the meeting.

- Monitor to see if discussions are related to the agenda topic. If a discussion is getting off track, stop the discussion and bring it back to the meeting's agenda. For example: "We are tight on time and need to focus on our agenda to finish our meeting. So let's get back on track."

- Before ending the meeting, summarize and verbalize the outcomes and next steps to all the meeting participants to make sure all attendees, especially people on the phone, are on the same page. If some team members have a different understanding, they have a chance to raise the issue and resolve it right away. And if some participants seem confused or disagree with the summary, discuss the issue right away and either come up with an agreement, a solution or at least the next step to resolve this issue. Don't leave the meeting with the issue in limbo. As soon as you can after the meeting, send out the meeting summary so everyone can refer back to if there's any question in the future. This will save you a lot of time from revisiting the meeting outcomes again.

- If you conduct the meeting with other attendees who are fluent in English or English is their native language while it's not yours, you need to make sure they understand what you're saying and as importantly, you need to understand them. If you are speaking, ask them if they have any questions or want more explanation from you. Remember to speak clearly and loud enough (don't mumble). If they ask you a question that you're not sure you understand, ask them to clarify. Likewise, if some attendees speak, ask them to repeat or explain if you're confused or don't clearly understand. When you conduct the meeting in English and you have people from different ethnic backgrounds attending for whom English is not their native language, be respectful to their needs. Remember to speak clearly and frequently check with them to make sure they understand what you're saying. Remind others in the meeting to speak clearly too.

- Using humour is a good technique to enhance the working environment, defuse tensions and promote teamwork. So be yourself and use your sense of humour at appropriate times in the meeting. However, be sensitive to people's feelings and don't offend them with dark humour or insensitive jokes, such as jokes about people's race, sex, physical appearance, etc.

Common Mistakes in Facilitating Meetings

- Too many people in the meeting. As a general rule, the larger the meeting, the less you will be able to get things done. If you have a meeting with too many people, determine who is really needed and disinvite people who are not. How many is too many depends on the context of your meeting. If it is a working or decision-making meeting, I believe less than ten is more conducive to having a productive meeting. If it is an informational meeting where no deep discussion or decision is required, a larger number of people can attend.

- Not keeping the meeting on track to be able to cover all the agenda items adequately, potentially resulting in sub-optimal results and rushed decisions. If you have to schedule another meeting because you weren't able to cover all the topics, you're taking more time out of your and other people's schedules. If you need to focus on facilitating the meeting and are not able to monitor the time, ask one of the participants to be a timekeeper for you.

- Failure to summarize key points, decisions, action items and next steps from the meeting. Forgetting or ignoring this important step can cause confusion or miscommunication. People are usually multi-tasking and probably don't remember all the details from the many meetings they attended. Having a written summary that team members can refer to will help save headaches and precious time.

- Failure to get full participation from the meeting participants. This is especially common when you have meetings with both people attending in person and people attending virtually. Keep a list of the virtual attendees and remember to repeat key discussion points and confirm their understanding. Also remember to check if they have questions or comments.

- Too many conversations are happening at the same time. If you facilitate a meeting from a remote location and the attendees are either on the phone or gathered in a conference room, the above practices are also relevant. However, since you are remote, you need to be more assertive in running the meeting. Listen for side conversations and put a stop to them; they are distracting to the meeting agenda. If multiple people are talking and making it difficult to hear, intervene right away. In addition, do your best to have video systems setup to enable people to see the meeting materials.

International companies with Western culture place a lot of emphasis on time efficiency. This counters many Asian markets that have flexible time handling approach. Develop excellent time management and meeting efficiency skills will set you up well within a multinational company environment.

PART 3
Collaborating

"The amount of meetings I've been in – people would be shocked. But that's how you gain experience, how you can gain knowledge, being in meetings and participating. You learn and grow."
— **Tiger Woods**

"Commercial cooperation must have three main prerequisites: first, the two sides must have the interests of cooperation, second, there must be a willingness to cooperate, and third, the two sides must have the intention of sharing common prosperity. All three are indispensable."
— **Jack Ma, Alibaba Founder**

Collaborate Successfully

- **Skills and qualities**
  - Adaptability
  - Communication skills ➔ Chapter 8
  - Negotiation skills ➔ Chapter 19

- **Strategies**
  - **Setup for good start**
    - Clarify goals to focus everyone
    - Align clear understanding of deliverables and timeline
    - Clarify individual tasks, responsibility, deliverables, deadlines
    - Understand dependencies
    - Team working model
  - **Clear documentation**
    - Project manager to send post-meeting summary
    - Central information bank
  - **Leadership**
    - Lead by example
    - Assist team members
    - Identify problems early
    - Focus on business issues
    - Compliment/reward members
    - Celebrate milestones
  - **Communications**
    - Seek and give regular feedback
    - Update managers on progress

- **Conflict resolution**
  - Deal with issues early
  - Don't make things personal
  - Identify root causes
  - Brainstorm solutions
  - Escalate for help if necessary

CHAPTER 13

How to Collaborate Successfully

Collaboration means to work jointly with someone or a group of people on an activity, especially to create or produce something. Regardless of your profession, it's rare when you work alone. You spend most of your time working with people in your company as well as external parties, including customers, suppliers, partners and consultants. These people play a key role in determining how successful you will be. In this chapter, I'll explain the importance of having good collaboration skills, the skills and qualities you need to be a good collaborator, as well as strategies and techniques you can develop and use in different working situations.

Why Having Good Collaboration Skills Is Important

Before we delve into the strategies, let's first understand the benefits of being a good collaborator.

- You normally spend a lot of time working with other people on a team project. Everybody needs to do their part and deliver on their commitment in order for the whole project to be successful. Because a project is only going to be as strong as the weakest link in the chain, team members are dependent on each other and need to work together closely. Collaborating effectively is the key to a successful project.

- Effective collaboration enables you and the team to work more efficiently. Teams who don't collaborate well often have miscommunication, confusion and conflict – all of which result in loss of critical time. For example, I have been on teams where we had multiple meetings rehashing the same topic, revisiting decisions or clarifying unnecessary confusion. Teams that work well together only meet as needed and use meetings to set goals, review project status and resolve issues. If you have good collaboration skills and use them to help your team work effectively together, you not only help your team but also yourself by saving time to work on other important activities.

- How you perform on a project and how you work with other people is a major factor on your performance review. Your team members and other managers' feedback have significant influence on how you will be evaluated. Positive feedback along with delivering excellent results will earn you good performance reviews, salary raises and consideration for promotions. I consistently noticed during my career that high performers share one common trait: the ability to work with people to get things done successfully.

- In collaborating with people, whether in a leading role or as a team member, you have a great opportunity to grow professionally, develop leadership skills, enhance communication skills and improve your ability to work effectively with others. Moreover, demonstrating good collaboration skills is a great way to make you stand out at work and get the attention of company executives.

- In today's professional working environment, oftentimes you'll work with people outside of your company, including customers, suppliers, partners and even your competitors. Your customers and partners especially can have different priorities from your company or they feel they have an advantage over you and, as a result, may make unreasonable demands on you and your company. In these situations, striving to achieve win-win outcomes is important and this will require great collaboration and negotiation skills.

Companies spend a significant amount of money to train their employees on teamwork. I once had an employee, Mark, who was an expert in his field, knew his stuff inside out but was not good at working with people and getting people to do what he needed to complete the project. If Mark could develop and improve this skillset, he would be a star. I sent him to a one-week professional development training programme at the cost of $5,000, not including hotel, travel and food expenses. This not only cost the company a lot of money, but more importantly, five days of productive work from him. If you had or developed these skills early in your career, you will have a leg up in your career and a great head-start over other people.

Let me explain how to effectively collaborate with other people and get them to collaborate with you.

Skills and Qualities Needed for Effective Collaboration

I'll discuss three important skills and qualities: adaptability, communication and negotiation.

- **Adaptability.** People you work with may come from different cultures, different backgrounds, have different personalities and working styles. Since there is no "one size fits all" approach to working with others and getting the most out of their effort, you need to be able to adapt to them. Invest your time on your team members to develop a rapport and understand how best to work with them – what motivates them, what work methods they prefer, what makes them tick, etc. Investing this time will go a long way in gaining their trust and set you up to work well with them.

- **Communication skills.** Having good communication skills goes hand in hand with collaboration skills. I covered this in detail in the "How to communicate effectively" chapter. Specifically, I talked about the importance of being a good listener. Moreover, I covered ways to communicate in different work situations. Lastly, I discussed the importance of maintaining professionalism, staying focused on the business issue and not reacting personally in difficult situations.

- **Negotiation skills**. This is the ability to influence people to achieve a mutually desired outcome. Even without being aware of it, we frequently negotiate. We negotiate with our manager on work assignments and priorities, with team members on project tasks and deadlines, with suppliers on material cost and delivery schedule, etc. Negotiating with other people plays a key role in collaboration. Refer to the "How to become a good negotiator" chapter for details. I describe a strategy and approach to use in any negotiation, the need to gather as much information as possible, to be creative, and most importantly, to achieve a win-win outcome.

Collaboration Strategies

Try these strategies for collaborating effectively on a team project.

- This is more applicable to the project manager, but even if you are not, you can play an active role in spending time in the beginning of a project to:

  ▷ Clarify the goals/objectives to make sure everyone is on the same page. If there is any confusion, this is the time to clarify and confirm project goals and objectives. If and when issues arise causing the project to get off track, going back to the project objectives is a good way to refocus everyone.

  ▷ Discuss and gain clear understanding of deliverables and timelines expected of the team. Moreover, it's important to align with management on the deliverables since they will hold the team accountable to these commitments. If the team cannot commit to the expected deliverables and timelines, they must negotiate with the management team.

  ▷ Clarify your specific tasks/responsibilities, negotiate and prioritize your deliverables and deadlines. Be thorough in assessing your tasks and schedules before committing. While you want to be aggressive, try not to over-commit to action items you don't have control over or confidence to deliver on time. All things being equal, it's better to under-promise and over-deliver.

  ▷ Understand your dependencies on other people and vice versa. Know specifically whom you need to work with to make sure they deliver to you what you need to complete your job.

  ▷ Determine how team members prefer to work together – method of communication, frequency of meetings, forums to resolve issues/conflicts, etc.

- Spend time to figure out effective ways to work with your team members as discussed in the "Adaptability" paragraph earlier.

- At the end of each meeting, make sure there is a meeting recap that summarizes decisions made, action items/owners and next steps. This helps eliminate confusion among team members and prevent wasting time from needing another meeting to clear things up. Confusion can easily happen when many topics are discussed at the meeting. To ensure team members are on the same page, the project manager should send out a summary message after the meeting.

- Create a central online shared workspace for sharing information, work in progress, and capturing up-to-date changes and status. This enables everyone to see the same work being done as well as changes made in real time and ensures everyone has the same information at all times. There are many online workspace tools available. Check with your company's IT group.

- Lead by example. Meeting your commitments and completing your deliverables on time gains you credibility and trust from team members. Moreover, looking for opportunities to put the team above individual results is a good way to show your leadership skills. For example, offer your team members a hand when they need help.

- Identify problems/conflicts early and resolve them as soon as possible. Refer to the "How to resolve conflicts and deal with difficult situations" chapter for ways to handle these situations. Focus on the business issue and not on personal matters.

- Seek regular feedback from team members and give constructive feedback as appropriate. This enables any confusion between team members to get cleared up and gives everyone the opportunity to make improvements on their work.

- Keep your manager updated on the project status and your progress. This enables your manager to keep the upper management team up to date and allows you to seek help if and when you need it.

- Know when to escalate for help. You need to use your judgment here. While we may want to try to solve problems ourselves, sometimes we need help. It's always better to ask for help than to miss your deadline. Your manager would much prefer to have you ask for help than hear the bad news about the project. Your boss' obvious question then would be: "Why didn't you ask for help sooner?"

- Compliment and reward people for excellent work and teamwork effort. People appreciate being recognized for their work, so even a small gesture of sending an email to thank them for their effort and copying their manager goes a long way in building strong team spirit.

- Celebrate key milestones and accomplishments. Many of us put our heads down to finish our work and then move on to the next project without taking time to celebrate the team's accomplishments. It's an opportunity to catch our breath, enjoy each other's company and recognize our own contribution to the success of the project. Moreover, it offers a great way to gain visibility and recognition.

Resolving Conflicts and Challenges

Inevitably, there will be conflicts or issues that arise during a project. The team's ability to stay on track and complete the project on time depends on the team members' ability to address and resolve these issues in a timely and productive fashion. Here is a summary of the steps to follow when a conflict arises:

- Recognize the issue early. Don't ignore and hope it will go away.

- Focus on the work issue and not personal issues.

- Identify the root causes of the issue – be honest and objective.

- Once root causes are identified, hold frank discussion to brainstorm potential solutions.

- Decide which solution is best to implement. If need be, escalate to management for help.

Let's take an example. A team member is not meeting his commitment and that is impacting your work. Because your specific project deliverables are dependent on his deliverables, you cannot perform your work without his output. As a result, the team risks not meeting the deadline. You are in a bind. What should you do?

- Seek to understand the root cause. Talk to this team member to understand why he's not able to complete his work and help him understand that this is impacting the entire team's project. Don't make any assumption about why he is not delivering on his commitment and avoid making any accusations. Maintain your professionalism and focus on the business issue.

- Once you understand why, offer to brainstorm with him ways to help him complete his work so you will be able to do your work and the project can get back on track. Let's assume that he was late because he had to take time off to attend to a family matter. Knowing this was the reason and not his competence or motivation, you can offer to take on some part of his work so both of you will be able to catch up. This will earn you goodwill and trust that will be helpful in future projects. If you found out he was just lazy and not motivated to do his work or if he rejects your offer to help, you should escalate the matter to the project manager to help resolve the issue. Before escalating, let him know the step you plan to take. While he may not like this, he should understand you have tried your best to resolve the issue with him, but you must put the team first.

Think Win-Win in Collaboration

It's essential in a collaboration approach to avoid "zero-sum game" situations. Such thoughts would place the parties into competing mode. Alignment on common ground is an important early step to establish rationale for shared goals or gains. For example, instead of just thinking as competing soccer teams, a common vision of the competing teams coming together to create a championship league which would increase the fan base would be an example of win-win thinking in a competitive environment.

In the case of international collaboration (usually from the company's worldwide HQ with local Asian markets), it's important to know your value-add in the entire value chain. For example, your local market knowledge and access gives you credibility and a good starting point in the collaboration effort. In addition, smaller markets in Asia give us insight of the process end-to-end vis-à-vis larger homogeneous markets such as the US.

While I have covered collaborating in the context of a team project, many of these strategies and techniques also apply to other situations, including working one-on-one with people in other functions and third parties.

CHAPTER 14

How to Earn Trust

Even though we are in the digital world with a plethora of social media tools, face-to-face interaction between people at work is still the most effective way to collaborate and build strong working relationships. If you work remotely and face-to-face interactions are not practical, having phone conversations or video-conferencing is your next best alternative. Trust is another important factor in having a good professional relationship. Trust is defined as "firm belief in the reliability, truth, ability, or strength of someone". If your colleagues trust you, you are in a good position to work with them effectively and be able to get things done.

But how do you build and earn trust, especially if you are new to the team, to the organization or to the company? In this chapter, we will cover ideas you can apply to everyday interactions with your colleagues.

- **Meet your commitment**. First and foremost, you must do what you say. This demonstrates your reliability and dependability. It takes a sustained period of effort to earn trust but you can easily lose it. Regardless of how big or small your commitment is, if you commit to deliver a result or do something for someone, you must do your best to meet your commitment and follow through. If you realize that you won't be able to deliver on your commitment, let them know as soon as possible, fully explain and give an alternative option.

    My former manager, a Vice President, had a tendency to ask the same person on my team to complete a task for him. After seeing this a few times, I asked him why he did not ask other members on my team. He answered: "Because I know when Julie says yes to my request, I have complete trust that she will get it done on time, and more importantly, done right. I can go away and don't have to worry about it." One other thing to keep in mind before you commit is that you need to consider carefully whether you have the ability and resources to complete the task on time. If you're not sure about the deadline, give yourself some buffer in case of unexpected problems.

- **Honesty**. Simply put, you can keep a secret, honour someone's confidentiality and tell the truth. When you say, "Your secret is safe with me", honour it. Don't use someone's information shared in confidence against them. As a senior product manager working with my operational planning manager, Dan, on a production plan, I met with him to discuss my proposal. After our discussion, Dan agreed that it was a good proposal and he would support it. When I presented my proposal to the management team later, I received push back from the manufacturing executive about the proposal's feasibility. After listening to my explanation, the executive asked Dan for his opinion. Sensing his manager's hesitancy, Dan backed off his support and said he had concerns as well. Needless to say, I lost my trust and respect for him on that day. I confronted him afterward and he wimped out saying he wasn't very sure about his support in the first place. From that point forward, I avoided working with him and when I had to, I proceeded very cautiously.

    Having a hidden agenda is something to avoid as well. For example, proposing something that you say will be good for the team when it will only benefit you. As the old saying goes: "Fool me once, shame on you, fool me twice, shame on me." People don't want to look foolish or feel they have been taken advantage of. If your idea benefits both you and the team, explain how that will be a win-win. If you only highlight the benefits to the team, people will either see through it or will find out later. Either way, you lose credibility and trust. You may win this time, but in the long run, you'll find it more difficult to work with people and to achieve success for yourself.

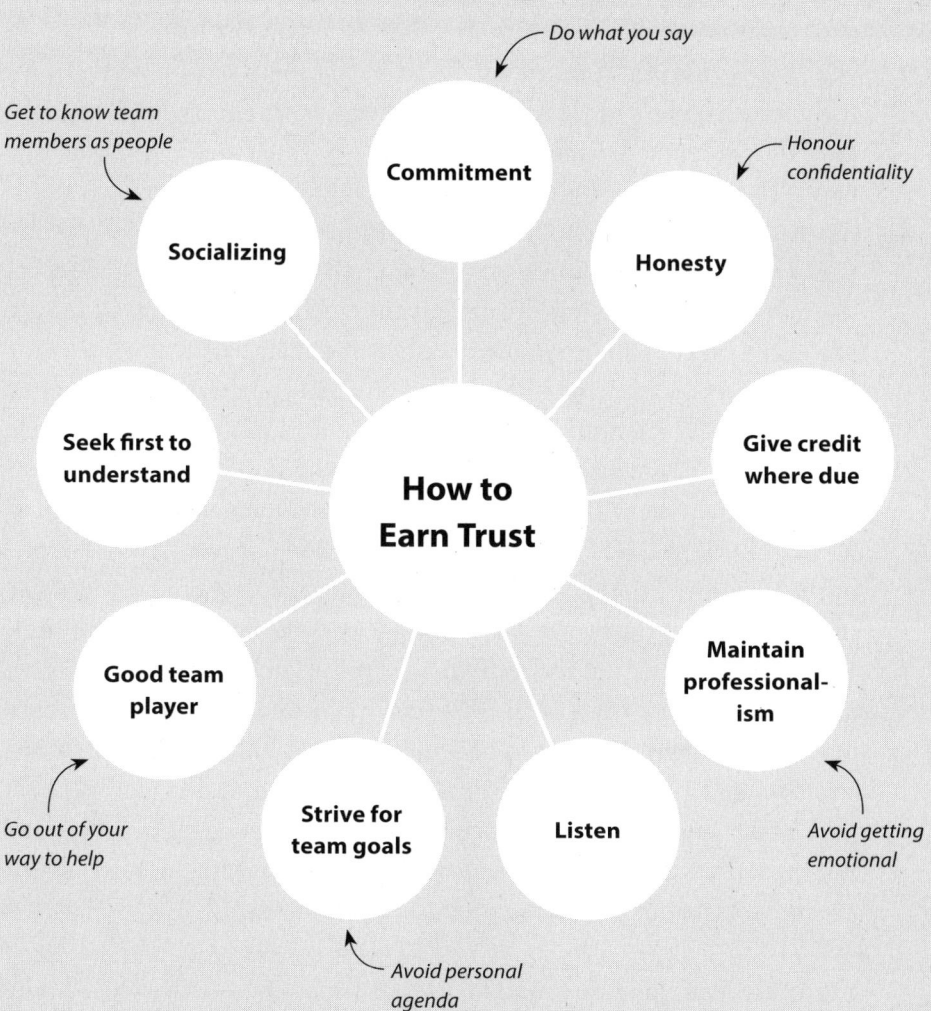

- **Give credit where credit is due**. It goes a long way when you praise or give people credit when they have earned it. It makes them feel appreciated and demonstrates your honesty and trustworthiness. Whether you're a team leader or a team member, focus on the team and not on you. It is better for team members to have others recognize them for their work. When people see that their work is recognized and appreciated, they're motivated and more willing to put their energy to the task at hand. Therefore, you should make a conscious effort to recognize opportunities to reward your colleagues for the job well done. A small gesture goes a long way. Something as simple as complimenting them and recognizing their work publicly during a team meeting or sending a message to their manager will do wonders for earning their trust.

  When I was working on data analytics, I received a request from a Senior Vice President to develop an IT tool for him to be able to access any key business metric he wanted. I solicited a couple of strong IT experts to help me with the project. When we presented the tool to him, he was impressed. He knew me but not the two IT specialists. At the end of the meeting, I thanked the team for going above and beyond to help me. When I told the Senior VP that they were the architects responsible for the development of the tool, they were very pleased with the recognition, especially from a high-level senior executive. I earned their trust and felt confident they would be willing to help me again in the future. Even though I did not publicly give myself credit, the Senior VP later told me he appreciated my leadership in recruiting the right people and getting it done quickly and successfully. In this project, I also earned the executive's trust by delivering on my commitment.

- **Maintain your professionalism**. At all times, especially when under pressure, maintain your professionalism. This means you should stay calm, poised, focused on the business issues at hand and not get personal. This is particularly important when you're leading a team or working on a team. During a project, inevitably the team will run into unexpected problems that may cause people to react emotionally. When we are emotional, we tend to get personal instead of focusing on the task at hand, show our tendency to be condescending, sarcastic and to blame other people. If you feel you are getting too emotional, excuse yourself and take a break to calm down. Or if you see others behaving this way, call for a break.

I saw first-hand an episode in a meeting my former manager attended with his boss and his peers. As he got heated, he made some out-of-character insulting comments about another VP, even suggesting that this VP should be fired. Well, it didn't go over well with the people in the meeting and a few weeks later, he was fired. Although the reason given for the firing was "organizational change", my boss and I knew full well that that was not the real reason for his firing.

- **Listen**. From my experience, I believe that if you are a good listener, people are more likely to trust you. This is because people feel you have taken the time to listen to them, to seek to understand, and are empathetic to their situation. When we fully listen to people, we develop and nurture a safe environment where they can open up and be themselves without fear of judgment. If we honour their confiding in us and keep it confidential, we will earn their trust even more. Take the time and make an effort to listen by asking questions so you can truly hear them. In addition, before you give feedback, seek to understand fully and accurately so you can give specific feedback. And when you do give feedback, focus on giving constructive feedback with examples instead of criticism. Refer to the chapter on "How to be give and receive feedback" for suggestions.

- **Striving to achieve team goals**. If you're leading a team, focus relentlessly on having your team achieve the common goals and persuading them that the team's success defines their success. If the team fails to meet the team goals, everyone fails. There is no room for anyone to feel they can deflect the blame for the team's failure by pointing fingers at other people. When your team sees that you don't have a personal agenda and you drive them to work together to deliver results, they will likely follow your lead. Even if you are a team member and not a leader, you can still play a significant role in helping your leader focus the team on achieving the team goals.

- **Being a good team player**. If you act and present yourself as a team player willing go out of your way to help team members get their work done, people are more likely to trust you. However, make sure you can complete your work before committing to help. Completing your work is your first priority. It's better not to commit than commit and not deliver. Knowing how to work efficiently will enable you to have time to assist your team. Being a good team player also means recognizing the team's weaknesses, bringing them to attention and finding ways to address them. The team is only as successful as the weakest link in the chain. By proactively addressing the weak spots – whether it's a specific area of the project or someone not delivering quality work – you help the team achieve the best results possible.

- **Seek first to understand**. If your colleague is delivering subpar work and that's hurting the team, seek to understand first and not jump to conclusions. Resist the urge to assume that he's a bad team player who's not fit to be on the team, especially if he has a good track record. There could be many reasons for this situation, such as personal or family issues, or too much work responsibilities that are spreading him too thin. Seek this person out to discover why he's not delivering his best work by listening and asking questions. Chances are he will be open with you if he knows that you sincerely want to help. Once you find out the root cause, then you can explore possible solutions.

    When I interviewed my former colleagues for this book, I heard an example from a person I had worked closely with for several years. Mary said during a big project she was working on, there was a team member who was delivering mediocre work results. There were several unhappy team members who were afraid this would reflect negatively on them. Mary went to this person and expressed her desire to understand what was going on and to help. She came to learn that the team member did not know how to say no to his boss, and as a result, kept getting work added to his plate. He was overloaded with work projects, felt overwhelmed and did just enough to stay above water. Mary helped him approach his manager to explain his situation. Together they helped the manager understand the risks and consequences to the team of not delivering on his commitment due to the heavy workload. The manager understood and removed some of the lower-priority tasks. As a result, he was able to get back on track. He thanked Mary, and from that point on, he was more open to confiding in her and seeking help before it was too late.

- **Socialize**. Get to know your colleagues. We spend so much time trying to get work done that we have little time for socializing, to get to know another side of the people we work with. I was guilty of this early in my career. I didn't spend enough time building personal connections with my peers. Developing and maintaining relationships with my peers sooner would have helped me work with them and get things done more effectively.

  Although time is valuable and we never seem to have enough of it to finish our work, make it a priority to get to know your colleagues. Start by showing your genuine care for them as colleagues and as people. Learn about their interests and hobbies outside of work. If you both enjoy the same sport – tennis, for example – invite them to play with you from time to time. Make an effort to have lunch with them instead of eating alone at your desk. Instead of taking a walk by yourself during a break, ask a co-worker to walk with you. And once in a while, organize a group happy hour after work where everyone can enjoy each other's company. This worthwhile time investment will enable people to feel closer and have more trust in you and each other, and help you to work even better with them and get things done more effectively.

Get People to Listen

Getting attention in meetings

- Understand the context of the meeting
- Prepare and act accordingly
- Listen, seek to understand
- Build rapport
- Seek opportunities to offer comment
  - *Make it a habit to speak up, and prepare potential comments*
- Know when to interject
- Express disagreement professionally
- Don't take negative comments personally
- Be comfortable speaking up:
  - Speak loud and clear
  - Establish eye contact
  - Practise for confidence

Qualities needed

- Build credibility with people you work with
- Earn trust with respect
- Be a good listener

CHAPTER 1.5

How to Get People to Listen

One question I frequently get from my students, employees and co-workers is: "How do I get people to listen to me?" Particularly in meetings, people have things to say and they get impatient when other people talk too much. They in turn may react by interrupting and speaking louder, resulting in a lot of people talking over each other and nobody really listens. Moreover, when in a large group meeting, we feel hesitant to speak up for fear of saying dumb things and embarrassing ourselves. We keep quiet while wishing we could speak up and get people to pay attention. I'll cover in this chapter the qualities needed and the best ways to get people to listen to you, especially in a group meeting setting. Many Asians need an extra push to speak freely. This chapter is critical for bringing your ability to an international level.

Here are the qualities needed to get people's attention.

- **Build credibility with the people you work with.** This doesn't happen on day one. This is something we earn over time. Credibility is earned by meeting our commitments, delivering results on time, being dependable, and helping out when needed. In addition, if you could develop a specific standout skill and use it to help people, you will go a long way in building credibility.

- **Earn trust by treating people with respect.** When you are a good team player who shows genuine care for your co-workers, they will tend to give you the benefit of the doubt because they believe you are honest and put the interest of the team ahead of your own. Respect what people say and genuinely seek to understand instead of being condescending or abrupt. People in turn will reciprocate that respect. When you speak up, people will listen, take your words at face value and not have to wonder if you have any hidden agenda.

- **Being a good listener.** This is a key part of communication skill. When we listen to people carefully, we understand their issues better and that helps us respond more appropriately. Moreover, it will encourage them to be more open to what you say. A good communicator is also an excellent listener. If you are new to the meeting and don't know people there, asking questions and listening to them is a good way to establish rapport.

How to Get People's Attention in Meetings

I'll focus on a group meeting setting for this discussion.

- **Understand the context of the meeting.** Is it a meeting where you're there to receive information, review a project's progress, solve a problem or reach a recommendation for management? Knowing the context of the meeting will help you prepare appropriately and identify ways you can contribute. If it's an informational meeting, you can participate by asking for clarification, praising the value of the information received and suggesting additional information needed. If it's a project status meeting, be prepared to review your own work progress, answer questions people may have and discuss your team members' work. If it's a meeting to address and solve a problem, you can play a mediator role to keep people on track, focus on the issue at hand and to offer potential ideas for people to consider.

- **Listen and pay attention to people's comments.** Before you speak, focus on listening to what people are saying. Is it clear to you? If not, ask them to clarify. Something like: "Could you clarify that for me. I just want to make sure I understand your points clearly." And if you want to respond or add to their comment, say: "What you're saying about XYZ is really helpful, and I would like to add to that."

- **Build rapport**. Ask for clarifications or rephrase their comment to avoid misunderstanding. This is a good way to connect with people and to show you are interested and engaged in their work. This will also help people feel more comfortable engaging with you. If you are new to the project and fear that you may ask a dumb question, you can preface your question by saying: "I'm new to this and sorry if this is redundant, but I was wondering if you could elaborate on that point for me."

- **Seek opportunities to offer comments**. Once you know the purpose of the meeting and have prepared yourself, look for opportunities to chime in. Keep in mind that having well-thought-out comments will give you credibility and the confidence to speak up. As you listen to someone in the meeting and decide you want to respond, wait until that person finishes his thought. Acknowledge his point and offer your own comments. For example: "That's a really good point, John. I would also like to add to that…" or if you're having a hard time chiming in, raise your hand clearly for people to see and firmly state: "I'm hearing a lot of good points and I also have a couple of comments I would like to share with you."

- **Know when to interject**. If you are in a contentious meeting where people are speaking over one another, it's fruitless for you to interject with your comments. At some point, the meeting facilitator should step in and take control of the meeting. Then you can take advantage of this opportunity to raise your hand and say: "I have a comment I would like to add." Then proceed with your comment. If the facilitator is not taking control of the meeting, wait for a good time to interrupt with a friendly but firm voice: "We're not making progress here when everyone is speaking at once. Let's have one person speaking at a time." Then gesture to the meeting facilitator to resume running the meeting. A simple gesture like that shows your assertiveness and also demonstrates your leadership quality.

- **Express your disagreement professionally.** Base your comments on the issue and not the person by focusing on what they do and not who they are. For example: "I believe your plan is missing some key details" as opposed to "You are clueless." Acknowledge their points before you express your opinions. For example: "I understand and appreciate your points and perspective, but I see the issue differently. Here's why...." When you're finished, you can ask for feedback: "Is it clear what I said? Any questions or anything you want me to elaborate on?"

- **Remember to speak up.** It's to your benefit to speak up in the meeting. If you don't, nobody knows who you are and what value you add. If you don't think you have any valid points to add, ask someone to elaborate on their points. At least this will allow people to see you, hear you and it helps you feel more comfortable speaking up later. Make a habit of speaking in a meeting at least twice, especially when you're in a meeting with your boss or company executives. This is your opportunity to be recognized, get visibility and to make a good impression with the management team. Thinking ahead of time about potential comments and insight that would be good to bring up in the meeting will make it easier for you to speak up.

- **Don't take people's criticism or negative comments personally.** Ask for clarification or specific details. Even when someone gets personal with you and makes condescending remarks, resist the urge to lash back. Put the ball back in that person's court by making them focus on the topic and the facts. For example, if Ted comments, "You don't make any sense with your analysis," you should reply with: "Ted, can you give me the specifics on the part of my analysis that didn't make sense to you." This puts the onus on Ted to give examples or risk looking bad with the people in the room.

- **Can you hear me?** When speaking, make sure you speak in a clear and loud enough voice for everyone to hear. In addition, look at the people you are talking to. This shows you are engaging actively and expressing your views confidently. Try to minimize word fillers such as "um" and "ah". They can make you appear timid and lacking conviction in your comments. If you have this habit, practise in a safe environment with friendly people you're comfortable with. If you are nervous, take deep breaths. With practice and repetition, you will be more comfortable speaking up. Especially if English is not your native language, you need to focus even more on speaking clearly and making sure people understand you. Make a habit of asking them if they have any questions or want you to elaborate on what you were saying.

CHAPTER 16

How to Give and Receive Feedback

Giving and receiving feedback is a regular practice in the corporate world, especially in Western business environments. Formal feedback takes place at annual or semi-annual employee performance reviews. This is when your manager solicits feedback from people you worked with throughout the year – your team members, co-workers, project managers, managers as well as people outside the company. Their feedback plays a significant role in how you will be evaluated. Delivering good results is only one part of your evaluation. How you work with other people is just as important.

As a manager, I was often puzzled when someone on my team expressed surprise at the feedback from their peers. If you have an open communication channel with people in the company and you pay attention to your working relationship with them, you shouldn't be surprised at the feedback you receive. Moreover, it shouldn't be that the first time you hear feedback is at your formal performance review. You should be asking for feedback from the people you work with and from your manager on a regular basis; this helps you address any issues that may exist, gives you a chance to clarify and take corrective actions when things are still fresh for both sides. In addition, if you are able to resolve these issues in a timely way, chances are these issues will not reflect negatively on you when your peers give their feedback for your formal performance review. Better yet, they will more likely appreciate your proactive effort to reach out and improve your working relationships with them.

Mindset reframe

- Feedback is not criticism
- Regular formal feedback
- Poor feedback could be improved

Give and Receive Feedback

Giving feedback

- Give feedback on specifics
- Appropriate time and space
- Right state of mind
- Prepare constructive message
- Listen

Receiving feedback

- Be proactive in seeking regular input
- Listen calmly, don't be defensive
- Reflect with open mind
- Validate the specifics
- Take corrective actions if feedback is valid
- Get back to show feedback taken seriously

Other managers will also ask you to give feedback on their employees who have worked with you over the past year. Well before the employee evaluation meeting, I would ask for feedback on each of my employees from people who have worked with them. Knowing how to receive and give feedback is an important skill. The good news is this skill is not difficult to learn. In this chapter, I'll share the best ways you can use to receive and give feedback, and have this skill as another tool in your toolbox.

Giving and receiving feedback is important for several reasons:

- Helps your team members be better at their jobs. We all want to improve our job performance and any help we can get to help us achieve this would be welcome.

- A good practice to build and maintain relationships if giving and receiving feedback is done the right way.

- Effective way to ensure you and others are on the same page. Any conflicts are brought up and addressed promptly.

- An excellent way to recognize someone for their good work as well as an opportunity to influence and persuade them.

- A great practice for you to continue to develop your interpersonal and communication skill.

Many of us view feedback as unpleasant and associate it with criticism. However, it should be seen as a positive communication vehicle. Simply put, feedback is not criticism. Criticism is being negative, and it comes across as judgmental and even personal. Moreover, it tends to make the person on the receiving end defensive and as a result, inhibits productive discussion. Feedback, on the other hand, is positive communication with good intentions. It's constructive and collaborative. It's intended to recognize others for their good work and help them improve their performance.

How to Give Feedback Successfully

Follow these steps to help you prepare and give feedback constructively.

- **Think about what you want to give feedback on**. What were the specific issues that triggered your desire to give feedback? Is there anything you need to clarify? Do you need to check with anyone else to validate the issues? The more specific the issues, the more effective you will be able to give feedback.

- **Pick an appropriate place and time to meet.** When you want to give someone feedback, it's best to have the conversation between just the two of you. This promotes an open environment for dialogue, especially if you don't know how sensitive the other person will be. You want to avoid any risk of embarrassing them in front of other people, even if that was not at all your intention. In addition, be aware of their mood and state of mind before you start. If they seem under a lot of stress, unhappy or on a tight work deadline, wait for another time. If you're not sure, check if this is a good time to talk: "Kelly, is this a good time to talk? I was wondering if I could have a few minutes to share some feedback with you."

- **Prepare your message**. The message should be constructive, not critical. Stay on the issue, on what that person did and not who they are. Bring specific examples to clarify your points. For example: "Tom, I've been thinking about your recent report on the team project. The report made some really good points. I also have some ideas and feedback to help make the report even stronger. Would it be okay for us to discuss them?" This focuses on the report Tom wrote and nothing about him personally. Of course, any smart person would accept your invitation to offer ideas and feedback. Contrast that comment with: "Tom, I don't know what you were thinking when you wrote that report. It makes no sense. You have a lot of work to do to fix it. I have some ideas." This is derogatory and insulting since it implies Tom is stupid. Starting with this comment will not likely result in a good, productive discussion.

- **Listen.** A key part of giving feedback is listening to the other person. Allow them time to reflect on your feedback and to respond. Ask them if what you said was clear or if they need you to clarify. Listen carefully to their response. Don't get defensive if they're not taking what you said seriously. Don't get rattled if they take it personally and react emotionally. Try to understand their reaction. Ask: "I'm sorry you seem upset. Was there something specific about my feedback that made you feel this way?" Then listen. Affirm with them that your only objective is to be constructive and to help. Before you end the discussion, ask them for their opinions on the way you gave feedback and how you can give feedback better next time.

- **Know the person you want to give feedback to.** While the steps I mentioned above are very effective in giving feedback, it's good to take into account the person you're giving feedback to may have a different personality, background or come from a different region/country with a different culture from yours. They may interpret what you say differently from what you meant or react to your feedback in unexpected ways. Therefore, it's to your benefit to get to know your colleagues (as I mentioned in the "How to earn trust" chapter), so you can be prepared in giving your feedback. And if you have their trust, they would take your feedback more seriously.

This skill will stand you in good stead if and when you become a manager. One of the responsibilities managers have is to coach their employees, which involves giving feedback. Your employees will want and expect to get feedback from you on a regular basis.

How to Receive Feedback

In addition to willingly sitting down with your co-workers to receive their feedback, it's even better to proactively seek them out. This shows you are taking the initiative to continue to get better. It puts people at ease knowing that you welcome and look forward to their feedback. By asking them, you let them know you give them the green light to be frank, you value their feedback and you want to build a good working relationship with them. Here are some of the best practices for you.

- **Listen**. If you initiate the conversation, let them know at the beginning of the meeting that you appreciate their time and you value their feedback. You especially look forward to receiving constructive and productive feedback to help you improve. Also be specific about what issue you are asking for feedback on. Is it about a recent presentation you delivered or an analysis you recently completed? Is it about your participation or interaction with the team members of the project? Is it about how you handled a recent conflict?

    Whether you asked for or agreed to receive feedback, the first and foremost important thing is to listen. Listen carefully to what they say. Try not to get defensive. Repeat their comment to make sure you understood. For example: "What I hear you say is that my presentation was good but was missing supporting data. Did I hear you correctly?" Or ask them to clarify if you are unclear about their comment: "I just want to make sure I understand what you said. Can you elaborate on your comments for me?" Make a note of the feedback so you can reflect on it at a later time. This is especially useful for critical feedback because we may get defensive when we first hear the feedback and not consider it objectively.

    If you feel they are being personal and criticizing you, stay calm and try not to take it personally. Instead, ask them for specific examples. This will confirm if they are being constructive or just wanting to give you a hard time. For example: "How is what you just said related to what I did? Can you help me understand?" Or: "Julie, I'm not sure I understood clearly. Could you give me a specific example of what I did?" If Julie is still vague and making general comments, suggest that she come back with some examples: "Julie, it would help me if you could think of a specific example. We can get together later when you're ready." Now the ball is in her court.

- **What to do with the feedback you received.** First of all, with an open mind, reflect and consider the feedback. Was it constructive? Was it valid? Was it specific enough? Did you agree with it? Was it something you can act on? If there were other people involved and they have knowledge of the situation, you can also cross-check with them. You don't need to reveal the identity of the person giving you the feedback. You can mention that you recently received some feedback and wanted to validate it with them. For example: "John, I received some feedback on my presentation in our meeting a couple of days ago and I would love to run it by you to get your thoughts. I want to make my presentation better and your feedback would be great. Would that be okay?" Then describe the feedback and listen for his response.

Next, decide what you would like to do with the feedback. Do you think it was valid and want to make corrections or implement their suggestions? Or do you decide to do nothing because the feedback did not have validity? If you decide to take actions based on their feedback, take an opportunity to get back to that person and let them know. They would appreciate your taking their feedback seriously.

- **Make it a habit to seek regular feedback as appropriate.** Your manager is an excellent person to give you feedback. Seek opportunities after a key project is completed, when a key milestone is achieved or after your presentation that your manager attended. If important stakeholders will read your written report, ask your manager to review it first. If you seek feedback regularly and take positive actions, you increase your chances of getting a good performance review because you will be able to demonstrate your effectiveness and success in working with people. Moreover, you are less likely to be caught blindsided during your performance review.

- **Mentor/reverse mentor.** From my experience, it is very beneficial to invest in such partnerships. Once you have such an arrangement, it would be much more natural to have conversations. This kind of relationship also provides a safe environment to practise feedback techniques and expand the scope of topics. With increased comfort level, individual personal pride and concerns no longer present a challenge to engaging with our partners.

CHAPTER 17

How to Handle Conflicts and Difficult Situations

When I joined an aerospace company as a new engineering graduate, I encountered a volatile situation at work during my very first project. Each of the software engineers on the team, which was tasked with delivering a test program for a fighter aircraft, owned a specific software module of the overall program. In order for the program to work properly, all the modules had to integrate seamlessly and work flawlessly together. When I and another senior programmer – Jim, who had been working at the company for several years – tried to integrate our respective modules, they failed to work. This was a bit of a disaster since other team members couldn't move forward without our successful integration. When this failure occurred, Jim's face turned red and he began yelling at me, blaming me for the failure and saying my program was a piece of "crap" (he used a more colourful word).

Throughout your career, you will face difficult situations –work conflicts, unexpected events or surprises that will test your ability to stay calm, hold your poise under pressure and think on your feet. These situations could arise from any number of circumstances, from dealing with co-workers and company management to managing external parties, including customers, partners and suppliers.

While it is impossible to anticipate and prepare for every situation, there is a basic approach you can apply to most situations. In this chapter, I'll discuss the general best practices and behaviour we should utilize when facing

Handle Difficult Situations

Common approach
- Professionalism
- Focus on listening to understand
- Prepare in-depth
- Define problem clearly; logical approach

Dealing with

Difficult customer
- Listen and understand the problems
- Own the problem for the company
- Potential turn around with resolution
- Treat customer engagement for better understanding

Conflict with co-workers
- Stay calm; don't get emotional
- Clarify and understand the issues
- Focus on issue resolution

Conflict with boss
- Read Chapter 22 "How to Say No Smartly"

Situation with executives
- Anticipate executive-level questions
- Clarify questions, definitions, assumptions
- Buy time to respond
- Handle questions/objections professionally

Last-minute surprises
- Expect the unexpected
- Plan for contingencies

a challenging situation. In addition, I'll cover some specific scenarios, their unique differences and the best ways to handle them.

Common Approach

Whether you're facing a conflict with a co-worker, your boss or a customer, there is a set of best practices to follow:

- **Keep your professionalism**. Stay calm and resist the temptation to give in to your emotions. If someone is yelling at you or making demeaning remarks, it's easy to return the favour and lash out at them. If you do that, the two of you will appear to other people like unprofessional people behaving immaturely. In Eckhart Tolle's book, *The Power of Now*, he talks about handling your emotions and controlling the urge to lash out (Tolle, 1992). While it may make you feel good temporarily when you lash out, it may damage your chances in the long run of having good working relationships.

    The first step is to acknowledge the emotion you're feeling, such as anger. Just acknowledging your feelings will help you calm down and reduce your urge to strike back. Also keep in mind that when you let your emotions dictate your actions, you are giving your "power" to the other person. Ask yourself if the other person is that powerful for you to lose your control and give him the power over your reaction. The answer is most likely no. Avoid an unnecessary emotional confrontation by walking away, even for just a few minutes. Take deep breaths to calm yourself down. If you're not familiar with this kind of self-control practice, continue to patiently work on it, and over time you will gain more emotional discipline.

    From my experience, taking a step back helps to clear my mind and allows me to dissect and clarify the situation. This may lower the "temperature", enable us to defuse a tense situation, and maybe allow us to reach a viable solution.

- **Focus on listening**. When faced with a conflict, we have a tendency to jump to conclusions and solutions right away without understanding first. Lack of communication or miscommunication often is the root of conflict. When people are talking over each other instead of stepping back and listening to what the other person is saying, confusion and misunderstanding can arise. Then as things escalate, they become more personal, emotional and before they know it, things have blown up into a real conflict. Sometimes what we thought we heard is not what the other person meant. To avoid this, ask: "What I hear you say is ABC… Did I hear correctly?" or "Can you give me an example…?" When you ask for clarification, you put the onus on that person to explain. Moreover, when people see that you're listening, they feel assured they're being heard, and this helps create a good communication channel which encourages them to be open to your views.

- **Prepare as best you can.** In any conflict or difficult situation, the more details we know about the situation, the better we are at keeping an open mind and being able to use our creativity to come up with the best solution possible. Some of the situational details include the nature of the conflict, possible causes, people involved, any impact on them and external factors. With the knowledge and information we have, we are in a better position to help get everyone on the same page and work to come up with the best solution. Spend time upfront to really understand the issue by talking and listening to the key stakeholders.

- **Use a logical problem-solving approach.** The first step in solving any problem is to define clearly what the problem is. It's not uncommon to see some people on the team trying to solve a problem while others have a different understanding of what the problem is. It's important to make sure everyone has the same understanding. This misunderstanding happens often in business negotiations where one party is working on one issue while the other party is focusing on a different one. Secondly, once the problem is understood, find out possible causes of the problem. The third step is to work with key stakeholders to brainstorm possible solutions and weigh the pros and cons of the different options. And finally, choose the best option among the ones considered.

How to Deal With Difficult Situations

Now, let's look at several different scenarios and discuss them in more detail using the suggested approach above.

1. **Difficult customer.** A customer is unhappy because your company didn't meet its commitment and they may make life difficult for you when you meet them. It may be obvious but needs to be repeated that it's especially important to be professional and use your listening skills in this situation. Let the customer vent; listen and make sure you understand their issues. Moreover, when you interact with them, remember you're representing your company and not just the department you work in. Avoid blaming others in the company or being defensive that the customer is taking it out on you when it's not your fault. The customer doesn't care about your company problems and since you represent the company, you need to answer to the customer. Moreover, you need to be clear on the resolution or the next steps before you leave the meeting and make sure you follow up accordingly.

   Let me repeat a story I told in the "How to communicate and present to different audiences" chapter. I once took a customer visit trip with the purpose of getting their input on a future printer technology. Per my request, the account Sales Representative (SR) set up the meeting for me. When a co-worker and I arrived and met a couple of executives from the customer's company, they proceeded to lay into us about issues they had with their computer systems and their dissatisfaction with our company. We could sense their frustration and anger as the volume of their voices got louder. We were caught completely by surprise since we had no prior warnings from the SR. To make the situation worse, he wasn't there to handle these issues with the customer and since we were from the printer business unit, we were in the dark about their computer system issues. There was only one thing we could do – we sat down and listened patiently. We asked questions to make sure we captured their problems accurately. When they were done venting and giving us a list of items they wanted answers on, we calmly thanked them for their feedback. We told them that although we were not involved in these issues, we would make sure that the right people from the company would work on their request and get back to them quickly.

After this resolution, the customers felt their concerns were heard and were satisfied with the next steps. They calmed down, listened and discussed our company printing technology and even spent an extra hour with us on this topic. I also learned a good lesson from this visit: I should have talked with the SR to understand more about the customer and any potential issues I needed to be aware of and to address before I met them.

2. **Work conflict/difficult situation with co-workers**. One typical scenario here is you and other people are working on a project in which everyone's work is an important part of the overall project and if one person delivers subpar work, the whole project would be negatively impacted. You discover a co-worker's deliverables are not up to the team's standard. You want to let him know but you also know he has a big ego, is sensitive to criticism and does not have to answer to you. What do you do?

We'll apply the approach we discussed at beginning of this chapter. In this situation, focus on the business issue at hand. The key here is trying to understand, giving constructive feedback and emphasizing his ownership of the team's goals.

Approach the person to confirm or clarify his understanding of the team's goals to make sure that you are both on the same page. If he doesn't have the same understanding of the team goals, that could indicate the root cause of the problem. The team project's goals should be clearly written and communicated to everyone on the team. Go over these goals with him if you need to. Before discussing his specific work, ask for his feedback on the status of the team project and suggestions for improvement. Then tell him you have some constructive feedback and suggestions for his work. The key word here is constructive feedback, not negative criticism. Again, focus your feedback on his work and not him as a person. Give specific examples. For example: "The ROI analysis was missing key assumptions to validate the results" as opposed to "You completely missed the boat on the ROI analysis." Emphasize to him that everyone's work is critical to the overall project and if someone doesn't deliver their best work, the whole team suffers. Then offer your help and close the meeting with the timeline for him to review his work with the team again. If your message doesn't get through, suggest to him that the team may need to ask management for help to make sure they deliver the best results possible.

Let's take another real-life example related to me by a friend and former colleague. Henry worked as software (SW) Test Engineer on an engineering team. The team was on the hook to deliver and launch a new application on schedule. When going through the testing, Henry discovered the program was buggy and had logic errors. One of the SW programmers he needed cooperation from was very protective of his work and sensitive to criticism. Tom, a senior SW engineer, had been with the company for several years and believed there was nothing wrong with his work. He didn't want to cooperate and would get offended if the test team approached him about his software code. The test team thought it was possible the issue could be his code but not sure. How would you handle this situation? Would you take him to the woodshed and read him the riot act? Or would you escalate the matter to management immediately and force him to cooperate.

I asked Henry how he handled this situation. He said he approached this with an open mind without assuming that the issue was Tom's code. He dealt with this difficult situation professionally and focused only on the business issue. He approached Tom to explain that the overall program was not working and it was critical to find out the root causes so the problem could be fixed. Henry then asked him for his thoughts on the possible causes and how to go about diagnosing the software bugs. This assuaged Tom from getting defensive or feeling he was being blamed. At the same time, Henry put the onus on him to get involved. Tom's demeanour changed and he suggested a couple of good ideas to go about discovering the bugs, including comprehensive integration testing of everyone's code. Henry then confirmed with Tom that the testing would include his code as well. The lesson here is by focusing on the business problem and having Tom involved in helping find the solution, Henry was successful in addressing this sensitive issue with him.

Let's assume despite all the effort from Henry, Tom remained stubborn and uncooperative. I would suggest the next step is to escalate the issue to management for help. Henry should also let Tom know he is bringing the situation to management. At least Tom would be in no position to complain since Henry is not going behind his back and he knows Henry had tried his best reaching out to him.

Regarding my situation where my co-worker Jim was blaming me and throwing me under the bus, it was just as easy for me to point fingers back at him and get into a pissing contest. However, I chose to keep my cool and waited until he had yelled enough. Then I calmly told him that the yelling was unprofessional and wasn't going to solve the problem. I then told him we needed to find the root causes so we could fix them. And if it turned out it was my work, then I would be happy to acknowledge my error and fix it. He was taken somewhat aback that I didn't lash back at him and he seemed a bit embarrassed. After working together for the next couple of days, we were able to diagnose the problem, fix it and move the project forward. The next day, he apologized to me for his outburst. After that incident, Jim was more aware of his behaviour and controlled his emotions better, at least with me. We continued to have a good professional working relationship. By not reacting badly back at him, I gave him an out and that enabled us to continue our working relationship. I was in control of the situation.

3. **Conflict or difficult situation with your boss**. A conflict arises when your boss assigns you additional work when you are completely swamped. You might feel upset that your boss doesn't appreciate you have too much work already. You may feel you're being taken advantage of and your boss doesn't care he's driving you too hard. You don't want to take on this new assignment. How would you handle this?

Treat this as a negotiation session on how to say no. Refer to the "How to say no smartly" chapter for details. The key again is to focus on the business issue and not get personal or emotional. Don't assume your boss knows how much work you have on your plate. Give him the benefit of the doubt. He is likely busy and not always able to keep tabs on your workload. The way to approach this is to give your boss visibility of your workload and have him prioritize for you. This gets him involved in solving the issue with you.

First, explain all the tasks you have on your plate, the effort and time they require, and be clear with him that it is not possible for you to take on more. However, you would be happy to take this work on if you can drop something else off your plate. Next, ask him to prioritize how important his request is relative to your current tasks. This forces him to evaluate carefully. If he prioritizes his request higher than your other assignments, then it would be reasonable to delay or drop the less important priorities. You need to be firm on this – if you take it on, something has to go. Or if he sees that his request isn't important enough, he can assign it to someone else who may not have as much going on.

4. **Pressure situation with executives**. There will be times in meetings when management may grill you with tough questions or challenge your work. Normally, they're not doing this to be mean to you. Rather, they want to test if you have done your homework, thought things through and can back it up. How well you prepare for meetings like this will determine how you perform. If you are prepared, you will come to the meeting with confidence and that will carry you through. Refer to the "How to communicate and present to specific audiences" and "How to organize and develop presentation content" chapters to help you prepare and conduct yourself in meetings.

To prepare for answering questions from executives, put yourself in their shoes and ask what tough questions you would ask yourself. Since you know the content of your material, think about where you are vulnerable and where the potential holes or weaknesses are. Ask yourself tough questions about those areas and figure out how you would answer them. Executives tend to see the big picture and ask open-ended questions such as: "Where do you see the risks of your project?", "What if things don't go as planned?"," What is your contingency plan?", "What are your key assumptions?", "What key stakeholders have you talked to?" and "What are the key requirements to achieve success?" Some executives are number-centric and will focus on your analysis to test for discrepancies. While you can't anticipate every question, preparing yourself with these questions and answers will give you the confidence and ability to think on your feet when you get a question you had not thought of.

If you get questions from the executives, don't appear ruffled, even if you feel tense and nervous. Remind yourself that you have done your best to prepare and to project confidence. Appearing timid or unsure about your recommendation will not inspire confidence in the executives. Even if you're coming to the meeting not fully prepared and hoping the management team will give you a pass, you need to do your best to maintain your poise. Here are some ways to handle yourself professionally in this type of situation.

▷ If you get a question where you don't know the answer off-hand but can get the answer later, you could say: "Good question. I don't have the answer off the top of my head but I can find out and get back to you after this meeting." That is a perfectly fine answer.

▷ If you are asked to give an opinion but you want to think about it before answering, you can buy some time. For example: "Great question. I'd like to give that some thought. Can I think about it a little bit and get back to you?" While the meeting is going on, you can think about that question in the back of your mind and get back to the questioner later in the meeting when ready. This is a good and professional way to handle this type of question.

▷ If an executive expresses doubt about your analysis or recommendation, don't get defensive. Focus on the business issue. Ask for clarification from the executive, such as: "Can you help me understand the specific area of your concern?" or "What I heard is that you're not sure about my conclusion on ABC because I didn't show enough data to support it, is that right?" When you get the clarification, you will more likely be able to respond better. Don't get flustered when they push you. Sometimes they want to see how strong your conviction is on the recommendation. If you did not have enough data or analysis to support your argument, acknowledge their question and propose to come back with more analysis. For example: "Thank you for the question. Let me look into this further and get back to you with a more detailed analysis."

- If an executive starts to drill down on your data, try not to get dragged down this path. It's a no-win situation and distracts everyone from the meeting's objective. Instead of focusing on the results, focus on your assumptions. For example, you may say: "Since the outcomes of the analysis are the results of the assumptions, let me show you my assumptions to get your thoughts and we can debate on the validity of these assumptions." By definition, assumptions are your educated guesses on the future or on the unknown, so they are not right or wrong at the moment. Therefore, the assumptions are open for debate and you can modify your analysis if the assumptions change. By handling things this way, you're being mature and professional, and you show you are open to people's opinions. If some assumptions need to be modified, thank the executives and say you will look at the analysis again based on the new assumptions. In this process, you have gotten the executives to get involved and take some ownership of your work.

5. **How to handle surprises in real time**. Last-minute surprises are toughest to handle. One of my former companies hosts an annual customer event where a couple hundred executives from Fortune 1000 companies are invited to come for updates on the company's future plan and strategy. We usually offer simultaneous sessions for the guests to choose which ones to attend. One year, our server business unit was allocated a big portion of the agenda to present to customers and we planned to have three speakers for this talk – two co-workers and me. On the morning of the presentation, the two co-workers were nowhere to be found. Moreover, the presentation materials the team worked on were on their laptops. We received no answer calling their hotel rooms or cell phones. Then we received a 15-minute heads-up and my manager was now in full panic mode. We asked another business unit to present in our time slot but they weren't ready either.

Out of desperation, I told a Sales Account Manager I had worked with about our predicament and asked her if she had any ideas. She thought for a couple of minutes and then suggested I could buy some time by opening the session and inviting the customers to give feedback on any topics they wanted. And it would be a great opportunity for the company top executives to hear their feedback directly. That was as good of an idea as any and I informed my boss of the plan. To my pleasant surprise, the feedback discussion went on for over an hour and was so successful I had a difficult time stopping the customer discussion so we could proceed with our presentation. The two missing speakers finally made it there after 30 minutes into the session. Afterwards, many of the customers thanked my boss and even suggested that every future session should allocate time for customer feedback. We heaved a sigh of relief because of how close we cut it.

The lesson learned here is to think of possible unexpected events and to prepare for them as best you can. And if it does happen, stay calm and keep your poise in order to think creatively and engage the right people for help. These are just some real-life examples of typical difficult situations you may face at work and while there will be many other situations you'll encounter throughout your career, keep in mind the Common Approach I described above: keep your professionalism; focus on listening; prepare as best you can; and use a logical problem-solving approach. Applying this Common Approach strategy to any challenging situation you face will give you a greater chance to solve it effectively, gain credibility and trust, and establish yourself as a true professional who's unruffled and poised in any pressure circumstances.

How to Deal with Difficult Co-workers

CHAPTER 18

While we all want a friendly and productive work environment, there are people of all types and personalities, and the difficult ones can make things uncomfortable and not fun for other workers. For the most part, we cannot control people or choose whom to work with. It's easy to work with reasonable, professional colleagues who put team goals first. However, if we know how to handle these difficult workers, it reduces the frustration and more importantly, allows us to get our work done while keeping the work environment as friendly and enjoyable as possible. In this chapter, I'll cover effective ways to manage and deal with difficult co-workers. If you work or want to work for a multinational company in the US (or in a Western country) with a different business culture from that of your country's, make sure you also read the "How to handle workplace politics smartly" chapter. It gives you insight into workplace politics and that will help you manage difficult work situations and co-workers.

1. **Party Pooper**. This person is Mr No. He presents an impediment to what you want to do. He doesn't like anything he sees and shoots down your work. He looks for what can go wrong with your plan and potential negative outcomes. While it can be useful to have a set of critical eyes examining your idea, he only sees failure, and does not offer constructive feedback or useful suggestions. His main message is that your plan has

no chance to succeed. His comments can be condescending, for example: "You did not think this through."

With this type of person, you need to stand up to him. However, stay calm and keep it professional by focusing on the issue. The best way to respond is to put the ball in his court and force him to respond to the topic at hand instead of just shooting down your plan. For example: "Give me specific examples of my plan that you don't think are good", and wait to hear from him. If he's being vague, repeat your question again with: "I can't improve on my plan unless I can get specific examples from you." If he gives you some useful examples, thank him and follow up with: "Can you give me suggestions on how I can improve my proposal?" If he asks to get back to you later, be sure to follow up with him. If he was just shooting off his mouth, he looks foolish and loses credibility.

2. **Downer.** This person is not a happy person generally and lives by the motto "Misery loves company". She is a glass-half-empty kind of person who looks at the negative side of things. For example, when company management is having an employee communication meeting, she tends to draw negative observations and cast suspicion on management's intention. Being around this person too much can bring you down and make the work environment less enjoyable. This type of person wants to draw you into their company and share their negative attitude.

Since people like to be listened to, try to listen for a little bit but don't get drawn into a conversation. You can say something like: "That's an interesting point and I didn't think of it like that, but I would rather talk about something else." Or if you feel the need to refute her, say: "I hear what you're saying, but I really didn't take it the same way." Or if you have more time, you can ask for specifics: "Give me an example of why you feel this way." Responses like these let the person know that while you want to listen and understand where they are coming from, you have a different view. Then ask to talk later since you need to get back to work.

3. **Bully**. This person uses strong-arm tactics. Intimidation, thinly veiled threats, pressure and name-dropping are some tactics he uses. He tells

How to Deal with Difficult Co-workers: Suggested Responses

Party pooper
Mr "No!"
- → Need to stand up
- → Ask for specific input
- → Follow-up closely

Downer
Sees mostly the negative side
- → Listen but don't be down

Bully
Intimidates, threatens, strong-arms
- → Avoid engaging emotionally
- → Ask for specific input on task
- → Highlight request to manager

Bragger
Exaggerates and name-drops
- → Look beyond BS for content

Exploiter
Takes advantage of others
- → Avoid distractions with negative impact on own job performance
- → Be clear and firm on own priorities

One-upper
Needs to step on you to look better
- → Seek clarity on critique
- → Let objective stakeholder judge

Gossiper
Negative and not focused on work
- Avoid distraction and feeding into his acts
- Speak to him if a rumour is about you
- Seek clarifications and engage direct with the source of information

Hidden dragon
Fails to respond
- → Request clearly in writing
- → Set clear timeline and cc team/manager
- → Track timeline with reminders and escalation

Avoider
Does the bare minimum
- → Set fair and clear actions from him
- → Track timeline and escalate if needed

"Yes Boss" only
Responds depending on your rank
- → Request clearly in writing, including team
- → Track timeline with team reminders and escalations to boss

you if you don't do what he says, bad things will happen to you. Your job performance will take a hit, you will be perceived negatively by other managers or he will let important people in the company know it was your fault the work didn't get done. He tends to come across as having power, self-perceived power, over you and other people and as being well connected in the company.

While it's easy to get angry and let this person get on your nerves, or worse, you feel intimidated or victimized, do your best to resist this. You may feel the urge to tell this person to take a hike, but there are better ways to handle him. Similar to the above example, stay professional by addressing the issue at hand and nothing else. Remind yourself that he's not worth wasting your energy on. A good response technique is to pepper him with questions to force him to be explicitly clear on the what's and the why's. This way you let him know you're not intimidated and won't just follow his instructions blindly. Ask him for the specifics of the task – why the need to do this, what problem he is trying to solve, what the goals are, and why this task is more important than other tasks that are being worked on. Force him to answer these tough questions. It's also important for you to understand how this request fits into the priorities that you and your manager have agreed on. Then with confidence, you can say no by explaining this doesn't fit into your priorities at the moment. However, if you think this is a big-enough deal, be sure to let your manager know in case it comes back to your manager later. If the Bully pulls the name-dropping card or uses threats, calmly tell him that you will be more than happy to discuss this with your manager and together will make the call on the priority. Then discuss this with your manager.

4. **Bragger**. As the name implies, this person is a talker who is all about "me", who likes to brag about himself, puts himself in the centre of attention, and has a tendency to embellish and exaggerate. He's also prone to name-dropping to show his importance, but generally is harmless, although he can be quite annoying.

The trick here is to look beyond the braggadocio, focus on the substance and judge the value of the content yourself. Ask for facts and tangible results and don't take his words at face value. When it's not a topic related to you, just ignore him. There's no need to set him straight or make his head any bigger.

5. **Exploiter**. This person takes advantage of your generosity. Once you helped her, she'll keep coming back, knocking on your door with more requests for help. She can appear needy, making self-pitying comments, and is especially good at making you feel guilty if you turn her down – "If you don't help me with this, I'll get in big trouble with my boss." This person uses your generous nature against you to get you to do what she wants.

   As much as we like to help and don't like to say no, there are times we need to say no because otherwise, we can't get our work done and it will negatively impact our own job performance. If we were to help someone complete their task but got behind on our work or delivered less than stellar results, we only hurt ourselves and would get no credit for helping others. Remember, before we can help people, we need to take care of our own job first. Refer to the "How to say no smartly" chapter for how to respond. I would suggest listening to the request, then telling her you empathise with her situation, but your plate is full with tight deadlines and your manager wants you to focus on these priorities first. As a result, you cannot help but you may have more time later when you finish your work. Be firm with your answer.

6. **One-upper**. This person has a need to be better than you, especially if you are in a similar job. No matter how good your work is, she needs to find weak spots to pick on. This trait is a little bit similar to the "Party Pooper", but this person is not just critiquing your idea but also wants to show that her work is better. You would hear comments such as: "I don't see clear benefits of your plan," "This plan is confusing," "This plan requires too much time to implement," or "It's not very useful."

   Let me share with you an example. The pricing team at a previous company developed a tool that allowed the users – Product Managers (PMs) – to easily and quickly run different pricing scenarios and compare the results. This tool was best for "what if" analysis, a key part of a PM's role. Previously it would take days to run this kind of analysis, and now it would take minutes to see the results, thus saving a huge amount of time. However, it would require the PMs to invest some initial time to learn how to use the tool. When the pricing manager, Mark, explained the features of the tool to the product management team, one of the managers in the meeting, Jane, shot it down, saying: "This tool is really complex and difficult to use and is not foolproof and prone to people making mistakes." Jane then brought up her own tool she has been using and compared against the pricing team's tool. It turned out her tool was good for her own specific use but not for other PMs, whereas the pricing team's tool was designed for multiple uses by different people.

The way to respond to this person is to seek clarity of their critique first. Avoid getting defensive. Instead, focus on the subject matter. If it turns out that their work is better or can improve yours, acknowledge and thank them. Otherwise, let others make the comparison and decide. From my example above, after asking Jane for more details, the pricing manager explained that his goal was to create a tool that met different needs of the Product Managers, and they should use whichever tool was best for them. Then he opened up the discussion to get other people's feedback. A couple of managers thought the pricing tool was a good fit for their needs and they didn't think it was too complex. In addition, they also thought Jane's tool was too limited for their needs. They then suggested having their teams try both tools and then give an assessment after a few days. After the testing was finished, they chose the pricing team's tool. The key point here is to let objective stakeholders be the judge.

7. **Gossiper**. This person talks to you about other people and maybe to other people about you. He likes to start or spread rumours and engage in conspiracy theories. The gossip often is personal. He sometimes pits people against each other. Even on company issues, the Gossiper often engages in company rumours such as potential reorganizations, firings and promotions. Although the gossip can be about any number of things, most of them tend to be negative. This person doesn't seem to focus on the work

at hand but enjoys mingling with people. This not only makes you feel uncomfortable, but also distracts you from doing your work.

The way to deal with this person is to avoid engaging if you can. If you have no choice but to listen for a few minutes, just listen but don't participate. Don't give your opinion or ask for more details. Look for a break in the conversation and excuse yourself to go back to your work. If you really feel uncomfortable about the topic and don't want to hear the gossip, just be honest and say you prefer not to know because it makes you uncomfortable.

If you find out from reliable sources that the Gossiper has been gossiping bad things about you to other people, one way to handle this is to confront him directly but professionally. State that you heard from other people what he had said about you and you want to confirm if that is true. If he admits it, ask for clarifications. Regardless of the explanation, you can be direct by saying that you absolutely prefer to talk directly with people who have things to say about you, that you welcome and want to hear feedback but not second-hand. Moreover, express that in the future if he has something to say to you, even negative things, you would like him to talk to you directly.

8. **Hidden Dragon.** This person disappears, remains silent and doesn't get back to you on your question, message or inquiry. She does not keep you updated on her work progress that impacts you and she doesn't share relevant information with you. For example, you send her an email message asking for a date that she can give you the result of her work so you can do yours. One day, two days, three days go by and no answer. You resend the message and still no response. You see her in the hallway, ask her about it and she says she will get back to you. We can speculate why she is this way – maybe she is absent-minded, disorganized, inconsiderate or irresponsible, but whatever the reason is, it's not important to you.

The way to handle this person is make sure you have your question or message in writing. If she was assigned an action item that you depend on, make sure the deliverables and the due date are clear to her. Send a confirmation message to her, copy other team members and her manager.

The day before the due date, forward your previous message to her with a reminder of the action items and due date. She may find this annoying but will get the message. If she still doesn't deliver, you can escalate to her manager and you have evidence to support your escalation.

9. **Avoider**. This person is a master of delegating work to others, deflecting his responsibilities and not taking accountability. He's good at coming up with excuses to avoid taking on action items. He does the minimum to get by and is prone to point fingers when something goes wrong. He may also use "Not in my work scope" to avoid doing tasks. He only has his own interests at heart and is uncooperative in areas not totally aligned with his personal interests.

    Similar to the "Hidden Dragon", clear and written communication is key to dealing with this person. If you are the project lead or even just a team member, make sure that the work is assigned fairly and everyone has action items. The way to handle his attempt at avoiding work is to give him a choice: "We all have to share the work, so you can take on action item #1 or action item #2," and you move on only after this is decided. Then make sure the expected results and deadlines are clear. Summarize all the action items and send a summary message to him, copying team members and his manager.

10. **"Yes Boss" Only**. Hierarchy motivation drives his action with "rank" in mind. He only listens respectfully to the boss or higher-ranking managers. And then he turns around and is nasty with other co-workers. He often takes credit for work done by others and is good at hiding this character trait from his superiors.

    The key here is to keep paper trails. On important things and work you've completed and want to share with your colleagues and managers, write and send out email messages, copying relevant people. Since this type of person tends to avoid challenging work, follow the suggestion from #9. Make sure he's assigned appropriate tasks and hold his feet to fire.

These are just some real-life examples of typical difficult colleagues you may face at work. Keep in mind some key points in dealing with these situations: focus on the business problem at hand and not let it turn into a personal conflict, keep your professionalism and try your best to not lose your cool, putting the onus on that person to give examples. You will come across as an ultimate professional who is effective in working with different colleagues to get work done.

PART 4

Negotiating

"Winning isn't everything, but wanting to win is."
— **Vince Lombardi**

"Whoever wants the pearls must be brave to dive in the deep sea."
— **Soekarno, 1st President of Indonesia**

Good Negotiator

Who, What, Why

- **Who?**
  - Internal: Co-workers, other teams, manager, executives, HQ
  - External: Customers, suppliers, service providers, partners
- **What?** Money, terms & conditions, time, job assignment, other non-monetary items
- **Why?** Strive for win-win

Analysis approach

- True issues and parameters
- Assess possible trade-offs
- Determine boundary conditions:
  - Desired outcome value
  - Walkaway value
- Best guess of other side's walkaway value

Create win-win

- Build trust
- Ask lots of questions – knowledge is power
- Create trade-offs
- More than 1 option at the same time

Tips

- Maintain professionalism
- Respect cultural differences
- Document progress and status
- Don't over-promise
- Think long-term

Common mistakes

- Wanting to win at all cost
- Win-lose assumption
- Taking information at face value
- Not considering other's perspective
- Over-confidence

CHAPTER 19

How to Become a Good Negotiator

Negotiating means having a formal discussion with someone in order to reach an agreement. Even if we don't realize it, we negotiate frequently. We negotiate with people at work, our friends, family members and even strangers. We negotiate on all kinds of activities such as where to go eat, which movie to see, where to shop, what to buy, which work assignments to work on first, and how much salary is fair. Being good at negotiating is a valuable skill in any job and position in the company. The more responsibilities you have as you move to higher positions, the more critical your negotiation skills. Good negotiators get results, achieve win-win outcomes and build productive working relationships. You will find that successful employees and managers are very good negotiators.

What Do Negotiations Involve?

Money comes to mind when we think about negotiations, but there are many other items we negotiate over. I'll describe some common ones here.

- **Money**. This is a popular negotiation term. When we go shopping, we may bargain over the price of an item. Buying a car is synonymous with negotiating. I remember being afraid of getting ripped off, and having to negotiate in order to not pay too much for my car at the dealership.

- **Terms and Conditions**. When we rent an apartment or buy a house, we need to come to an agreement with the other party over items in addition to money. One such item is called "Terms and Conditions" (T&C). If you are renting an apartment, the T&C to negotiate include the duration of the lease, number of people living in the apartment, early lease termination and alterations to the apartment. While the landlord may be firm on some of these items, they could be open to negotiation on other items.

- **Time.** I hire a general contractor to build an additional room to my house and I want the project to be completed in two months but the contractor has a much longer time frame in mind. A similar situation at work would be if you're starting on a project for which your boss has a deadline in mind. As you're scoping out the project schedule, you realize you need more time. Or you would like to take your vacation on a certain date and your boss is afraid that the project may not be completed. These are examples of negotiating over the time component.

- **Job assignments**. Job assignments are another item you may negotiate over. Your boss has a list of job assignments that he would like you to take on; however, you're already working on other projects and can't take on additional tasks. Or you're working on a project and the project leader is discussing with you about your deliverables. However, certain tasks on that list you don't find interesting and you would rather take on other more exciting tasks.

- **Other non-monetary items.** You can exchange one item for another, or exchange your service for something tangible or the service of another person. For example, you propose to fix a friend's car and in exchange, he agrees to build you a storage cabinet. Or in negotiating a job offer, you may want to take less pay in exchange for a more flexible work schedule. And if you represent a professional union, you may negotiate over health benefits.

As you can see, negotiating situations can occur in our professional life or personal life, at work or at home or practically any place, even online.

However, for the purpose of this chapter, we'll focus on work situations. My objective here is to provide you a successful negotiation approach to any work situation.

Whom Do You Negotiate With?

- **Inside the company.** This includes anyone employed by the company such as co-workers on your team, co-workers on other teams, your manager and the executives of the company. Keep in mind that if you work for a multinational company that has business offices in other countries also, you need to be aware of cultural differences and language barriers when negotiating.

- **External party.** This includes customers, suppliers, service providers, competitors, industry partners, government agencies, etc.

What Is the Goal of Negotiating?

The goal is to reach an agreement that is better for you than without an agreement!

- **Strive for a win-win.** Contrary to what many people believe, the purpose of negotiating is not to get the best deal for you at the expense of the other party. You may wonder why this is not a good thing. After all, doesn't it demonstrate how shrewd you are in getting the most for yourself? And if the other party wasn't smart enough to look out for themselves, well, that's not your problem. While this may give your ego a boost, it's not a successful strategy in the long run, especially in the workplace. If the other party realizes they've been had or taken advantage of by you, they likely will carry a grudge and are much less likely to negotiate with you in good faith in the future. If they do, it would be under a cloud of suspicion and mistrust, which is not a good recipe for achieving a good, professional working relationship. The ideal outcome is a mutual agreement that both parties are satisfied with. In many Asian cultures, negotiation is a way of life in certain markets and regions. Negotiation combined with "face-giving" practices forms a key part of the win-win outcome and promotes sustainable partnerships.

Analysis Approach for Successful Negotiations

As described in the book *Negotiating Rationally* by Max H. Bazerman and Margaret A. Neale (Neale, 1993), here are the key steps to help you conduct negotiations successfully.

1. **Understand the true issues and parameters of the negotiation.** While it might have been clear to all parties involved, people may get off track and forget what they were negotiating about as discussions drag on and nerves get fragile. When I was a project lead negotiating with an international company, BTP Inc., to produce a printing product for my company, I thought we were clear on the negotiation goal – to come to an agreement to design and manufacture a printing product for my company. The true negotiation issue was the price and the parameter was the volume of units. As the negotiation dragged on, got more intense and emotional, BTP's CEO went off on a tangent and accused my manager of being a bully, not interested in their proposal and just toying with him. This had nothing to do with the negotiation issues. Finally we had to take a break for both sides to cool down, and when we reconvened, we reminded both my boss and the CEO what we were there to negotiate on.

    I have also seen situations where both parties started negotiating on one issue, then got sidetracked and began negotiating on something else. Labour union negotiations are perfect examples of this. Without a clear understanding of the main issue and its parameters at the beginning of the negotiation, it is difficult to get both parties to focus and, as a result, the negotiation faces the risk of getting derailed.

2. **Assess where possible trade-offs exist.** While the parties may only talk about the factors they want to negotiate on, they may not realize

there may be other variables they might want to consider trading off. In the example I cited above, BTP's executive was focusing on the highest price he could get for the product, even though there were other possible tradeoffs that would be worthwhile to consider. For instance, by partnering with a bigger company and a well-known brand, his company could get much more marketing exposure than he could on his own. Moreover, my company could help them with their quality process to achieve higher production yields as well as connect them to a broader community of material suppliers who could provide his company the same components to build but at a lower cost. So don't get fixated on one variable in a negotiation and remember to consider all possible variables to trade off.

3. **Determine your desired outcome value and the walkaway value**. This helps you stay disciplined and not be swayed by your emotions or the excitement of the negotiation. Of course, these values are not carved in stone, but it should take something significant for you to change them. Usually a negotiated agreement comes somewhere between your desired outcome and your walkaway value. You must be certain about your walkaway value and willing to end the negotiation with no regrets if you cannot at least achieve it. The useful question to ask yourself is: "What do I do if I don't reach an agreement?" or "Would I be better off not having an agreement if I don't achieve my walkway outcome?" If it's not better, then you need to rethink your expected outcomes.

   To determine your outcomes, especially the walkaway value, you need to understand your situation, your priorities and your tradeoffs. With our negotiation with BTP, the main variable was the price of the product and we had determined that our walkaway value was the breakeven price where we would not lose money selling the product. Since we believed this product would help sell other products our company produced, we were willing to set the walkaway value at the breakeven price. At anything below this price, we would be better off walking away instead of having an agreement that would cause our company to lose money.

4. **Make your best estimate of the other side's walkaway value**. This can be difficult to predict and is an educated guess. If you have a good idea

of the other side's walkaway value, you can try to validate your educated guess. If you find out that you are in the ballpark, you are more likely to succeed in reaching a negotiated agreement. Keep in mind, however, that the other side's value may change during the negotiation, depending on what information they learn or what additional tradeoffs exist. After discussing the possible tradeoffs my company could offer to BTP, including more market visibility for their brand, better production yield and lower cost from suppliers, they seemed more flexible on their pricing stand. Sensing this, we tested their possible walkaway value and were able to make an educated guess on their price.

Strategy for Creating Mutually Beneficial Agreements

I'll discuss here how to put the Analysis Approach into practice and describe the best ways for achieving a win-win agreement.

1. **Build trust**. This is an important criterion for a win-win negotiation. When the other side trusts you, they are more willing to share information, more open to possible options and more willing to reach a mutually beneficial agreement. Spend lots of time getting to know them. People in general love to talk about themselves and their world. Don't rush into negotiation right away. When you feel you have built a rapport, proceed with the negotiation. If you find them hesitant to talk, be patient. One good way to break the ice is to share with them some information about you. This usually enables them to be more comfortable and open up. Moreover, have these social talks outside of work where people tend to be more themselves in a relaxed setting.

2. **Ask lots of questions**. The goal here is to find out as much as you can. Information is power. The more you know about the other side's business – their priorities, challenges, needs, weaknesses, flexibility, etc. – the more you will be able to propose meaningful options for them to consider. While you probably won't get information directly from them, through the course of talking you may be able to infer and draw insight.

Over several conversations, we learned BTP was at risk of losing a major OEM (original equipment manufacturer) and that loss would cut significantly into their company's revenue stream. With this knowledge, we believed they would be motivated to reach a deal with us and use our company as leverage with this OEM. Moreover, we learned their product profit margin had been declining due to their high component cost. All this information was valuable to us and helped us understand why they focused so much on the product price. In addition, it helped us think creatively about solutions that would help address their needs and enable our company to be profitable at the same time.

3. **Evaluate between expectations and risk preferences to create trade-offs**. All of us have different levels of tolerance for risk. If you tend to be more risk-averse, you may want to take a more "sure thing" deal while compromising on other terms. On the other hand, if you're a risk-taker, you may be willing to take a deal with less certainty of results but potential for bigger returns. Knowing the other side's expectations and risk preferences will greatly help you formulate your strategy. Again, the way to formulate an educated guess of this is by talking to them and asking lots of questions. With the BTP negotiation, we speculated that, given their company's vulnerable business situation at the time, they would be more likely to accept a low-risk deal in exchange for a lower price and better terms for my company. Given this, we came up with a few options.

4. **Make more than one offer at the same time**. This is a good practice to implement. If you offer only one option, the other side has limited options to respond. They either accept or reject your offer, or they can propose another deal. By offering more than one option, you have control over the options, all of which should benefit your company and achieve a possible win-win outcome. If you offer only one option and they reject it, you have reached an impasse. If you come back with a better option, they know your interest level and they can negotiate for an even better deal. If they counter-offer, they likely will counter with more favourable terms to them.

    By offering multiple offers, the other side is under a certain pressure to choose and less likely to reject all options and propose their own counter-offer. You can even ask them to rank your options in order of preference and that will give you more insight into their thinking. We offered BTP three options: (1) Guaranteed large number of units at a low fixed price; (2) small initial unit volume with a higher price and then a lower price if we exceeded certain volume levels; and (3) a higher fixed price with no guaranteed unit volume. Moreover, all these options included our company's additional benefits to them – more marketing exposure, better production yield and lower supply chain cost. As we suspected, they chose option #1 since it guaranteed them a revenue stream. At the same time, with a lower price, our company would be able to achieve profitability.

Common Mistakes in Negotiating

- Desire to win at any cost. Keep in mind that this is not a competition and you should keep an open mind and be flexible. I was involved in a bid against other competitors to acquire a company's product. Because this was an important product, I felt a strong sense to win the bidding war. As a result, the bidding price kept going higher, reaching a point of being unreasonable. In the end, one competitor apparently had an even stronger desire to win and ended up bidding a very high price to win the deal. This turned out to be an expensive purchase for their company. If my company had won the bid at that price, we would have lost money selling that product.

- Assuming your gain must come at the expense of the other party. This does not achieve a win-win outcome. In addition, it limits your creativity to find beneficial tradeoffs and explore all possible options. While it may be a short-term win for you, it's not beneficial for future working relationships.

- Taking certain information at face value. Keep in mind that the information presented by the other side can be skewed. Treat the other side's information and initial offer with some healthy skepticism. Instead, take their information and do your homework to validate and verify its accuracy.

- Not thinking about the other party's perspective. A key requirement for being a good negotiator is being able to seek information from the other side to help you better understand their situation and anticipate their offer or their response to your offer. Without having some idea of their perspective, you're operating in the dark and hoping for the best.

- Being cocky about attaining outcomes in your favour. This is a dangerous trap. Overconfidence induces complacency and inhibits thorough research and possibilities for creative solutions. Remember you are trying to get the best possible win-win outcome.

Additional Tips

- Maintain your professionalism. Don't get emotional or personal. Negotiation can get intense and contentious. There usually is a lot of ego and personal pride involved. You must be able to control your emotions, even when the other party is trying to provoke you through snarky remarks or put-downs. You don't have to take it lying down but you should also try not to lash back at them. Instead, channel all your energy to the issue being discussed. If you are not successful getting the negotiation back on track, maybe it's time to take a break so everyone can cool off and resume the discussion at a later time when ready.

- Understand and respect potential cultural and language differences of the other party if they are from a different country or background. Before engaging in the negotiation, take a little time to learn about their culture and how best to work with them. One of the common-sense practices is to avoid using your language's jargon or slang since they may not understand and may even see that as a lack of respect.

- Document the progress and status of negotiations in writing to avoid potential confusion or disagreements. At the beginning, document the negotiation issues and the parameters for both parties to make sure everyone has the same understanding. Document key milestones achieved or any changes to the negotiation issues. And if there are any disagreements, documenting them allows these to be brought up and resolved right away.

- Do your best to achieve a win-win agreement. This creates positive professional relationships and sets you up for productive future negotiations.

- Do not make promises you may not be able to keep. Don't agree to a deal if you need final approval from company management, even if you are very confident you have gotten a great deal. When I was a product manager in my early years of employment, I once agreed to purchase a large volume of a computer component for my company. I was very confident that my company would be able to sell and, better yet, it was at a great price from this supplier. I later informed my manager that I had agreed to this deal and just needed his signature on the contract the supplier would send over the next day. To my surprise, my manager was quite upset I had committed without clearing it with him. I then learned that this business division, as a business practice, does not commit to that kind of agreement since the risk could be high due to unforeseen factors outside the company's control.

  As a result, I had to go meet with the supplier's sales manager the next day and renege on my agreement. After some tense discussions and my sincere effort to explain, the sales manager reluctantly agreed to void our agreement. Technically, I wasn't legally bound to the agreement since the contract had not been signed, but my words were good enough for him. Needless to say, I was embarrassed and lost credibility with the supplier. It took a lot of effort to rebuild my credibility with them again. It was a good lesson learned.

CHAPTER 20

How to Negotiate a Job Offer

This chapter focuses on multinational companies whose headquarters are based in the United States or in other Western countries. Other companies may have some differences in their hiring process. However, they're likely to include many elements of the hiring procedure and process described here.

One common question graduating students ask me is if they should negotiate when they get a job offer and if yes, how to do it. My answer is you should absolutely negotiate, especially if you have multiple offers. The best time to negotiate for the best compensation package, of which salary is a big component, is when you receive the job offer because that is when you have the most leverage. By making you an offer, the employer showed that they wanted you more than the other candidates. They would not want to lose you over the compensation package terms and they will more likely do what they can to get you to say yes.

While salary is the most significant variable, there are several other components to a job offer. A job offer includes salary as well as other incentives such as stock options and a sign-on bonus. With respect to salary, each job position is associated with a job level and each job level has a predetermined range of salary from which the HR manager and hiring manager can decide on the amount to offer. The salary offered would likely be somewhere in the middle or in the lower half of the range. This leaves room for negotiation if necessary and for future salary increases for the employee. If they offer you a salary near the top end of the range, the manager has limited flexibility on how much salary raise he can give you in the future. The company also has guidelines on the flexibility of the other benefits, such as how much cash to offer for sign-on bonus.

The Human Resource manager would likely be the person you negotiate with since HR has the final approval on many of the offer terms. The HR manager consults with the hiring manager and makes counter-offers based on the hiring manager's input. However, there may be other components that make sense for the hiring manager to negotiate with you directly.

Companies may differ on the degree of flexibility of the offer components. Some companies are firm on salary but flexible on stock options or sign-on bonus. Do your best to find out where they are limited and where they have the flexibility. Here are some of the typical job offer components:

Monetary Components

The HR manager plays a major role here in helping the hiring manager.

- Base salary.

- Stock options. These are shares given to you that you can exercise over a number of years at a given price. For example, 5,000 shares at $30 per share price vested over four years. If you sell all 5,000 shares after four years at $40 a share, you gain $50,000 pre-tax.

- Restricted stock units. These are shares given to you outright ($0 cost) vested over a number of years.

- One-time sign-on bonus. Typically 1–3 months of the base salary.

- Relocation expenses. This covers your moving expenses if you have to relocate from another city or state.

- Temporary housing. This covers you for a temporary period while you try to find permanent living arrangements.

Negotiate a Job Offer

Should you negotiate
- If you have multiple offers
- 10% higher starting pay is equivalent to 2–3 years of increments

How to negotiate
- Understand the parameters
- Assess possible trade-offs
- Determine desired outcome and walkway value
- Estimate company's acceptable limits
- Counter-offer options

What to negotiate

MONETARY
- Starting base salary
- Relocation expenses
- Temporary housing
- Stock options
- Restricted stock units

NON-MONETARY
- Work schedule flexibility
- Job responsibilities
- Travel requirements

Tips
- Don't come across arrogant
- Don't issue ultimatums
- Don't be confrontational
- No "fake news"
- Be professional and positive
- Don't burn bridges

Let me explain the importance of the starting salary. Companies determine employee salary raises and bonuses as a percentage of the employee's base salary. For example, if your starting salary is $70,000 a year and you get a 5% raise and 10% bonus after one year, you receive a $3,500 raise and $7,000 cash bonus. On the other hand, if your starting salary is $80,000 and you get the same 5% raise and 10% bonus, you receive $4,000 raise and $8,000 cash bonus. Comparing the two scenarios, you receive $1,500 more with the higher starting salary. Assuming you stay in this job for 3 years and get the same 5% raise and 10% bonus every year, you will earn a total of $4,500 more. So if you were able to negotiate for a higher starting salary, you not only get paid more in your base salary but also more in raises and bonuses.

One more point. Typical salary increases are small because they're based on the overall company's performance, projected budget and the entire employee population. Typically, an average salary increase is in the range of 2–5%, not very much. Because of this, negotiate for the best salary you can in the beginning.

Non-monetary Components

The hiring manager is likely the decision-maker on these items and the person you would talk to directly.

- Work flexibility. For example, how often you can work at home.

- Job responsibilities. In addition to your core job responsibilities, are there other exciting and interesting projects you can be a part of? Can you get assigned to a company-wide project where you get more exposure to other aspects of the company? Is it possible to work on a temporary project in another country, if that's what you like?

- Vacation benefits. If you move to this company after a long period of employment with a previous company, you probably have less vacation days. You can negotiate to get more vacation days than the company policy allows. However, this tends to be a handshake agreement between you and the hiring manager and not something that would be in writing. The downside is, if your manager leaves the company, you may lose this benefit. Also note that many companies now have the "unlimited vacation" policy. There is no set amount of vacation days for employees and approval for taking vacation is between the manager and the employees. Obviously, for these companies, vacation benefits are not a negotiating term.

- Travel flexibility and requirements. Do you want to travel more or less? If you prefer to travel less than what the job stipulates, you may be able to negotiate for less business travel or travel to business locations closer to home. Before you consider negotiating on this term, make sure you are clear on the importance of business travel in your job. If this is a critical part of the job, it may not be an option for you to negotiate.

Case Study Example

Let's examine and negotiate a job offer scenario.

- You are a new college graduate and recently received an employment offer as a Business Analyst from an HR manager of Stay InTouch Inc., a social networking company.

- The manager expressed in the offer letter that the company is very excited to have you join its family. The company's offer includes $70,000 a year in base salary and 2,000 shares of stock option.

- You will need to relocate to another state to join this company.

- The offer seems low to you.

- The job market is good for new college graduates this year based on credible market information. However, you don't know for sure but guess that the company has other candidates in the pipeline.

- You currently don't have other offers, but you had excellent interviews with two other companies and received positive feedback.

- You want to negotiate a better job offer.

How I Would Negotiate This Offer

Let's review the Analysis Approach described in the "How to become a good negotiator" chapter.

1. Understand the true issues and parameters of the negotiation.
2. Assess where possible tradeoffs exist.
3. Determine your desired outcome and the walkaway value.
4. Make your best estimate of the other side's walkaway value.

I'll use these steps to help me with my approach:

1. Understand the true issues and parameters of the negotiation. I am negotiating the job offer as a package, not just the salary, although it is a big factor. While only salary and stock options were listed in the offer, I want to think about other components that are important to me. I am currently tight on money; I would need it for my move and to find temporary living arrangements when I start my job. In addition, I'm interested in international experience and I want to explore the possibility of working overseas on an interesting project.

2. Assess where possible tradeoffs exist. From my thinking in #1, the variables I want to negotiate on are, in order of importance: salary, relocation expenses, sign-on bonus, stock options and opportunity to work on a temporary assignment overseas. Therefore, I want to negotiate for a higher salary and relocation expenses/sign-on bonus in exchange for receiving a smaller number of stock options. Working overseas is a bonus and I can ask for it if I cannot get an agreement on other components.

3. Determine your desired outcome and the walkaway value. Before I do this, I need to find out as much information as I can from the company and research thoroughly about the job market. Specifically, I need to talk to the HR manager to find out how flexible they are on the offer terms and whether they are open to other items not mentioned in the offer letter. To do this, I need to ask a lot of questions:

    - "I'm very interested in joining Stay InTouch and I'm doing my due diligence to gather as much information as I can to help me with my decision, and given my understanding of the job market, the salary offered seems low. Do you have any flexibility on the salary figure?"

    - "Can you let me know where the company is more flexible and where it's not?"

    - "Are there other items not included in the offer the company would be open to discuss?" Be prepared to give your own suggestions if asked.

    - If the manager does not bring up the items you have in mind, ask: "Does the company have the flexibility to provide relocation expenses and a sign-on bonus?"

    - I generally find employers are willing to share information with you because they want you to join them and would try to make it work for you. I would also talk to the hiring manager and ask about the flexibility on the work items that I wanted. Let's assume that I found out the company has a little bit of room to increase the salary, no flexibility on the stock options, and is willing to offer relocation expenses and sign-on bonus. Typically, the hiring manager owns the budget for some of these expenses and he has to decide how much he can afford to spend on me. In talking to the hiring manager, I also found out that he's open to a temporary overseas assignment in the second year, depending on my job performance.
    With my knowledge about of the company's flexibility and my

own assessment that I may get at least one more offer from another company, I come up with my desired and walkaway value. My walkway value is: 5% above the offered salary, 2,000 stock shares and $5,000 relocation expenses. My high value is: 20% above offered salary, 2,000 stock shares, $5,000 relocation expenses, and 2 months of salary for sign-on bonus. I want to shoot for achieving the final agreement somewhere in this range. However, because I like the company a lot, I would accept an offer closer to my walkaway value if that is the best I can get. I also understand that I'm willing to turn down the offer if I don't achieve at least the walkaway value because I feel confident I can get a better offer from another company.

4. Make your best estimate of the other side's walkaway value. Based on the information I have, my best guess of the company's lowest acceptable value is somewhat higher than my lowest acceptable value, but since I'm not absolutely certain, I am comfortable keeping my current walkaway value.

The final step is to make a couple of counter-offers that are attractive to me. By offering multiple offers, I encourage the HR manager to consider which one of the counter-offers is best for the company. This is better than offering only one counter-offer which the HR manager has to either accept or reject or come up with another offer that may not be ideal to me.

Additional Tips

- Don't be arrogant or give the impression of arrogance. Coming across as a hotshot and having an "I don't need this company" attitude is a real turnoff. Even if you end up joining the company, you're not starting off with the best impression.

- Don't give ultimatums. "Take it or leave it" or strong-arm tactics usually don't work. There is no need to do this, especially since you don't know for sure where the company is flexible or firm. If your "take it or leave it" offer doesn't work for the company, the negotiation is over. Keep in mind no one is irreplaceable in the company, not even the CEO, and you're not a must-hire. Companies almost always have other candidates to choose from. If you do decide to use this tactic, be sure you're ready to walk away. But my recommendation is to stay away from this tactic.

- Don't be confrontational or adversarial. Keep in mind this is one of the companies you want to join and they also want you since they have made you an offer. Maintain your professionalism and cordial discussions in your negotiation. Don't push them into a corner, use unprofessional language or an accusatory tone if you don't like the offer terms or feel the company is not accommodating. Even if the company plays hardball, stay calm and don't let your emotions get in the way. After all, this is a business negotiation.

- Don't lie. Don't make up stories or offers you don't have in order to gain leverage. The business community can be a small world where people know each other, and if you're caught lying, the company may rescind the offer and you have a black mark on your reputation.

- Don't push past the limit and try to go for every last dime you can get. If you have an offer that's in the range between your high and lowest acceptable value, consider taking it and not pushing it further. You need to use your judgment here. If you and the company have gone back and forth a few times and it feels like they're running out of patience, it may be a good idea to accept. Keep in mind the adage "Penny wise, pound foolish". It's more important to start off on the right foot with a good impression than to get a little more money and leave a bad perception.

- Be professional in your communications with the company. When in doubt, ask for clarification. Maintain a positive attitude and show the company representatives that you very much are interested in joining the company. Even if things do not work out or you decide to take another offer, explain to them honestly and professionally. If you have conducted your negotiation in good faith, the company representatives would understand if you have a better offer they could not match. Keep in mind to never burn bridges because you never know if you will cross paths again with them.

- There are good websites offering useful information about specific companies. For example, in the US, Glassdoor.com site provides information on a specific company's annual salaries by job titles, feedback on the management team, etc. Check for similar websites for companies in the region you're applying in.

CHAPTER 21

How to Ask for a Raise

Before we discuss the question of how to ask for a raise, it's important to understand the salary structure and the impact that performance review has on salary increase. In this chapter, we will cover how performance evaluation impacts salary review as well as examining reasons that may merit a raise and an approach you can use when you meet with your manager.

In a typical salary structure of a company, each job is associated with a job level that is tied to a salary range, i.e. the salary of all employees with that job level falls in that range. Different job levels have different salary ranges and the higher the job level, the higher the salary range. When you're hired, your salary is likely to be in your job level's salary range. As long as you are in the same job level, your salary increase cannot push your base salary above the upper limit. If you're near the upper limit, in order to increase your pay significantly, you need to be promoted to the next job level.

Understanding How Performance Review Impacts Salary Increase

Formal job performance and salary review is usually done once a year and changes in salary are based on how the employee is evaluated. Many companies still use the forced distribution ranking system where employees are ranked relative to their peers, while other companies evaluate employees individually instead of relative to their peers. Regardless of evaluation method, you are evaluated on two dimensions: (1) the results you produced versus expectations; and (2) your effectiveness in delivering the results. The outcome of your performance review plays a key role in how much salary increase you'll get.

HR provides guidance for managers to manage the salary increase they give to their employees based on their evaluation. The salary increase guidance can be changed year to year, depending on a number of factors, including company business results, market condition and competitive environment. Another thing to be aware of is that your manager has a fixed budget to administer the salary for all his employees. He has to decide how to allocate salary increases so as not to exceed his budget limit. While this is not your concern, it's good to be aware of the constraint your manager faces.

The amount of your salary increase is determined by two factors: the outcome of your performance review, and where your current salary is in your job level's salary range. I think employees put too much emphasis on salary increase. Generally, the salary increase is not significant. If you are ranked in the middle of the pack or you delivered results that met expectations, you may get a 2–3% raise, nothing to write home about. If you are ranked in the top 25% or you delivered results that exceeded expectations, you may get a ~5% raise – a little more but not a huge increase by any means. For example, if your salary is $80,000, a 5% raise comes out to $333 more per month pre-tax and deductions. It's an okay raise but nothing too exciting. The way to significantly increase your salary is to get promoted to the next job level, where it's not uncommon to see a 10% salary increase.

Possible Reasons to Justify a Raise

Before you sit down and request your manager for a raise, you need to be self-aware and objective about the reasons to justify a raise. "I am not able to keep up with my bills so I need to get paid more," "My friends are getting paid more than I am" and "I haven't gotten a raise in a while" are not relevant reasons to justify a salary increase. Achieving a high ranking or an excellent performance review is the best way to get a raise. Do your best to maximize your chances of getting an excellent review. Before you approach your

How to Ask for a Raise

- **Understand increment factors**
  - Salary structure
  - Performance review
  - Promotion — *For larger jump in pay*

- **Reasons to justify**
  - Pay under minimum wage
  - Uncompetitive pay vs peer companies
  - Uncompetitive pay vs peer employee — *Not easy!*
  - Performance review done "unfairly"

- **Approach (good negotiator)**
  - Understand the issues and parameters
  - Establish desired outcome and walkaway value
  - Estimate acceptable range
  - Explain information to gain manager support
  - Listen for manager's response and options
  - Gain clear "next step" and timeline — *Minimum to highlight concerns and gain extra attention*

- **Tips**
  - Prepare with research from web resources
  - Personal hardship not a reason to justify
  - No "entitlement" mindset
  - Avoid ultimatums or threats
  - No lies!
  - Don't over-push the line

manager, examine closely the possible rationales to support your request for a raise. Here are the possible reasons:

- You are underpaid for your job level in the company. One way to determine if your salary is within the salary range of your job level is to ask your HR or your manager for this information. The company should have a salary table showing the salary range for each job level by job function in the company. Although it's not common, I have seen cases where an employee's salary was below the minimum range of their salary level. If this is the case, it needs to be rectified.

- Your pay is not competitive. Comparing to your peers in other companies in the same industry shows that you are paid less than they are. You need to do your homework to obtain the information and industry salary data to back your claim. Online resources such as Indeed.com or Glassdoor.com provide useful information on the salary compensation and benefits of different companies. However, this is a difficult sell because it's not a straightforward comparison. The HR manager would want to compare the total compensation package and not just the base salary. This includes, among other things, bonus, vacation days, stock incentives, 401K matching and health benefits. Because it's difficult to get accurate data from other companies to support your claim, this would be a tough hill to climb.

    However unfair it may seem, companies usually are not inclined to change your salary in this case for a couple of reasons. One, your company already has a salary structure and as long as your job level's salary is within the designated range, there is no problem to be corrected. Secondly, if the company adjusts your salary for this reason, it may open up a can of worms for other employees in the company. As a result, it's unlikely your company will accommodate your request. The one situation your company might be more open to re-examine your salary is when you receive a better job offer from another company. That may be your best chance to negotiate a better salary. Refer to the "How to negotiate your job offer" chapter for more details. Due to the need to hire strong employees, companies need to be competitive in their offer. This can create an undesirable situation where current employees are paid less than new employees in the same job level. Unfortunately, this is a fact of life. There may come a point where the only option you have to increase your salary significantly, outside of getting a promotion, is to look for a job with another company. When you receive a better offer from another company, you can decide whether to accept or use it to negotiate a better salary with your current company.

- You are paid lower than your peers in the same job level. An example of this is when a new employee joins the company with a base salary higher than yours even though that employee has the same job level as you. Unlike you, this employee has not contributed to the company; so it seems grossly unfair that you get paid less. Another example: a co-worker is doing a similar job and has the same performance ranking as you but received more pay raise than you. One likely reason for this is that her starting salary was higher than yours when she joined the company and the salary increase is a percentage of the base salary. While both cases have a reasonable argument, you're unlikely to be able to convince the company to make the changes. As I discussed earlier, employers compete for workers in the market place and at times they have to pay a high salary to get the candidates they want.

- Your salary increase was negatively affected because you were "unfairly" evaluated. It's best to prepare your manager to represent you fairly before he goes into the evaluation meeting with other managers. Or if the company evaluates employees individually, prepare your manager thoroughly before he sits down to review your performance. It's much more difficult to change the review outcome once the review results are completed. The one recourse you have is to convince your manager you deserve a better performance review outcome and to negotiate with him to make an exception and give you more of a salary increase than your review result allows. However, if you feel strongly about this and you're not getting satisfactory answers from your manager, you may want to escalate it to a higher management level. Your odds are long here, but I have seen a few cases that worked out in the employee's favour.

How to Approach Asking for a Raise

You have done your homework and determined you have a strong case and want to move ahead. You should consider asking for a raise if you have confidence that your manager values your work and wants to keep you on his team. Think of this as a negotiation and make sure you read the "How to be a good negotiator" chapter to help you develop an effective game plan. Here is the approach to use in negotiating:

1. Understand the true issues and parameters of the negotiation.
2. Assess where possible tradeoffs exist.
3. Determine your desired outcome and the walkaway value.
4. Make your best estimate of the other side's lowest value.

Let's apply this approach.

1. **Understanding the issues and parameters**. The issue here is clear. You want to negotiate for a salary raise and are equipped with information, rationale and data to support your case.

2. **Assess where possible tradeoffs exist**. From your perspective, think about possible tradeoffs you can make. Be creative. Instead of a raise, would you settle for stock options, a cash bonus or other non-monetary items such as extra vacation days, opportunities to attend popular industry conferences, or a new project that will give you more visibility? From your understanding of the manager and his flexibility, think about the possible areas he may be willing to compromise. You may not have a lot of insight here, so when you sit down to talk with your manager, ask questions to find out as much information as possible. This will help you think of potential options you can propose.

3. **Determine your desired outcome and walkaway value.** This is an important step. Based on all the information you have so far, think about these two values. The walkaway value is especially important to consider since you are willing to walk away if you get less than this outcome. To

help you determine the walkaway value, think about the lowest outcome you would accept before you would be willing to look for another job. Let's assume that you are generally satisfied and like your job, the company and the people, and even if you didn't get what you wanted, you would be willing to stay put. In this case your walkaway value is status quo – no change to your current situation. Or you are willing to search for another job and join another company if you don't get some compensation above what you are currently getting. Give serious consideration to what your walkaway value is.

4. **Make your best estimate of the other side's lowest value.** If you don't really know, ask yourself questions that may give you some clue. Questions such as: "How much does your manager value you and your work?" and "How willing is he to lose you, and how hard would it be to replace you if you leave?" may give you some clue about his flexibility. If you believe that he doesn't value your work enough to try to keep you if you leave, then you may not want to go through with the meeting. On the other hand, if life would be really difficult for him if you leave, you have leverage here to negotiate since he's more likely to accommodate.

When it's time to sit down with your manager, follow these steps:

- Explain to him that you have been putting your best effort into your job and contributing to the company as much as you can. You have given it a lot of thought and believe your salary is low and would like to request a raise. Here is an example of what to say: "I have been with the company for a while now and I have always given my best effort to contribute to the company. I have been giving my salary situation a lot of thought and I believe my salary is not competitive with the market and I would like to request a raise. Let me tell you why." Then give the manager the reasons, data, and any information from your research to support your case.

- Ask him for his thoughts. Listening to his comments will give you some ideas of where he stands. If he's open to your request and asks what you have in mind, be prepared to give him a percentage raise and explain why. If he says he has no flexibility, ask him to explain and then probe for areas where he may have more flexibility. Ask: "If it's not possible to give me a raise, which areas do you have flexibility?" and listen to what he comes up with. If you don't hear anything meaningful, ask: "Is giving stock incentives an option? Do you have any flexibility on that?" or "What about a cash bonus?" If he is open to these ideas and says he will check with HR, let him know you appreciate the effort and ask for a follow-up time. In general, if your manager values your work and wants to keep you, he will look for some ways to appease you, even if he cannot give you a raise or much else.

- Your objective of the meeting is to get closure or the next actionable step. The outcome of the meeting should be: (1) yes, your manager agrees and supports your request and will ask for approval; (2) no, there is nothing he can do or seems willing to do for you, which tells you where you stand; (3) he's open to consider your request but needs to look into it; or (4) he cannot give you a raise but is open to other ideas. Don't end the meeting until you are clear on the next step. Ask and clarify the next step if you're not sure, and confirm when he will follow up with you.

Even if you don't get your wish, your manager is likely to keep your request in mind, especially if your case has merit. At the next salary review time, he may be more flexible in giving a higher raise than he normally would, assuming that you get a decent performance review.

Additional Tips

- There are websites offering useful information about specific companies' salary compensations and benefits. For example, on Glassdoor.com, you can get information on a company's annual salaries as well as details on company benefits.

- Don't use personal hardship or financial difficulties as justifications for your request, such as "I cannot afford to make ends meet or pay my bills," or "My husband is unemployed and I need to make more." Companies focus on business issues so you should focus on the business justifications.

- Don't be arrogant or give the impression that your case is so obvious, you should not even have to ask for a raise, or come across as "I am entitled to a raise". It's a real turn-off.

- Don't give an ultimatum or threat. It doesn't serve any purpose other than push your manager into a corner. If you do decide to use this tactic, be sure that you're ready to walk away.

- Don't lie. Don't make up stories or data you don't have in order to give yourself leverage. If you're caught with a lie, you will lose credibility and trust from your manager and it can hurt your case in the future. He will be less likely to give you the benefit of the doubt.

- Don't push past the limit and try to go for every dime you can get. If you can get something between your desired and walkaway value, consider taking it and not pushing it further. Keep in mind the adage "Penny wise, pound foolish".

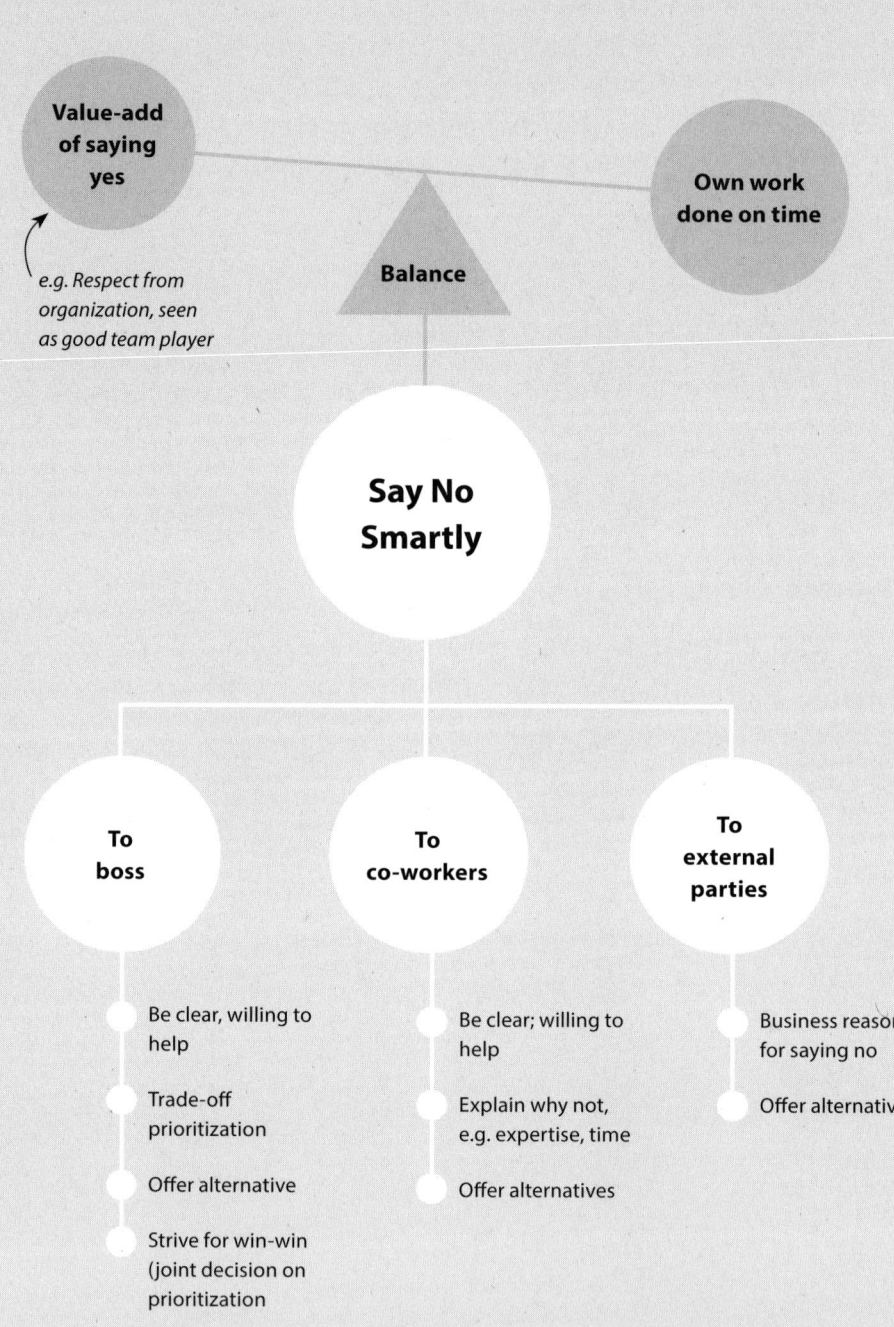

CHAPTER 22

How to Say No Smartly

Most of us have good intentions. We want to help and please people. We want to say yes to their requests and hate to say no because we don't want to disappoint them, even sometimes at our expense. We want to be a good team player. However, in work environments, requests and demands of your time have no boundaries. Many people are not aware of or sensitive to your time constraints, even though they work with you and see first-hand how busy you are. They want to satisfy a need they have and they assume you would let them know if you cannot accommodate.

Having co-workers value and respect you is important and is a key factor in your success at work. As I talk about in the chapter "How to stand out and promote yourself", showing ability to work well with people and being a good team player who provides value to the company is a big plus for you at performance reviews. Even more importantly, when promotional opportunities open up, you would be in a select group of people considered. After all, who doesn't like someone who goes out of their way to work with them and help them succeed?

However, the trick is to balance between getting your work done and helping other people. First and foremost, you must get your work done on time and do an excellent job before you can help others. If you fail at doing your job or are perceived as ignoring your work, your boss is not going to be happy. The ability to prioritize and balance between getting your work done and helping other people is important to your success. Be clear at all times about your job priorities, deliverables and deadlines. When you get an unexpected request, you are in a position to assess objectively your availability.

The ability to say no while expressing a sincere desire to help is a good skill to have. In this chapter, I'll offer ways and suggestions on how to say no smartly.

How to Say No to Your Manager

Throughout your job and career, you should expect unplanned requests from your manager to take on certain projects or short-term tasks. If you can accommodate and the request is important to your boss and gives you good visibility, by all means say yes. However, before you agree to take it on, make sure you understand clearly the task's objectives, expected deliverables and timeline. If you're unclear, make sure you ask for clarification. If you don't feel confident about the timeline or your ability to deliver some of the expected results, this is your opportunity to negotiate. You can negotiate to extend the deadline, reduce some of the deliverables, or ask your manager for additional resources in order to complete the task. Make sure that taking on this request will benefit you as well in some ways – whether you will get visibility with upper management, credit from your manager, or a chance to learn other skills you don't have. This is not being selfish, but achieving a win-win situation for both of you.

Sometimes, however, your manager may get a request from her boss or other executives and ask you to take it on for her. In these instances, even if the task is trivial and doesn't offer much benefit to you, you may want to take it because she's doing her boss a favour and you want to make her look good.

If you're already swamped with work and feel you can't accommodate her request without jeopardizing your own work, you should say no. You don't like to disappoint our manager. But when you need to say no, there are ways to say no and still come across as a team player. Here's how:

- Ask for details of the requests, including goals, expectations and deadlines. By listening first, you show that you care and want to know as much as you can before considering. So if you end up saying no, at least you have considered and not dismissed her request out of hand.

How to Say No Smartly

- Be clear that you want to help, but given all the work on your plate, you cannot do so without making changes to your priorities.

- Put the ball back in your manager's court by having her help you prioritize how important her request is relative to the tasks you currently have on your plate. Don't assume that she knows all the things you're working on. Chances are she doesn't know the full picture. Explain by giving her a full run-down of what you're working on, how much time and effort they require and how much longer they will take. Then ask your manager to prioritize her request against your tasks. If she prioritizes her request higher than some of your tasks, you can agree to take it on, but only after getting her agreement to drop or delay the other less important work. If she deems that her request is not as important as your work, then she has answered her own question and, as a result, will take back the request or consider some other ways to get it done.

    Be clear that it is a zero-sum game: if something gets put on your plate, something else must come off. Don't give in. If your manager is still pushing, push back by saying: "You know I'm swamped already and if I take one more thing on, I will squeeze everything in and end up doing a half-baked job and delivering poor-quality work, which is bad for me, for my team and a bad reflection on you, and I don't think we want that to happen."

- Offer alternative ideas if possible. For example, do you know someone who is capable and may be available to help your manager? Or is this something that your boss can hire outside help for, such as contractors you may know who can do the job.

- Strive for a win-win solution. The idea is to involve your manager in coming up with a solution so you don't feel you have to make the decision on your own. This way, once a decision is reached, she will have taken some ownership in the decision. And even if the decision is no, you still are perceived as a team player and you don't have to feel bad or disappointed that you let your boss down.

    After the decision is reached, write a short email message to your manager confirming the decision. This is to make sure that both of you are on the same page and to avoid any miscommunication later on. It eliminates the "I thought we decided that you would do it." If that happens, you can clarify by referring back to you email message. Managers are often busy and can be forgetful.

Let's look at an example. Your manager asks you to take on a project. You learn that it will take 25% of your time for three weeks. You ask for the details, timeline and expectations. You realize you can't take this on as your plate is full. The question here is how to say no. Let's apply the steps described above.

- "I would love to help taking this on, but I am not able to, given all the things I have on my plate. Here are the major projects I'm working on currently: task 1, 2 and 3." Describe each project briefly, focusing on expected deliverables, timeline and amount of time required. Summarize by saying: "These projects are taking 100% of my time at least for the next four weeks."

- "Can you help prioritize your project with the projects I have on my plate? Is it more important than some of the projects I'm working on?" This puts the ball in your manager's court to prioritize for you. If she confirms that this is more important, then you can suggest: "How about I take this project on and delay project xyz which has lower priority until I finish this new project?" Or after understanding all your projects and the manager decides that her request is not as important, she will withdraw her project and you have your answer. Then you could offer some alternatives, such as: "I know a couple of people who would do a good job for you and they may be available. Would you like me ask them?" Or "Maybe this is something we can outsource to some of the contractors we have used in the past."

Whatever your manager decides, it's an acceptable outcome and you come away looking good since you presented yourself as a team player.

Sometimes you're available to take on a last-minute request, but the deadline is unrealistic. Don't assume your boss knows how long it takes. She knows when she wants the results, but not necessarily what is needed to get the job done. You need to set the right expectation. It's not good if you commit but cannot deliver. If you think it will take longer but you're not certain, tell your boss that you will scope it out, see what is required and come back to her with a timeline. If you learn that it actually will take longer than she would like, explain why and support your assessment with data and solid reasons.

My boss came to me one afternoon and asked me to do a professional services analysis to see if there could be an opportunity for the company to generate more revenue by offering value-add services to customers. When I asked her for the deadline, she said her boss would like to receive it by the end of the next day. While I wasn't certain how long it would take to get the data, I had a feeling that it would take longer. I told my manager I would do a quick assessment to see what is required. I then went to an IT expert in the company to get an idea. I learned it would take about three days to get the data manually because the company did not have an automated system to extract the data. I explained this to my boss and clarified that it would take five days to complete a thorough analysis with a full written report. Although it wasn't the answer my manager wanted, she understood and was able to explain to her boss. It's better to set an expectation and beat it than over-commit and miss the deadline.

How to Say No to Co-workers

Showing ability to work well with people and to be a good team player who provides value to the company is a big plus at your performance review and when a promotion or better job opportunity becomes available. If you could help out without compromising your work, you would earn goodwill, credibility and visibility with your colleagues and their managers. You also have chips you can cash in when you need them in the future. However, if you can't accommodate the request without compromising your own work, you need to say no. Here's how to say no smartly in such situations:

- Listen to their request and ask for details and timeline to determine if you can help. Before you say no, it's important to have a good understanding of the request to help you decide. This also helps the other person know that you listened and considered their request.

- Be clear that you want to help, but can't. If you don't have the expertise to help them, let them know. They would appreciate your honesty. If you can't because you don't have time, explain that you have so much on your plate at the moment.

- Offer alternative ideas. For example, can they wait until you finish some of your tasks so you will have more time? Do you know someone else who is capable and maybe available to help? While you're saying no, you are giving your co-worker options to consider. Even though you turn them down, you come across as a team player willing to help.

Word of caution: think carefully about accommodating other people if there are risks of compromising your work. You will not get extra credit from assisting other people if you don't do a good job with your own work. We may have a tendency to think that we can take our work home and do it later, so we say yes to our co-worker. Doing this over and over a long period of time can add more stress to you and increase the risk of getting burned out.

How to Say No to External Parties

If your job involves working with suppliers or partners, you probably have developed professional relationships with them over time. After many hours working together and getting to know each other, you may develop a personal connection and trust with them. This sometimes can put pressure on you to say yes because you don't want to disappoint them. Here are some suggestions to keep in mind:

- Listen to their request and ask for details and determine whether you can help. If you turn them down, at least they know you have listened and considered their request.

- Focus on the business reasons for saying no. It should be why it doesn't make business sense or it's not a win-win for both of you.

- Offer alternative ideas and solutions.

The situations described in this chapter give you an idea and approach on how to say no professionally. It's an important skill that successful people I know and have worked with possess.

CHAPTER 23

How to Stand Out and Promote Yourself

Not surprisingly, this is one of the most popular topics people asked me to write about. Many of us, whether because of our culture, the way we were raised by our parents or influenced by important people in our lives, believe that if we work hard, stay humble, don't complain and let our work results speak for themselves, we will be rewarded accordingly. This can be especially challenging in Asian cultures. Well, most of us eventually learn that we aren't going to get very far in our career with that belief. I was one of those people. From day one in my new career, I was all heads-down doing my job. I was a good worker, never complained, created trouble or bragged about my work. I also wasn't too excited about public speaking and I stayed away from speaking opportunities, especially with customers. Instead, I was happy to have my co-workers presented to the company executives and customers about our project, which I had been a key part of. And of course, my team members ended up looking good and getting the credit, at least in the executives' minds since they didn't really know of me.

I remember, to this day, about a meeting I had with my manager and her peers. When I was finished and started walking back to my office, I heard one of the managers commenting: "Michael just does his job, does what we ask him and never complains." I think they meant that as a compliment, but looking back, that didn't do justice to my career. Since they figured I was low-maintenance and not one to complain, they didn't know about my

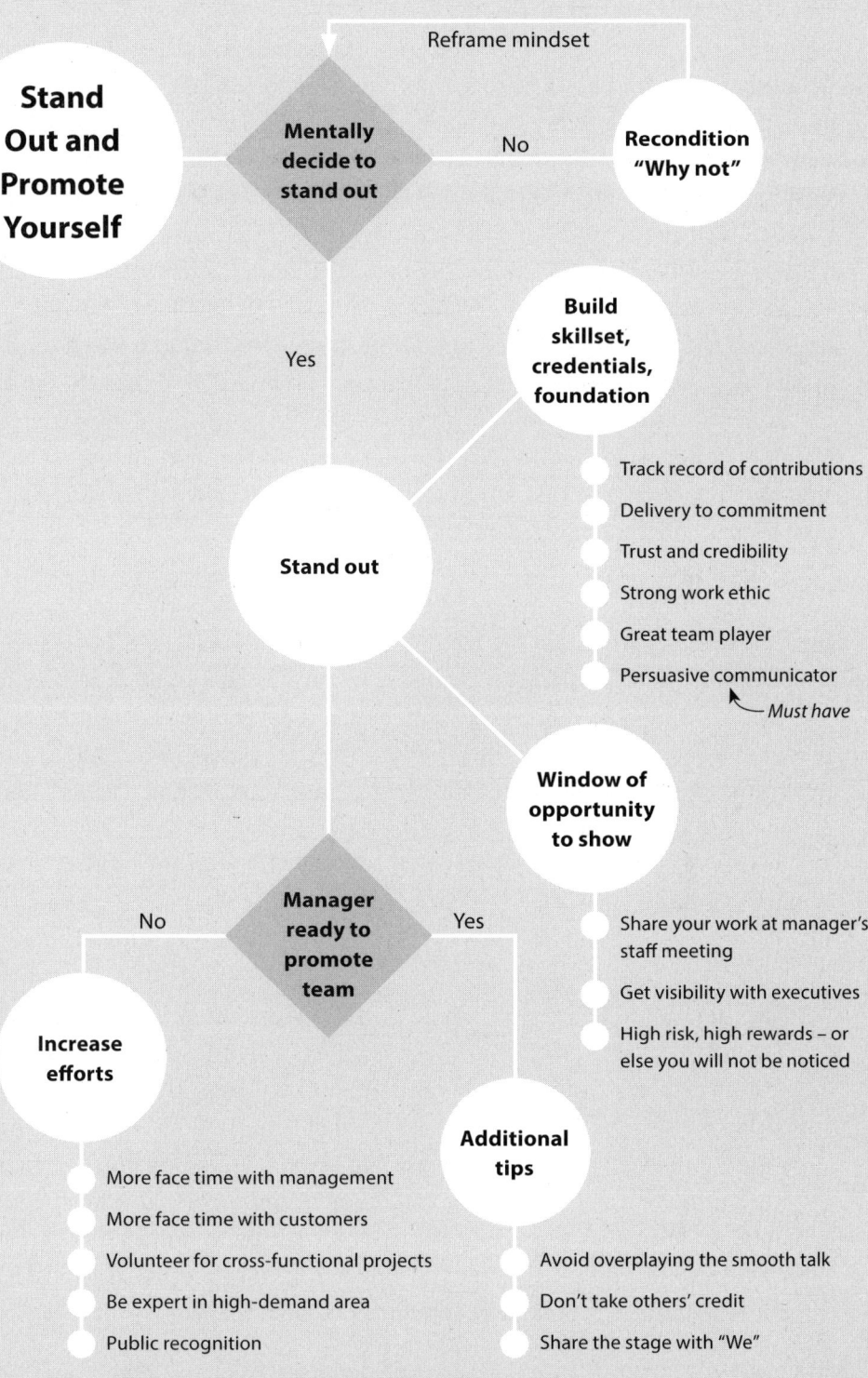

aspirations and felt little motivation to promote me when they already had people banging on their door for promotional opportunities.

Another example: After having been in the job for three years after graduating, I sat down for my annual performance review expecting a really good ranking. To my dismay and disappointment, my manager, Cindy, told me I was ranked in the middle of the pack, a mediocre ranking even though I delivered excellent results. According to her, other managers said they weren't aware of my work and the results I produced. Basically I was invisible to them and they would not agree to give me a higher ranking. It was a humbling and painful lesson for me. It taught me that I needed to take charge of my career and to make sure my work was known, valued and appreciated by not only my peers, but my manager, her peers and other executives. Over the years I got better at this as I observed and learned how other successful people conducted themselves.

With greater exposure to international media and newer international education approaches, Asians are now more open and relatively more outspoken; however, it's still a lagging factor on the international stage. For Asians working for multinational companies, you have to adapt and consciously practise standing out. While you may feel this is beyond your comfort zone, do your best to step out of it. This is critical to your career. You could be the most outspoken in the "pond" of your school, but in international companies, the competition is an "ocean".

In this chapter, we'll discuss how you can go about promoting your accomplishments, making yourself standout in the workplace while still maintaining respect and healthy working relationships with your colleagues.

- **Nail the basics**. Before you can be considered a standout performer and a star in the workplace, you must establish a strong work foundation with your peers, your manager and other executives. This strong foundation means you establish a track record of being reliable, delivering on your commitments and doing what you say you will. This must be your work ethic and not something you do once and forget. You must continue to deliver on your commitments. Continue to build on the trust and credibility with the people you work with. Once you have established and maintained your strong work ethic reputation, people will take you seriously when you want to promote yourself and management will be willing to give you more important and high-profile projects which give you more opportunities to stand out and shine.

- **Be a great team player.** Go above and beyond to help your team complete the job, deliver results and meet their commitments. Go out of your way to help your co-workers when they really need it, as long as you don't compromise your work. By doing this, you establish yourself as an important team player who puts the focus on the team and in turn, creates a positive impression in people's minds. In addition, take the time to give credit and praise to your team members when they achieve a key milestone or do something well. A simple thank you or acknowledgement message to their managers would be greatly appreciated.

- **Become a persuasive communicator and presenter.** This is a must. I have highlighted this skillset throughout this book and I cannot emphasize this enough. In order for you to promote yourself, you must be visible. How you communicate, speak and present to various audiences determines to a great extent the impression people will have of you. If you are articulate and a good presenter, people will be impressed and form a positive image of you. I have seen numerous instances where company executives were effusive in their praise about someone who delivered an outstanding presentation for the first time in front of them. This positive impression will likely be a positive factor in that employee's next performance evaluation. If you believe communication is a weakness for you, make it a priority to work on improving. Without this ability, you will face a steep uphill battle to get noticed. If you demonstrate this skill, it will go a long way to help you achieve a successful career.

- **Look for opportunities to show your work.** If your work affects other teams or provides value to them, look for opportunities to share it with them. Request time in their manager's staff meeting for you to come in to discuss and present. Although one of your objectives is to gain visibility, keep in mind that what you present or discuss must be of some interest to the audience. The topic should have a positive impact on the audience. Another idea is to use the time in the meeting to seek their input on something you and your team are working on. If some people in the audience have also been working with you, use the opportunity to give them credit and visibility in front of their manager. In the process, you are also making yourself stand out because you're the one presenting. Make a point of doing this with different teams periodically.

- **Get face time with executives**. When you're working on team projects, inevitably you and your team will be asked to review your project or give updates to company executives. When you have these opportunities, jump on them, prepare and deliver the best presentation you can. These are your chances to shine. Of course, it is a high-risk and high-reward situation. However, if you hit it out of the park, you will earn great stripes and valuable credit. If you perform poorly, it can have the opposite effect. It is a risk, but if you don't take advantage of it, you will never be noticed. So embrace the opportunity, make sure you are prepared and give your best effort. Continue to look for opportunities to get in front of the executives to discuss specific ideas you have or are working on.

    During my time as a Marketing Operations Director, I had a new manager after the previous manager took another position in the company. During the one year with the previous manager, I didn't meet or present to company executives at all. A month into her new job and after I reviewed my work with her, Bridgette set up a meeting for me to meet with a high-level executive team – a Senior VP, several VPs and Senior Directors – and to share with them the detailed worldwide business analysis I developed. That gave me a golden opportunity to highlight my work and get great visibility. At the same time, my new manager knew my work would be of interest to these executives who had wanted a simple way to regularly assess the company business worldwide, but had not been able to. I knew the subject matter well and I prepared thoroughly for my presentation, and as a result, my boss and I had a great meeting. The Senior VP commented that he didn't even know the company had some of the data I presented and asked to be updated on a quarterly basis. I had a manager who not only highlighted my work to her management team, but in the process, also impressed her boss and other executives.

If you don't have a manager with a keen eye for when to highlight the team, proactively work with your boss to identify opportunities to get in front of company executives. You can achieve this by showing your manager how your work is addressing a business need and would be valued by the executives.

- **Seek more face time with executives and other management teams**. Another way to get face time with executives is to ask your manager to take you to certain meetings she has with the executive team. You're not looking to present, but to be there to support your manager, to be her right-hand person. Whenever I had meetings with company executives to review progress of my team's project or to update them on an initiative, I would take one or more of my employees with me. I would introduce them to the executives, let them know that my team was doing the work and they were there to back me up. Inevitably in the meeting, there would be times I needed them to provide answers to the management team. It was a win-win for my team and me. If your manager is not intuitively looking at these opportunities, take the initiative to encourage her to do so.

- **Get face time with customers**. If your job allows opportunities to meet, present and discuss company plans or other topics with customers, take advantage of it. Customer opinion carries a lot of weight with key company stakeholders, including sales people, their management team and executives. When you meet and present to customers, the Account Sales team is usually present, and frequently company executives would be there as well. You're seen as a subject matter expert and if you come across as knowledgeable and skilful in managing customer interaction and you delivered a strong presentation, you will be sought after. Sales people aren't shy about giving feedback and if you can help them with your ability to interact and communicate with customers, they will let your manager and the company executives know. A good reputation with the sales force is one of the best ways to help you stand out. The sales teams will make sure you get the recognition you deserve. Moreover, they will seek you out for more customer engagements. While this is a good thing, you need make sure this doesn't take away the time or distract you from your core work responsibility.

When I was a product management manager, my new manager was not keen on having me travel to meet with customers. She was focused on cutting expenses and had not seen me present in front of customers to have confidence in my ability. On a customer event, we met with CIOs and IT managers to update them on the company plan and future technologies. In my presentation session, the Sales Executive team was present as well as my manager and her manager's boss – Executive VP of Enterprise Group. A short time after I wrapped up my presentation, my manager walked up to me and told me the Sales Managers were impressed with my talk and wanted to request me to come out to meet with their important customers individually. After that, she couldn't stop encouraging me to fly out to meet with more customers. Better still, the sales team's feedback was reflected positively in my next performance review.

- **Volunteer to lead an important cross-functional project**. This will enable you to demonstrate your ability to lead a team to deliver results. This may be a high-risk, high-reward opportunity and you need to have confidence in your skills and ability to successfully lead this project. Find out all you can and assess the feasibility of the project as well as your own workload before volunteering. If you want to take this project on and your plate is full, negotiate with your manager to remove some of the less important tasks from your plate.

One other idea to make a name for yourself is to look for opportunities to work directly with one of the executives on a project they need help on. For example, when I was a manager in the Product Operations group, I found out that the Senior Vice President of the Product Operations business unit needed someone to be a part-time Chief of Staff to help him manage his organization. I learned that it would take 10–20% of my time for six months. After discussing with my manager, who agreed to reduce some of my workload, I took it on and did it for a year until the Senior VP was able to hire a full-time Chief of Staff. The insights I gained on how a high-level executive worked with his team and other executives on decision-making process as well as how he dealt with organizational challenges and company politics was invaluable. In addition, I had great exposure and developed good relationships with people across organizations and those relationships paid dividends later on.

- **Be an expert in a high-demand area.** Many respected people who stand out in their company are also recognized for their expertise in a particular area. They could be recognized as an expert in a new and emerging technology, a master presenter or a business analyst guru, while someone else could be recognized as a creative marketing expert. These are the "go to" people who other people reach out for assistance. These are the people company executives assign important work. When I was in Product Operations, we had a person who was responsible for Business Analytics and Metrics. She was the person our manager and other executives went to when they needed a quick turnaround business report, a deep dive analysis on a business problem, or analysis to prepare them for upcoming meetings with industry analysts.

    Typically in your department, organization or company, there are "gaps" in one or more areas due to lack of people with the right skills, expertise or people with already too much work on their plate. By talking to your manager and other managers to find out what important areas are not being covered or, if they had the means, where they would invest the resources, is an excellent way to identify areas where you can take the initiative. Managers frequently are forced to focus on short-term goals that leave them with little time for longer-term priorities, such as what the company needs in the future in order to continue to compete successfully.

    In addition, in your research, you may discover an innovative idea that will help improve your company's business. If you do, develop a proposal and discuss it with management. If they find it compelling and believe it would contribute significantly to the business, they may agree to fund the initiative and appoint you to lead it. One of the customer support engineers on my team came up with an idea to improve customer experience by reducing the time required to set up a networking system. Kent discussed it with me and I set up a meeting for him to pitch the plan to our Senior VP. The pitch went well and Kent got the approval and funding to implement a pilot. After the plan was proven to be successful, he was put in charge of implementing it throughout the company.

- **Public recognition and reward**. Most companies on a regular basis choose employees to recognize for their outstanding work, such as excellent customer service, going above and beyond, innovation, teamwork, etc. Employees are nominated by their peers or their managers. This is an effective and public way to receive recognition and a potent way to promote yourself by letting others promote you. When you have one-on-one meetings with your manager, find out what you can do to be considered for this kind of recognition. And if you have done something worthy of the recognition, discuss whether it merits consideration.

Additional Tips

- Self-promotion is only meaningful if you have tangible, positive work results to show. Otherwise, you come across as an empty suit. It's true that we'll sometimes see people who have gotten by with self-promoting without having meaningful accomplishments because they were excellent smooth talkers. However, this tends to catch up to them eventually when they are exposed for who they really are.

- Don't take credit for other people's work. There is no faster way to lose credibility and people's trust. You may get away with it once, but good luck getting other people to work or collaborate with you in the future. It's reasonable and legitimate to get credit as part of the team. If you're the team leader, a good way to earn credibility and respect with your team is to give credit to the entire team and then recognize key team members for their unique contributions.

- As part of a team, learn to say "we" instead of "I" as much as appropriate. Say: "We got creative and found ways to finish our project ahead of schedule" instead of "I was the one with the creative idea…" I learned this lesson early on in my career when in one presentation to update the executive staff on a team project, I apparently used "I" too many times without realizing it. A manager from another department approached me after the meeting and told me that it was a team effort and I should try to remember to say "we" and give the team credit as appropriate in the future. I realized I was being selfish without doing it intentionally. I apologized to him and explained that it was not my intention and I would learn from it going forward.

PART 5

Managing Your Manager

"An overburdened, overstretched executive is the best executive, because he or she doesn't have the time to meddle, to deal in trivia, to bother people."
— **Jack Welch**

"I wouldn't ask anyone to do anything I wouldn't do myself."
— **Indra Nooyi**

"Leadership is the self-confidence of working with people smarter than you."
— **Azim Premji, Chairman of Wipro**

How to Manage Up

- **Mindset reframe**
  - Not butt-kissing
  - Build successful working relationship with superiors
  - Life skill to improve career opportunities

- **Complement your manager's weakness**

- **Help your manager work effectively**

- **Invite your manager to important meetings**

- **Make your manager look good**

- **Improving your position**
  - Be in most ready position for next promotion opportunity
  - Get a management mentor
  - Become a needed expertise
  - Act professionally, with respect and confidence to advocate views
  - Seek personal face time with key executives

Related topics
- Stand Out and Promote Yourself → Ch 23
- Working with Different Managers → Ch 25

CHAPTER 24

How to Manage Up

Some people view "managing up" with disdain, equating it to butt-kissing and playing politics. They hold low opinions of people who manage up well because, in their mind, these people don't really produce results and brown-nosing is the only way to climb the corporate ladder. This is certainly the case in many Asian regions where managing up is seen as bad behaviour, unproductive sucking-up. If you hold this negative view, I want to persuade you to see it in a more positive light, as an effective method to get work done successfully and help make yourself stand out at the same time. By the end of this chapter, I hope to have convinced you that shifting your mindset to balance negative views with positive ones of managing up is the right way forward. And the sooner you start, the better.

What does it mean to "manage up"? One common definition is to build a successful working relationship with a superior or manager. I would describe managing up as working to help your management be successful and for them to help you do your job effectively. Most people confine managing up to only their manager, but I think this is too narrow. Managing up includes having a good working relationship with other managers as well as executives. In order to be promoted, you need to show you already know how to work with management, how to communicate with them and how to handle yourself in their company. It's another skillset to learn and have in your bag.

Moreover, it's a skill you can apply throughout your career as you interact with executives from different companies, or in the future if you decide to go out on your own, to interact with high-power clients. It's a skill you can learn, practise and continue to improve on. In this chapter, I will discuss effective and practical ways to manage up from any position you hold in the company. In addition to reading this chapter, I encourage you to read the "How to stand out and promote yourself" and "How to work with different types of managers" chapters as they contain complementary information to what we will be discussing here.

Follow these best practices to manage up:

- **Help your manager work effectively and efficiently.** By understanding your manager's management style, you can help her be effective and successful by adapting to her management style. Managers seem to not have enough time, and they would appreciate your proactive effort to work with them. In your initial meetings with your manager, discuss how she prefers to work with you – getting updates, her hot buttons, one-on-one and team meeting structure, annual plans, etc. By proactively doing this early on, you create an environment for your manager and you to work efficiently together and reduce wasted time by eliminating guesswork and miscommunication.

- **Complement your manager's weaknesses.** Like all of us, every manager has weaknesses. For example, some managers are disorganized, some don't have good analytical skills, and some aren't good at creating compelling presentation slides, while others are not good with details. If you can discover your manager's weakness and have the skills to complement it, you will become valuable to her.

    Let me give a couple of examples. I had a manager who wasn't great at and didn't want to deal with the detailed, nitty-gritty part of managing the department budget. I was good with numbers and ended up taking over this responsibility for him. It relieved him of a burden he didn't enjoy doing, and at the same time, I earned his trust and confidence by having the skills to handle the budget for him. Being disorganized was another manager's weakness. She wasn't good at organizing, following up on meeting details, and had a hard time keeping tabs of her action items. Recognizing this, one of my colleagues, who had great organization skills, volunteered to help her. Kim helped the manager come up with meeting agendas, arranged all the logistics for our department meetings, kept track of the action items from our staff meetings, her manager's meetings, and organized employee ranking sessions. This relieved her manager from having to do something she was not suited for, and Kim became her right-hand person.

- **Make your manager look good.** One of the best ways for a person to stand out is to let others sing their praises for them. Look for opportunities to do this for your boss, but make sure you do it when warranted and not just shamelessly sucking up to her. During one meeting with the US and international marketing regions to discuss an upcoming product launch, I presented the marketing plan to several Vice Presidents of Sales and Marketing. I pointed out to the audience that my manager was instrumental in helping to create a successful plan and working extremely hard with the CEO executive staff to secure a significant amount of funding for each international region. The international VPs were immensely impressed with the plan and effusive in their praise and appreciation. The Senior VP of marketing was at the meeting and heard directly from these sales VPs. My boss looked good to a very high-level executive and to other executives who would be influential when it came time for her promotional consideration. She earned the praise she received and in turn appreciated my effort to give her the credit she deserved. At the same time, I also gained her confidence and loyalty.

- **Invite your manager to important meetings**. Invite your manager to meetings where you believe she would receive useful information and be able to use it to help her with a key project she has been working on. At the same time, you may be able to gain her support for what you're working on. You may think managers have visibility and know about all the important meetings to attend; however, keep in mind that your manager can't possibly know about all the meetings you and the team have, not to mention which ones to attend. When I was working on a proposal to get money to build a number of product prototypes to promote and train our resellers, I realized that it might be an uphill battle since we had a tight budget and the company was looking for ways to cut expenses. I invited my manager to a meeting with the reseller representatives to discuss their needs for a successful channel programme. In this meeting, she heard directly from these representatives why they needed the prototypes and how the programme would help them sell the product successfully. In addition, they provided her with insight into other important business aspects, which she could incorporate into an overall channel business strategy she had been working on for the company. Walking out of the meeting, she thanked me for inviting her and appreciated the insight she received from the group. It was a win for me as well since it helped me get the funding I needed.

- **Get a mentor who can be your champion**. This should be a must requirement on your career development checklist. A mentor who is a member of the management team can provide you honest advice on how to manage up, interact with other executives, respond to different situations as well as give you visibility to a broader group of company executives. When I first met with my mentor, a Vice President in another function my boss suggested to me, I told him that I didn't really know what managing up meant or how to do it. Through talking with him regularly, observing his interactions with people and practising what he suggested, I came to understand managing up better and more importantly, how to do it effectively.

- **Become a needed expert**. One of the great ways to manage up is to become an expert in an area that adds value to the company and helps other people do their job better. This will put you in a high-demand position and provide you with valuable opportunities to interact with the management team. When you're able to offer help to the executives, they're more likely to become advocates for your ideas and have your back when you need it.

    But how do you become a valuable resource if the executives don't know you? The answer is to find opportunities to show your work and demonstrate how it can help them. When I started my new job as a Pricing Strategist, I developed a regular business dashboard for the product management teams to use. The dashboard showed company business results, trends and potential challenges. I explained to my boss how this dashboard would enable her and other managers to make more informed business decisions by providing real-time analytics and insight. She bought into it and invited me to present at her manager's staff meeting. The management team loved it and they wanted the dashboard to become the standard reporting tool.

After that I was known as a Business Metrics expert. Over time, several executives came and asked me for help with their business problems, and as a result, I gained a lot of experience working with them and earning their support. I remember distinctly a meeting when a colleague and I were to present a new initiative to a group of managers. I was nervous walking into the room because I knew several high-level managers would be in attendance and I only knew one of them, Richard, a Senior VP of Customer Solutions whom I had worked with on a business issue a year ago. At the start of the meeting, each of us introduced ourselves, and when my turn came up, Richard piped up and told everyone in the room that I was an expert at analyzing business problems and that I was the go-to person for anyone with a business challenge. Needless to say, the rest of the meeting went very well and we had full support for our proposal. Although I felt we had a strong proposal, having Richard's support helped greatly.

- **Act professionally**. In your interactions with your manager and other executives, respect their status and give them the reverence their position deserves. At the same time, don't feel that you're in a subservient position where you need to do everything they ask or agree with everything they say. You need to have the confidence to push back, to advocate your views or ideas in a polite and respectful way. Be professional and never get personal. In a meeting with a group of managers, maintain your poise and don't get rattled when they question you. Refer to the "How to communicate and present to specific audiences" chapter for suggestions on how to handle meeting situations with executives. The impression that people form of you is mostly optics – how you come across in your expression, your behaviour and what you say. For example, if you disagree with a manager's conclusion in the meeting, push back with something like: "I understand and appreciate your point. However, based on the information I have, I have a different view on it. Could I share my view?" Then go ahead and explain. Remember to back up your response with facts and solid data, as appropriate.

- **Seek personal face time with key executives.** When you have one-on-one time with your manager or other managers, they can be more themselves, and more comfortable revealing the side that you may not have seen before, and you may get a better understanding of them as people. These kinds of insight are helpful as you learn how to work with them effectively. It's difficult to get this kind of interaction but seek out opportunities. As a young Product Manager, I sometimes met with the General Manager and his staff to present recommendations on business issues such as the forecast for our products. During one meeting, the GM felt the forecast was too high and should be reduced. After I explained my rationale to him, he still was not quite sure about my forecast. I then jokingly suggested a bet – the one who lost would buy the other dinner. To my surprise, he accepted. Well, I was lucky enough to end up winning the bet. He took me out to dinner and I had two hours of his time to myself. I learned a few important and interesting nuggets about how his mind worked, how he worked with his staff and managed up to his superior. At the risk of overstaying my welcome, I suggested having dinner periodically if he was available. To my surprise, he agreed and we had dinner 2 to 3 times a year for a couple of years.

    Seek out a couple of key executives that you would like to have a one-on-one lunch with and send them a request. It makes it a bit easier if you already have a rapport with them through meetings that you attended or presented. They may surprise you and accept your invitation. After all, some executives want to keep their finger on the pulse of the company and would welcome opportunities to hear from employees. Other executives, from time to time, have open invitations where you can sign up to have lunch and discuss company business.

- **Manage up to a promotion.** Hopefully, your managing up effort to earn the management's support will pay dividends for you in the future. By demonstrating your contributions to the company, helping the management team succeed and making yourself stand out in a professional way, you put yourself in a position to be considered seriously for promotions when the opportunity arises.

CHAPTER 25

How to Work with Different Types of Managers

In the 25-plus years of my professional career, I have had 15 managers, the shortest stint being three months and the longest four years. They all had different managing styles and personalities. This averages about one manager for every two years. There were a multitude of reasons for having gone through this many managers: changes in my job, my manager's job or the company organization. Some management changes were my choice while others were not. In talking to other professionals, I found my career situation was quite similar to theirs, and I suspect yours will not be too different. It's not unusual to have many different managers in your career. While your career may not have the same frequency of management turnovers, don't be surprised if you have a new one every couple of years. If someone tells you that only you can control your career success, it's only half the truth. In addition to your talent, effort and hard work, situational dynamics and upper-level managers are important factors as well. While this seems unfair, the fact is life can be unfair. Your managers are an important factor to your career's exposure, opportunities and growth. Learning to embrace and work with this reality is as important as doing your work.

You seldom get to pick your manager. Of the 15 managers I had, there were only two that I knew and wanted to work for. Accept the fact that throughout your career, you likely will work for many managers with

Different Types of Managers

Bully manager
- Lowers your morale
- Impacts self-confidence
- Could damage your career and life quality

Handling unfair treatment
- Keep it professional, not personal
- Document paper trail
- Start with annual plan – deliverables and timelines
- Know how to utilize HR
- Copy HR and next-level boss
- Negotiate: exit/stay/move to another team

Difficult managers
- Hands-on/micromanager — *Give proactive frequent updates*
- Clueless manager
- Absent manager
- "Go where the wind blows" manager
- "I'm smartest" manager
- Disorganised manager

Develop self-help options

Work successfully with your manager
- Adapt to your manager's style
- Be low-maintenance
- Make manager's life easier
- No surprises
- Complement manager's weaknesses
- Approach with solutions

different management styles; therefore, to be successful in your career, you need to know how to earn their trust and work with them effectively. In this chapter, I'll share the best practices to work with managers in general, regardless of their specific management style. Then I'll cover specific types of managers and how best to work with them.

Best Practices to Work Successfully With Your Manager

- **Adapt to your manager's management style**. Many problems occur between employees and managers as a result of miscommunication or misunderstanding. Your initial meetings with your manager are good opportunities to figure out how to work effectively with him. Ask your manager about his managing style, "hot buttons", expectations and how he likes to work with his employees. Find out if he prefers to communicate via email or face to face, how frequently he likes to have one-on-one meetings with you, how often he wants to be updated on your work, what kind of information he cares about and how other successful employees have worked with him. Having this meeting to hear straight from the horse's mouth will save you headaches and frustration later on. Once you have a good idea of his management style, write down what you have learned and store it somewhere you can easily refer to later.

- **Low maintenance**. Because managers need to do their own individual work as well as manage a team of employees, they're quite busy. Just attending all the required meetings as part of their management responsibilities consumes a significant amount of time. As a result, managers love low-maintenance employees – employees who don't require a lot of time from their manager, are not frequent complainers and don't need a lot of hand-holding to do their job. This, however, doesn't necessarily mean that a high-maintenance employee is a low-performer or that a low-maintenance employee is a high-performer. I have had employees who delivered good results but were frequent complainers and needed a lot of TLC (tender loving care). These employees can drain a manager mentally and soak up his energy. If you are self-motivated, can stay focused regardless of distractions, and work independently when given direction, guidance and support from your manager, he would appreciate you immensely.

- **No surprises**. This is one of the biggest pet peeves managers have. They don't like to be caught off-guard, especially with bad news. If your manager's boss asks him about some bad news that he wasn't aware of, he comes off as not being on top of things and looks bad. This is not going to make your manager happy. Tell him. If your project is running into a major problem, risking delays and you're unsure of what to do next, let your manager know and ask for help sooner rather than later. Resist the urge to solve it yourself. You may feel you are failing if you can't find a way to solve it on your own; however, that is what a manager is for. Chances are he has been through these experiences and can help you. It's better to escalate to him now than for him to find out through his peers, or worse, his manager. In addition, keep your manager in the loop on important matters. If you're asked to meet with his boss or with other executives and you're not sure if he was also invited, let him know about the meeting, unless you were asked to keep it confidential.

- **Make your manager look good**. Making yourself successful and stand out at work also helps your manager look good. A manager, to a great extent, is a reflection of his team. If the team is doing well and getting the recognition from other managers and executives, the manager looks good and gets the credit as well. If you and your team receive recognition for a job well done and your manager played a role in helping you, thank him. Show your appreciation for his support and make sure his boss is aware of it. Moreover, avoid undermining your manager or throwing him under the bus. When you and your manager are in a meeting with other managers and executives, try not to contradict him directly. Before the meeting, you and your manager should spend a few minutes to make sure both of you know the purpose of the meeting and are in agreement on potential issues. If you hear your manager make wrong statements, determine if you can wait to correct him after the meeting to avoid making him look bad in front of people. However, if you believe you must correct him, do it diplomatically. Don't say: "You are wrong. That information is not correct." Instead, try something like: "I'm not sure if you have the most updated information, let me double-check on that for you." This gives the manager a way out by deflecting the incorrect information off of him.

- **Don't come to your manager with just the problem.** While there can be exceptions, don't come to your manager with just the problem, but come with possible solutions as well. Or at least be prepared to discuss potential options. When you have a business problem you need to bounce off your manager, you can help make the meeting more productive by discussing the problem and then presenting potential solutions you have in mind. This gives your manager options to think through and give his opinions. Furthermore, it shows your proactive effort in addressing the problem and trying to come up with solutions. Good managers know to not give their employees answers but help them get to the answer on their own. If you're about to discuss with your manager a business proposal but you're not sure about your recommendation, share with him the potential ideas you're considering and ask for feedback to help you form a solid recommendation.

- **Make your manager's work life easier.** Managers have a lot of things going on and would appreciate your effort to use their time wisely. There are ways you can help them. For example, when you have a one-on-one meeting, optimize the time with him by being prepared. Before the meeting, send him an email asking for anything specific he would like to cover in the meeting as well as prepare a list of topics you want to discuss. If there are any decisions or follow-up actions, send him a short summary message afterward to ensure that both of you are on the same page. When it comes to performance review, do your homework to prepare him as best as possible to give you a fair review.

    If he is a visual person and understands better with graphs instead of numbers, show him your analysis in graphical form. If there are meetings you can attend without needing him there, let him know and then give him an update afterward. Your manager would appreciate the extra time to do his work. For meetings you need him to attend with you, make sure you spend a little time with him beforehand to brief him on the topic, objectives and any requests you have for him. This will help prevent confusion or miscommunication between you during the meeting. If he doesn't have time prior to the meeting, see if you can walk with him to the meeting and use that time to brief him. My manager and I used this practice quite a bit in my previous job and it worked out well for both of us.

- **Complement your manager's weaknesses**. All of us have weaknesses and managers are no different. Some managers are not well organized, some are not analytical, some are not skilful at creating compelling presentation slides, some are not good at handling details, some are good at managing up but not their employees, etc. If you can discover your manager's weaknesses and even better, if you have skills to complement them, you will become valuable to your manager. For example, if you sense your manager is not good at organizing and managing the details of his department meeting, offer to help with organizing the meeting, creating the agenda, taking notes and keeping track of action items discussed in the meeting. A tactful question such as "I notice you have a lot of things going on, would you like me to organize our staff meetings and manage the meeting agenda going forward?" offers him a solution to consider without admitting his weakness. One of my former managers, a Vice President, was a straight-shooter. He spoke to company executives the same way he did to his employees, without trying to be diplomatic. In a work environment, this sometimes created ill-will even though it was not his intention. One of my roles was to be a sounding board for him in these situations.

    You can also be a good partner who watches out for your managers and helps them out of unpleasant situations. I recalled an incident where a team member of mine, Dae Hwan, helped me defuse a situation. In a tense moment of business review cycles, tempers flared and voices were raised. Dae Hwan initiated a sideline call with me. He then advised me to play the good cop and let my other team members to do the tough challenging. It was great advice from him. By watching out for your manager and serving as sounding board, you are not only helping the team, but also helping your boss. It will go a long way to earn their trust. Dae Hwan and I remain great friends and business buddies.

How to Work With Difficult Managers

My focus here is to describe the different behaviours of managers and offer suggestions on how to work with them. It's not my attempt to try to understand or explain their behaviour.

- **Hands-on/Micromanager**. This is one of the more common management types. Throughout your career, you either have experienced or will have the unfortunate experience of working for a micromanager. This manager is a control freak who looks over your shoulder and wants to know everything you're doing, who needs to review your detailed work and often tells you how to do your job. This manager seems to have difficulty figuring out what he needs to know or focus on, so instead, he tries to know everything. First-time managers managing a team of employees, who were their peers, often exhibit this type of behaviour. As they gain more experience and grow into their management role, they may change or moderate their management style; at least we hope, so for the sake of their employees. This type of manager may seem to contradict my contention that managers are busy and don't have time to delve into their employees' detailed work. However, this type of manager cannot seem to help it, even if they're overwhelmed.

    Although it's easy to feel frustrated and not empowered, the way to work with a hands-on manager is not to fight him since it will create a lot of tension for both of you. Instead, take a proactive approach. In your initial meetings with your manager, discuss the best way to work with him. Here you may learn more about his hot buttons and come to an agreement on working together. He may not reveal his micromanagement style, but at least you are encouraging him to communicate how he would like to work together. At least he knows that you're being proactive and that you want to work with him and not against him. In the initial period, update him on your work regularly (daily, if you need to), via email or face to face, whichever works best. Instead of resisting him, ask him for his opinion and be open to his comments. Once he feels comfortable that you are open and proactively working with him instead of keeping things close to the vest, he will start trusting you more, easing up and giving you more space. Also by overwhelming him with updates, he will likely reach a point where he needs to back off, physically and mentally.

Due to an organization change, I once moved to a team with a hands-on manager. Neither of us knew each other much. Initially, she was critical of my work, didn't seem to trust me and wanted me to update her with every single detail. I had always wanted to work independently and felt that I did my best work without the pressure of someone constantly looking over my shoulder. Following the advice of a co-worker who had successfully dealt with this manager before, I made a conscious effort to meet with my new manager frequently, several times a week, to explain my work and ask her for feedback. This routine went on for a few weeks and as she started to feel more comfortable and gained more trust in me, she eased up. Although she was never fully hands-off, we eventually achieved a balance in our working relationship.

- **Clueless manager**. This manager is all talk and little action, all style and little substance. He talks a good game and speaks management speak, but there is no real substance in his words. He doesn't seem to have the skills to run the business and doesn't possess the judgment required to make good decisions. This kind of hiring could be a result of a manager getting promoted into a new function even though he had little knowledge of the new organization. Or he was brought in from another company without much knowledge or experience in the new company or industry. I have seen this happen multiple times in my career. Sometimes an executive wanted to bring in his buddy to run a department, regardless of the person's background or experience. When I was a member of the product marketing team, the GM of our business unit brought in an engineering manager to run our team when our previous manager left the company, even though she had no marketing skills or experience.

Moreover, there are different types of clueless managers. One type is a "Clueless but Harmless" manager who knows he lacks the business experience; so he leans on a few strong people on his staff to help him run the organization. The other type is the "Clueless and Dangerous" manager who does not seem to be aware of his lack of business skills and experience, and often makes decisions on the fly, sometimes depending on whom he heard from last.

At one company I worked in previously, I was Chief of Staff for a Senior VP in the Product Group. He was initially hired to run the engineering department and when his boss suddenly left the company, he was named the acting head. Three months later, his boss appointed him to be the permanent head of the Product Group. Coming from another company in a different industry, his background was in engineering and manufacturing and he had little industry knowledge or business experience. Yet, from day one, he expressed a lot of arbitrary opinions about the business and made rash, ill-informed decisions. He came across as forceful, and people were too timid to push back. He disregarded recommendations from people who had extensive knowledge of the business and, instead, reacted and made decisions based on the crisis of the moment. Because of the lack of experience and judgment, he changed his mind frequently when things did not turn out right, but he continued to make bad calls that cost the company millions of dollars. On top of that, he also had selective memory and was good at deflecting blame onto others. I witnessed this first-hand for almost a year. Whether he realized it or not, he was in over his head and made bad and costly decisions for the company. After three years, when the company reorganized, he was finally reassigned to do "special projects". To me, it was three years too late.

How should you handle this type of manager? Since he craves public attention and has a big ego, try to work with him behind the scenes and persuade him to change his mind and adopt your well-thought-out ideas as his own. Don't contradict or undermine him in public and do your best to not get on his bad side. With the example above, I made the mistake of correcting the Senior VP a couple of times in his meetings and that didn't sit well with him. In my career, I unfortunately have seen some of these managers stick around for years because they were very good at playing politics. My advice is to be patient and find better opportunities outside of his control. But remember to leave amicably and not to burn any bridges.

- **Absent manager.** This is the opposite of the micromanager. For many different reasons, this manager is not very engaged with you or the team and does not seem interested in your job details or the team's. As long as things are going smoothly and there is no major crisis, he's happy not getting involved in your job. You don't have much interaction with him, other than the infrequent one-on-one meetings or when a crisis occurs. I have observed some managers who fit this category over the course of my career – some became jaded in their job, some reached a dead end in their career and were lost, some were too busy to be involved or, worst of all, some used their position's status to pursue other self-interest goals.

  I remember one specific example where a manager moved from another function to manage the team I was on. She had no marketing knowledge, no experience running a product management team, and from the beginning, she did not seem interested to learn. It didn't take long for the team members to see that she was only interested in looking out for #1 – to manage up and make herself look as good and as visible to the General Manager as possible. She latched onto and took the lead on a PR (Public Relations) initiative aimed at promoting the company's leadership position in the industry, and by extension, making the company executives look good as well as getting her name out. She hired a PR consulting firm and spent her time working with them, the GM and his staff. It was crystal-clear she was only using this campaign as a stepping-stone for her career. Her team operated mainly on its own as she spent little time with them. Fortunately, we were senior product marketing people with a lot of experience and didn't need much help from her. If we were a less experienced team, we would've been in a real tough situation.

  However, the danger for you with these managers is that they won't care much about promoting their teams or helping to remove obstacles for their employees. In addition, they may not have much influence over their peers, which obviously can affect your success and standing in the company, especially when it comes time for employee reviews or promotions. The downside for the team and me was that she didn't represent us well in the performance ranking meetings because she knew very little about our work, and as a result, we felt we didn't get ranked fairly.

If you have this manager, look for a better situation to move to because this manager will most likely be of no help to you. Meanwhile, you should take control of your own career and do your best to stand out and promote yourself. You can't rely on this kind of manager to look out for you. If you are new in your career and need your manager's support or guidance, my suggestion is to seek out a highly regarded mentor with knowledge of your job functions and lean on this person for guidance and support. Meanwhile, make sure your work is visible to your manager and her boss by updating them regularly on the progress and results of your work. Look for opportunities to meet and present to your manager's boss.

- **"Go where the wind blows" manager.** This type of manager goes with the crowd and has no strong ideas or convictions on how to make decisions or how he wants to operate his organization. He is easily influenced by "key" people outside of his organization and often acts according to whom he last spoke to or who was in his ear the loudest. This manager does not appear to be very self-confident and comes across as paranoid, even emotional at times. The difference between this manager and the "Clueless and Dangerous" manager is this type of manager realizes what he doesn't know and is reluctant to make decisions whereas the latter has no qualms about making decisions, even though they often are ill-informed.

  When I was in the marketing organization, I had a manager who fit this type to a T. She would question what I did, get emotionally upset at me and accuse me of hurting the organization. When I was putting together a budget, I requested two million dollars for a product promotion programme in important international countries. When I met with her to go over the budget, she got upset without waiting for me to explain the rationale, and accused me of wasting company money. She then flatly rejected my budget proposal without further discussion. I was perplexed since this was the normal budgetary practice and was disappointed she didn't give me a chance to explain. Since I had had extensive discussion with the countries' managers to get their ideas for my promotional programme, I sent her a voicemail message suggesting she touch base with the country marketing managers who wanted to know why they weren't getting the funding they needed. A few days later, she approved my budget for the marketing programme. It turned out she spoke with the country managers and heard their opinions loud and clear.

A good practice in handling this kind of manager is, first of all, to remain calm in the heat of the moment and act professionally. Resist the urge to get personal or emotional. Secondly, this manager tends to be highly influenced by other stakeholders in the company. If some of these stakeholders are involved in your project, get them to be your advocates by soliciting their input and support for your ideas. When you go over your work with your manager, make sure to describe your involvement with the key stakeholders and ask your manager to touch base with them.

- **"I'm the smartest person in the room" manager.** This manager tends to be strong-minded, not easily persuaded and can appear intimidating, especially if he truly is smart. However, this style does not promote individual creativity and limits employee empowerment since they will just default to do whatever this manager thinks is best. I have seen instances where a Senior VP got into a deep discussion on data details with someone in the meeting in order to show he knew more than the employee, even though the analysis was not a significant part of the meeting agenda. His behaviour made the employee feel undermined and belittled, and did nothing to help the progress of the meeting.

    If you face a manager like this, you need to realize there is no benefit to getting into an argument to prove who was right and wrong. It can only create ill-will for you if you make him look bad; it's a no-win situation for you. Again, act professionally and let him have his way in the meeting. Take the high road. You don't have to agree with him, just acknowledge his assessment and move on. You can try something like: "Thank you for your comments. I'll check my analysis and get back to you later." Then verify your work and meet with him later to clarify. It could be that you missed something too. If you have a chance to go over your work with him before the meeting, take advantage of it because it's much better to resolve issues one-on-one than in a public setting. Make sure your work is solid so that he would have a difficult time poking holes in it. Moreover, avoid getting into a discussion about details. Rather, focus on your assumptions where you and other people can have a more productive and meaningful discussion. Another good practice is to persuade the manager to adopt your idea as his, which will make him look good while knowing you deserve the credit.

- **Disorganized manager**. This manager is not detail-oriented and not very organized in his own work, not to mention being organized with your work or his team's work. He tends to be forgetful, lose things or have a hard time locating important materials. Don't assume he has the information you gave him or remembers what you two discussed and decided previously. This is not helpful to you or your team, for example, when he has to meet with his boss to discuss the team's work progress.

    The way to manage this situation is to pretend that you are your own manager and you organize and maintain the records, documents and materials in a way that you can easily forward to him when he needs them. Take the employee ranking review for example. To help your manager prepare, gather all the pertinent information and materials. Then write a one-page summary of the key results, accomplishments, and people's feedback and any other pertinent information. Put them all in one electronic folder. When you sit down with your manager prior to the performance review meeting he'll have with other managers, use this folder to review with him.

    When you meet with him in your one-on-one meetings, find out what major meetings or reviews he has coming up and what he needs to prepare for. Then offer to help him organize the information and materials he needs for these meetings. Disorganized managers tend to realize this is a weakness and would appreciate your help.

How to Deal With a Bully Manager

You believe you have been doing your best, delivering results and meeting goals expected of you; however, you feel you are being treated unfairly by your manager. This manager seems to want to make your life miserable, want to get rid of you or make you into a "whipping boy" for whatever reasons. You don't have to put up with it. I fortunately have never experienced this in my career but have had several colleagues who came to me with this situation. They were miserable, their self-confidence was shot and morale was very low. It's an unproductive situation for both the company and the employee. A good manager should not mistreat his employees and should not get into this kind of situation. Whatever the core of the problem is, it should be addressed and resolved professionally. I don't attempt to know why managers exhibit such behaviour. However, I can suggest ways for you to deal with your manager.

One day I received a phone call from a former colleague, Kim. I knew her well as a professional and as a person. She sounded distraught when she told me how miserable she was in her new job of six months. When she interviewed for the position, the hiring manager told Kim she created this new position with a specific set of responsibilities. She received the job offer and transferred from her current department to the new organization within the same company. But shortly after starting her new job, Kim was told by her manager to stop working on those responsibilities and instead, to take on a new set of responsibilities that she didn't interview for, didn't have experience and hadn't been trained to do. When her manager told her about the new responsibilities, she did not provide Kim a new plan with clear goals, expectations and timelines. Kim asked for training but didn't get it. Then her manager began to demean her, criticize her work harshly in front of her peers and exclude her from the team and other company meetings, even the ones she was asked to attend by people who set up those meetings.

Up until then, she had received excellent reviews and compliments for her work from internal company partners – sales people and international field partners. She had been a high-performer; during her years at her previous organization, she was highly regarded and received a top employee ranking.

Then one day, Kim's manager called her into her office and told Kim she would place her on the Performance Improvement Plan (PIP). When a manager puts someone on PIP, it's usually a step before removing that employee from the company. Imagine the shock Kim must have felt. Here is someone who had been an excellent performer in the company and was now told that if she did not show expected improvement in 30 days, she would be fired. I knew Kim as a high-energy, driven, self-confident person but at that moment on the phone, she was a different person – depressed, hurt and confused.

Before I describe how to go about handling this situation, I want to emphasize one point. Before you conclude that your manager has been treating you unfairly and harshly, you must be completely honest and objective with yourself. You need to ask yourself questions such as: Have I been performing my job according to expectations and goals set out in my annual plan? Have I received at least satisfactory performance evaluation? If there were changes to my responsibilities, were they documented and updated clearly in my plan and did I agree and understand them? Have I received negative feedback since my last review about any issues regarding my job performance? And have I received warnings from my manager about my job performance and behaviour? The answers to these questions will help you make an objective assessment. If you have received good performance reviews and no indication or warning about performance issues from your manager, then you have a strong case.

Let's talk about how to handle this kind of unfair treatment from your manager. Let me tell you a secret about managers. They don't want to deal with employee headaches. More specifically, you can make your manager's life as miserable as they make yours. Managers are typically busy and stressed in their own work life with pressure from their boss, company executives, their colleagues and their employees. They don't want to spend all their time on paperwork and dealing with personnel issues. As an employee, there are ways to make your manager's life miserable. This is not revenge or payback, but a way to keep them honest and force them to do their job properly. However, when you get into this situation, try your best to reach a satisfactory resolution in the end.

- **Keep it professional, not personal**. Even if your manager is petty, condescending and behaves unprofessionally, you should maintain your professionalism. As difficult as it may seem, treat this as a business issue. After all, why waste your effort on someone who treats you like this? They are not worth spending an ounce of your valuable energy on. Don't burn any bridges with anyone, including HR personnel, co-workers or even your manager. This is a small world and you never know whom you will cross paths with in the future. I also view it as a generous gesture on your part to give your manager the benefit of the doubt that they will eventually recognize their mistake and change for the better.

- **Document everything**. You need to keep all the evidence and have everything in writing so you don't get into a "she said, he said" situation that is extremely hard to prove. This includes email messages. When you meet and discuss with your manager, write down the minutes, what was decided or not and next steps. Also keep a record of all materials, especially ones that support your performance and put you in a good light, such as thank-you notes, complimentary messages from people you work with, as well as the accomplishments you achieved – high employee ranking, employee award, recognition and performance review.

- **Start with your annual plan.** Managers are required to have an annual performance plan for each of their employees. The plan describes clear responsibilities, expected results, metrics and timeline for each of the key responsibilities. However, many managers do a cursory job of this just to have it on file with HR and to check off a box on the management list. If the plan is unclear with no specific deliverables and timelines, you can hold their feet to the fire and have great leverage. After all, managers would be hard-pressed to justify their actions toward you when they were unclear to you about your job and their expectations of you.

- **Know how to utilize HR**. Keep in mind that in a dispute between an employee and the company/manager, HR works to protect the company and is not there to help you build a case against your manager or the company. They are there to see if they can make the situation go away quietly. However, they are bound by law and company policies with regard to employment practices. Therefore, keep in mind what I mentioned earlier about the annual plan and having everything documented. In a conflict or dispute, HR's role is to work with the manager to resolve the situation. Moreover, companies typically want to avoid lawsuits, which are costly and can generate negative publicity. You should use HR as a third-party "witness", as someone who has visibility of all the communications between you and your manager, and as someone you can negotiate a solution to resolve the issue.

- **Copy HR and your manager's boss in your correspondence with your manager**. Managers don't want headaches from their employees. Your manager's boss definitely would not want to get involved with this headache either. Similarly, your manager would not want to look bad or have to explain to his boss about the "messy" situation. In addition to copying your manager's boss in correspondence between you and your manager, be sure to copy your HR representative as well as a high-level HR manager – Senior Director or VP level. This is for your protection since you don't know what your manager is communicating to HR about your situation. By copying your correspondences and showing proofs of your job performance, you give HR visibility of your side. HR is required to keep all records of the dispute.

    Regarding Kim's situation, I suggested she follow the above steps. Kim told me her manager did not reply to the messages she had sent previously. She then decided to follow my advice to copy her manager's boss. When Kim sent her manager a message describing the lack of a clear plan with no training provided and copied HR and her manager's boss, she received a reply from her manager within one hour. Her manager responded with a much more professional tone. After that, she copied them on everything. Her manager finally got the message that Kim was no pushover and she could make her life miserable as well. Her manager did an about-face and was more cooperative in working to resolve the situation.

- **Negotiate a best deal for you**. Refer to the "How to be a good negotiator" chapter for details. By and large, HR wants your manager to resolve the situation with you amicably, and if you are in the right and have leverage, you should negotiate a deal that is best for you but try to achieve a win-win agreement. If you decide you want to leave the company, negotiate a severance package that will also allow you time to look for another job while still being employed by the company. The terms of the package should include payment for a number of months (1–3), length of time to exercise your stock options if you have them, and medical benefits. Each company has different policies on severance packages and you need to get as much information as you can so you can negotiate effectively. If you want to stay in your current job or move to another job in the company, think about the type of job and responsibilities that fit your skills and interests. If you want to stay on the current team, think carefully about your working relationship with the manager and whether it can be repaired.

Kim's story had a happy ending. She decided to leave the company while working through the resolution with HR and her manager. They gave her time to search for her next job and she ended up getting a great job with a successful and up-and-coming company. As a bonus, she was also able to obtain a severance package. Most importantly, she got her confidence, self-esteem and self-worth back.

While companies may have somewhat different personnel procedures and operate a little differently, the approach described in this chapter should help you navigate a difficult situation in your company. However, to give yourself the best possible outcome, you need to understand your company's HR procedure clearly and more importantly, understand how HR and management handle employee-versus-manager conflict. One way to understand is to talk to employees who have been through a management conflict situation. Another way is if you have a friend or know someone you can trust who is in a management role, ask them for advice and insight on how management works with HR.

CHAPTER 26

How to Prepare for a Performance Review

Employee performance reviews play an important role in our career. How we are evaluated determines to a great extent our salary increases and our chances of promotion. Beside tangible rewards, getting an excellent job review is a major boost to our confidence and standing among our peers, although I would argue that we shouldn't let our self-confidence be affected by external factors we don't have complete control over. In this chapter, I will describe a couple of employee evaluation methods being used, how you can help prepare your manager to evaluate you fairly and how to respond to your manager when you receive your performance review.

Performance Ranking and Evaluation Process

Companies may differ somewhat on the method they use to rank or evaluate their employees. Typically, formal job performance evaluation is done once a year. Regardless of the methodology a company uses, employees are evaluated on two dimensions – what results they achieved and how they were achieved (the "what's" and the "how's"). The former are tangible, measurable results while the latter is based on the employee's effectiveness in working with other people to produce results. The feedback from peers, partners and other managers plays a key role in how the employees are ranked or evaluated.

Performance Review

- **Ranking approaches**
  - Forced ranking distribution
  - Individual absolute performance score
  - Individual value and impact to organization – no performance score

- **Discussion frequency**
  - Periodic
  - Ongoing year-long

- **Help prepare your manager**
  - Keep track record of results and feedback
  - Share and discuss with manager regularly
  - Provide list of people who know your work
    — *One month prior*
  - Summarize accomplishments, including examples of going beyond call of duty
  - Establish visibility to broader management

- **Handling different outcomes**
  - As good as or better than anticipated
  - Lower rating then you deserved
  - Very low rating
    → Performance Improvement Plan

- **Output**
  - **Pay increment factor**
  - **Career planning**
    - Promotion potential
    - Development plan
  - **Next year plan**
    - Scope
    - Above and beyond
    - Clear and realistic targets

There are companies who are going toward the concept of managers having year-round continuous conversations with their employees and with no specific rating scores. The goal here is to avoid demotivating factors in the communication with employees and have the discussion focus on coaching and development. However, pay/reward administration is still aligned to specific individual performance factors, such as results versus goals and objectives.

I'll describe two employee performance evaluation methods many companies employ: forced ranking and individual performance review.

- **Forced ranking**. Employees are ranked on their job performance for the past year relative to other employees in similar job junctions. These companies adhere to a predetermined ranking distribution known as the bell curve. Employees in similar job functions within a department are rated relative to each other. Each department is required to adhere to the bell curve distribution policy.

    Take one of my former companies for example. This company ranks employees on a scale from 1 to 5, with 1 being the highest rank and 5 the lowest. Approximately up to 25% of employees can be ranked with a 1 or 2 ranking, 50% with a 3 ranking, and 25% with a 4 or 5 ranking. Employees with high rankings receive bigger salary raises and other financial incentives, including stock shares. Lowest-ranked employees would be put on performance improvement probation and likely receive no raise or other financial rewards.

- **Individual performance review**. Unlike forced ranking, each employee is evaluated individually and there is no ranking scale. Each employee is evaluated based on their performance compared to expected results described in the employee annual plan and based on feedback from the key people they worked with in the past year. Each employee's results are compared to their annual plan to determine whether they met, exceeded or did not meet expectations. The managers have more flexibility to apply salary increases based on their evaluation of the employee.

How Managers Conduct Employee Rankings and Evaluations

- **Forced ranking**. Prior to the department ranking meeting, the manager should gather all relevant information on each employee on his team so he will be prepared to represent his team fairly in the ranking meeting. He compiles the results for each employee relative to the goals outlined in the employee's annual plan. In addition, he gathers feedback from people whom the employees worked closely with in the past year, including team members, co-workers, partners and managers from other functions. While all managers should follow this preparation practice, not all do. Some are more prepared than others. Needless to say, managers who are better prepared stand a much better chance to get a fair ranking for their employees.

    I'll describe one ranking scenario in an organization I worked in. At the beginning of the meeting, all managers give their ranking recommendation for each of their employees. Once this is done, each manager explains his ranking recommendation by summarizing the employee's results, the manager's own assessment and other people's feedback on the employee. A discussion follows among the managers in the room on whether they agree with the manager's recommendation. Based on this discussion, the employee's ranking may get moved up, down or stay unchanged. Other managers' impression of you can have a big impact on your ranking. For managers who did not have frequent interaction with you, their limited opinion may skew their overall assessment of you. While this may seem unfair, it's the reality and I have seen examples of it.

    When all the managers are done with the discussions, the revised rankings are compared against the bell curve policy and if the rankings are off, adjustments will need to be made. The variance normally happens at the top ranking and at the bottom ranking band. This is where tradeoffs and compromises are made. A manager may have to give up one of the high rankings to save an employee from being included in the lowest rank band unfairly. Employees who are not known or who are perceived negatively by other managers stand the greatest chance of being moved to a lower ranking band. This can be a painful and unfair part of the forced ranking distribution policy.

Once the rankings are finalized, each manager administers his employees' salary increase and other financial rewards based on their ranking and the company's guidelines. Finally, the manager completes a performance review report and reviews with each of the employees. This report also includes next year's plan.

I want to emphasize a point here regarding other managers' opinion of you. If their assessment of you is not fair or inaccurate, the way for your manager to counter it is to be thoroughly prepared with facts and feedback on their employees from others. This is where you can help your manager.

- **Individual performance review**. This process is much simpler and less controversial. Your manager is the only person evaluating you. He compares your results to the objectives described in your annual plan; this is the "what" part of the review. He also assesses how effectively you worked with other people to achieve the results; this is the "how" part of the review. He reviews the feedback on you from people you worked with over the past year. In assessing both the "what's" and the "how's" of your performance, your manager determines if you have exceeded, met or failed to meet expectations.

How Your Salary Increase Is Determined

Several factors go into salary increase considerations. First is the company's business performance. If the company is doing well, employees may get better raises. If not, employees may not get any raises at all. The second factor is the result of your performance evaluation – if the result is good, you'll typically get a bigger raise. The third factor is where your base salary is within the salary range of your job level. Per your company's salary structure, each job level has a salary range, and the salary for employees with this job level must stay within this range. If you are near the top of the salary range, you may not get much of a raise even if you received a good performance review. The best way to get a significant raise is to get promoted to the next job level.

How To Help Prepare Your Manager for Your Evaluation

While we all want to have an excellent review or a high rating, that should not be your goal. Your goal is to get as fair a ranking or performance review as possible. One more important point: you must take ownership of helping and preparing your manager and not assume he has what he needs. I learned this the hard way. As a product manager for a computer system company early in my career, I thought that if I put my head down and focused on giving my best effort, my manager would take care of me and reward me appropriately. I was managing a several-hundred-million-dollar server business, responsible for several aspects of the business, including working with engineering to enhance the products, providing forecast for manufacturing, setting pricing and solving customers' business issues. The product line business was successful and generating better-than-expected sales and profit. I was certain I would receive a high ranking.

I looked forward excitedly to the day of my annual performance review. When I sat down with my manager, Mary, she was very complimentary on my work and results. I was feeling good. However, my excitement came crashing down when she told me I was ranked a 3 (an average ranking on a scale of 1-5). In my dismay and anger, I asked her to explain. She told me she had wanted to give me a higher ranking, but other managers in the meeting told her they didn't have visibility of my work and my contributions to the company. She told me she had tried to fight for me but didn't have enough evidence to support her argument. In my anger, I thought about leaving the company. After all, I had busted my butt, worked days, nights and weekends to help the company succeed and my reward was a lousy 3 ranking – a ranking attributed to an average performer.

I took a few days off from work. The break gave me time to think, and after I calmed down, I realized I had no one to blame but myself. I had completely and blindly relied on my manager to know what I was doing and as importantly, to let other managers know my results and contributions. Although she didn't ask me, I did nothing to prepare her. I learned a hard lesson – I had to take ownership of my career and not rely on anyone else. Even though I didn't have direct control over my job performance ranking,

I had to make sure to help my manager be as prepared as possible and not assume she had it under control. In addition, I needed to make sure that other managers and key stakeholders had visibility of my work and my results. Refer to the chapter "How to stand out and promote yourself" for details.

Here are the steps to help prepare your manager to evaluate your performance:

- Keep an ongoing track record of your results and feedback as the year progresses. Don't wait until the last minute. This is too important to wait until just before the evaluation time to start writing down your accomplishments and other people's feedback. And in the rush, you may forget to include some key milestones as well as gathering feedback from all appropriate people.

- Review regularly your results relative to your employee plan's objectives. If and when your plan is revised due to changes at work, make sure you and your manager are on the same page, especially regarding the expected results. Be proactive and review this plan and your progress with your manager at least once a quarter. This is also an opportunity to capture and revise any changes in your plan if necessary. In addition, if you have been doing a good job on an important assignment that was not part of your plan, make sure you capture this accomplishment as "exceeding or going above and beyond your responsibilities" when you review your plan.

- Whenever you receive a positive message from one of your colleagues, managers, partners or customers regarding a job well done, let your manager know and keep a record. In addition, make a habit to seek out your peers and other managers for feedback on key projects you are working with them on. If they do want to give you feedback, they will appreciate your being proactive. Moreover, you get real-time feedback from them on things you can work to improve instead of hearing about it from your manager at your performance review meeting. And when it comes time for them to give feedback to your manager, they'll more likely give positive feedback on you.

How to Prepare for a Performance Review

- About a month before your ranking or evaluation meeting, give your manager a list of names of the people you want your manager to obtain feedback from. He may ask you for this list, but will appreciate if you took the initiative to provide him the list. These are people who can give your manager constructive feedback with specific examples from their time spent working with you. They include peers who worked closely with you on different projects and other managers who have seen your work and observed your teamwork skills.

- Provide your manager a list of your accomplishments since the last ranking or evaluation session or since you joined the company if you're new. Make sure to highlight the results compared to your annual plan – how the results impacted company business, whether the results met or exceeded the goals and/or timeline. In addition, if you took on additional important projects that were not originally in your plan, be sure to highlight this as "going beyond the call of duty" accomplishments. Among the criteria for getting a high ranking or excellent review is that you not only meet your job expectations, but exceed them. When you provide your manager the list, sit down and go over this list in person with him to make sure there is no confusion. Don't assume he will understand or remember. By going over it with him in person, you eliminate the risk of your manager reviewing your list at the last minute and having no opportunity to clarify any detail with you first.

- Take advantage of opportunities to get visibility with other executives. How other managers and executives perceive you has a significant impact on your review outcome. Look for opportunities to present in front of them and when you do, be prepared to give your best effort and make the most positive impression you can. I had one employee, Mike, who was very good at this. He would seek out opportunities to go into an executive's staff meeting to present his work or a team project important to the company. He not only gained visibility but also developed a reputation as an excellent presenter and a team leader. When I met with my boss to review Mike's performance later in the year, my boss not only agreed with my proposed high ranking for him but also wanted to give him even more raise and stock options than I had recommended.

How to Discuss Your Performance Review With Your Manager

You have done your best and given your manager all the ammunition he needs for your performance evaluation. Now the day comes for you to have your performance review with him. Once the ranking or evaluation result is final, it's very difficult to change. I have seen only very rare cases where a ranking was changed as a result of employee escalation. Here are suggestions on how to handle different evaluation outcomes in your review meeting.

- You received a lower evaluation result than you deserved.

    ▷ Maintain your professionalism. If you didn't get a fair ranking you anticipated, it's certainly understandable to feel disappointed and express it to your manager. While it may be difficult, be as professional as you can and resist throwing a tantrum or making comments you may regret later. But clearly express your disappointment. Take a break if you need to calm down.

    ▷ Focus on the two evaluation dimensions I discussed at the beginning of this chapter (the "what's" and the "how's"). Ask him to compare your results versus expectations in your annual plan. You want him to explain and give specific examples to clarify your evaluation results. You want to probe to understand (1) if your manager prepared himself adequately with the details you provided, (2) the specific reasons you fell short in not earning a higher evaluation result, and (3) what you could have done differently to achieve a better outcome.

    ▷ To find out if he was prepared, ask questions such as: "Give me suggestions on how I could have helped you better prepare for your management evaluation meeting" and "Of the materials I provided you, what was most helpful and what else did you need that I didn't provide?" To probe for more specific details, ask: "I would like examples in my job performance that held me back in my evaluation", "Please give me examples of what, if I had done differently, would have enabled me to get a better outcome" or "Give me an example of where someone was able to get a better review than I was." If he makes comments regarding not working well with others, say: "Please give me specific examples where I wasn't effective working with people to get things done" or "Give me examples where other managers had a negative impression of me." Conclude this discussion with a question on what else you need to improve going forward in order to achieve a better evaluation outcome next time.

- If you received a very low ranking or very negative review, your manager probably has begun working work with HR to develop a "Performance Improvement Plan" for you. This plan spells out specific tasks with expected results and deadlines you must meet. If you don't meet them in a given period, you manager will proceed to terminate your employment. Ask your manager to provide an objective assessment of your results versus expectations in your annual plan. Focus on the two evaluation dimensions I discussed above (the "what's" and the "how's). If you have been taking the steps to monitor your own performance and how others perceive you, you should not be surprised with the evaluation outcome. You can avoid getting into this predicament by paying attention to your manager's feedback in one-on-one meetings and proactively seeking other people's feedback. You then can take actions to improve your situation or consider other job options. By the time you hear this in your performance review, it may be too late.

    Note: If you feel strongly and objectively your evaluation result was unfair and unjust, you can escalate your dispute to HR and your manager's boss. Ask for a meeting where you can objectively lay out the facts to justify a better evaluation result. As I said earlier, you would face a steep hurdle to have this changed, especially if the company uses the "Forced Ranking" process. My advice on handling this dispute is to be professional and use all the facts you have to make your case.

- If you received an outcome you anticipated or even better than you had hoped, use this opportunity to find out what you did right in your manager's views and where you can continue to improve. Ask questions such as: "Can you give me examples of what you and other people see as my strongest areas?" and "Where can I continue to improve going forward?" You may also want to have a discussion on promotional opportunities. Ask questions on what the next steps are and what you need to do in order to merit promotional considerations. Look for concrete examples and suggestions.

- The next step in this meeting is for the manager to review with you your plan for the next year. The plan should include goals, deadlines and expected results from your responsibilities and the projects you will be working on. Ask for clarification on anything you aren't clear on and assess how achievable the plan is. What parts of the plan are within the scope of your job and what parts are "going above and beyond", where if you accomplish them, they would be a plus for your next performance evaluation. Most of all, once you have your questions answered and are clear on expectations, don't commit right away, ask for time to think about it. Even just for a day or so. You have a chance to step back, clear your head and assess more objectively. Ask yourself if this plan is realistic to complete as required. Keep in mind the importance of meeting your commitments. Not meeting your commitments will affect your review negatively. If the plan is not realistic, negotiate to reduce the plan's expectations, or change some parts of the plan from "Must" to "Want" deliverables.

- Some companies' annual employee plan also includes an employee development plan. This plan is intended to help employees continue to develop skills and grow in their career. Think about what you would like the next step in your career to be and draft a plan to support that. It may include trainings or classes you would like to take, or an assignment to participate in a company-wide initiative that would give you additional skills and knowledge. Or it could be to identify a mentor who can coach and help you in your career path.

One word of advice: many managers tend to pay lip service to the development plan and don't put in a lot of effort. Managers are not really evaluated or measured on this responsibility. You should own and drive your development plan for your own success.

Work with HR

When to engage
- Need information/clarification, e.g. on job or company policies
- Career counselling/advice
- Negotiate company offer
- Encountered issues:
  - Harassment/abuse
  - Medical treatment program
  - Dispute/conflict
  - Ethical

Understand HR's role
- Serves company's interest, *not* employee advocate
- Supports, advises management
- Recruitment/hiring
- Benefits/compensation
- Learning and development
- Implements organizational changes
- Facilitates performance review
- Career counselling

What not to expect
- Be your advocate against manager
- Answer to all your questions
- Advocate of change in company
- Honour your sensitive info
- Make decisions for you as employee

How to work with HR
- Proactively engage and learn about their roles and services
- Align with HR/company priorities
- Prepare your facts

CHAPTER 27

How to Work with Human Resources (HR)

Human Resources (HR) plays an important role in the company. HR advises the company management team how to strategically manage people as assets and resources. Among key HR functions are design and managing recruiting/hiring, training/development, salary administration, mediating employee conflicts, etc. In addition, from my management experience, HR also has an objective to protect the company and management team. If there is a dispute between an employee and a manager, don't depend on HR to play a neutral role or be on the employee's side. In these situations, HR is there to keep the company and manager from taking the wrong or potentially illegal actions, not to help the employee win their case. Realizing this helps you know how to work with HR and not get frustrated from unrealistic expectations of your HR personnel. In this chapter, I will describe the roles of HR and how you can utilize HR services.

HR's Roles

Here's a sample list:

- Manages the recruiting and hiring process. HR plays an important role in helping managers hire employees – recruiting, screening, interviewing, putting together offer packages and negotiating employment offers with potential employees.

- Recommends, designs and implements employee benefit programmes, salary and compensation structures for company employees.

- Recommends, designs and implements training and development programmes for employees.

- Implements and manages company organizational changes such as lay-offs and acquisitions.

- Mediates employee conflicts and facilitates performance reviews.

- Provides support and tools to managers and employees.

- Provides career counselling to employees.

- Serves company business interest. HR's loyalty is to the company, not to the employees. HR is not there to be an employee advocate. They will do what is in the best interest of the company.

- Serves a supporting and advisory role to the management team.

When to Engage HR

In general, HR is a great place to go to for information and clarifications of company policies and programmes – questions such as how to get information, what options are available from company programmes, clarification on particular company policies, etc. This kind of information or clarification is clear and unambiguous. You probably can find most of the information on the company website. If you can't find it, contact HR for answers. Below are some specific items you can go to HR for:

- When you need information regarding your employment, such as your job scope, available training classes and personal leave policy.

- You are a manager and you need to fill a job opening, understand the performance review process or training programmes for managers.

- If you face harassment or abuse at work.

- If you have medical-related issues and want to know what treatment and programmes are available to you.

- When you want career counselling and advice.

- When you want to negotiate the job offer you receive.

- When you have a dispute or conflict at work.

- When you face an ethical issue and want clarification.

What Not to Expect From HR

In general, you should not rely on HR on matters requiring them to give judgment, make decisions or take sides. You should not expect HR to be your advocate when it comes to disputes between you and the company. Here are some situations that show what HR can and cannot do.

- If you bring a dispute between you and your manager to HR, don't expect HR to be your advocate. Many employees don't understand that HR's priority and loyalty lies with the company. Instead, they expect HR to support and fight for them when they escalate a work-related issue with their management. Unfortunately, they end up walking away disappointed. Primarily, HR is there to listen and to keep management out of trouble.

- If you face harassment or abuse at work, by colleagues or managers, you need to escalate this to HR. They take this situation very seriously. Companies care greatly about public perception and don't want to be sued. Moreover, companies don't want to have the perception with their employees that they let these situations fester, and they don't want to risk causing morale issues in the workplace. HR will take action because it is in the company's best interest to have this addressed and resolved as quickly as possible.

- Don't expect HR to provide you answers to all your questions, especially if the information is sensitive or confidential. HR knows much of the company's sensitive information but is not allowed to reveal it to you. For example, if there's an impending change to the company organization, HR personnel would know this well in advance since they have to manage potential changes to employees' reporting structure, relocation and employment status.

- Don't expect HR to be a leader or a change agent in the company. They are there to primarily support company management. It is more of an exception when HR plays a lead role in making breakthroughs in the workplace. A common complaint many employees have had for years is the forced ranking distribution that managers have to adhere to. This type of ranking system creates unhealthy competition among employees and results in low morale in the workplace. This has been in place for decades, and only in recent years have companies started to change to a less restrictive evaluation process.

- HR doesn't necessarily need to honour the confidential or sensitive information you share with them. In some instances, HR is required to share the information with company management such as knowledge of employee harassment or illegal actions. If you want to share with HR in confidence, disclose the nature of your topic and confirm with them whether this will be kept confidential.

How to Work With HR

If you know how to work with HR effectively, they can be a good partner and good resource. Here are some suggestions.

- Understand what services HR provides. When you first join the company, take a little time to learn about their services and support resources, tools you can use, different processes to follow, etc. Many companies have an internal website where you can find all or most of this out. You should also meet with your HR representative to introduce yourself and learn about their role and effective ways you can work with them.

- Have facts and information in writing when you meet with HR, especially on a controversial issue. Typically you will meet with an HR representative and the person you have the dispute with. View the HR representative as a third-party witness you want there to have and record the information you present. Make sure you can support your position with facts. I had a colleague who felt that her manager was undermining her work and reneging on an agreement to have her work on a certain highly visible project. She requested a meeting with HR and her manager. Since she did not have the proof to support her claim, it became a "she said, he said" situation. She didn't accomplish much in that meeting. After that, she learned to document decisions, agreements and next steps in her meetings with the manager as well as writing down specific instances where her manager undermined her. Because the last escalation was not successful, he was overconfident and did not change his behaviour. A few months later my colleague escalated again to HR, except this time, she was prepared and able to back up her complaint. HR had no choice but get her manager's boss involved and he was reprimanded. He eventually left the company.

Rely on HR as a resource to support you, to provide suggestions, counselling and guidance, but don't rely on them to make decisions for you or to be your advocate in potential disputes between you and the company.

In China, those born after 1990 are known as *jiulinghou* – the post-1990s generation. I asked these young employees in China on what help they needed most when they first joined a new company. Top of mind is to better understand the company culture and how to blend in. HR is a great place to start for this. While we can learn a lot from our managers, HR has a more company-wide picture. For a newcomer, reaching out proactively to the HR team would add another source of information and networking, and very importantly, make a good impression as a keen learner.

> "I'm not concerned that I am not known,
> I seek to be worthy to be known."
> — Confucius

As a business leader, it's always at the back of my mind to work closely with HR in spotting talent. In this VUCA (volatile, uncertain, complex and ambiguous) world, potential is seen as more important that current capabilities. Early-career employees should value interactions with HR as exposures to talent scouting. According to my HR partners, they first look for motivation. Motivation is a stable factor and often comes across subtly. Also, potential could be the "engine" that propels top talent to perform. Therefore, we must look inside us to unlock the motivating factors. That will not only help us invest our energy in things that matter, but also help the HR community recognize the talent potential in us.

The other potential talent indicators often mentioned in talent conversations include curiosity, insight, engagement and determination (*21st-Century Talent Spotting*, Claudio Fernandez-Araoz). Once again, HR is a key partner here and can play a key role in helping you bring out these desirable qualities.

PART 6

Optimizing Your Success

"Control your own destiny or someone else will."
— **Jack Welch**

"You had better face your difficulties as early as possible."
— **Korean proverb**

"If you fail to change, someone will change you."
— **The Answers of AliRen, Alibaba Group**

Effective Time Management

Prioritize
- Prioritize "To Do" list
- "Urgent vs Important" 2x2
- "Do It Now" 2x2

Reduce unproductive activities
- Block 2 hours "Priority" time
- Learn to say no ➔ Chapter 22
- Discipline in attending necessary meetings only
- Align upfront for presentations
- Hide from desk interruptions
- Limit breaks
- Resist browsing
- Organize emails
- Stay healthy to minimize sick days
- Work from home

Avoid time-wasters
- Social media, cell phone, texting
- Gossip, socializing
- Internet browsing
- Excessive meetings
- Emailing
- Extra tea/smoke breaks
- Interruptions at desk
- Commute time
- Unexpected events

CHAPTER 28

How to Manage Time and Prioritize Effectively

To many working professionals I know, achieving work-life balance remains elusive and seems more like wishful thinking than a realistic goal. They never seem to have enough time to get work done even though they spend many hours at work and even take it home. With the availability of high-tech devices, they seem to be on call 24/7. As a result, they have less personal time and feel more stressed. They wonder how they can spend less time working and still get their work done in order to have more personal time. This is an essential life skill and habit. Much like fitness, this is a muscle set to build and develop. It will also get better with practice and regular conditioning, so it pays when you start this early in your career. Tight timelines and limited support resources are common situations in business. However, you can learn to manage effectively. I have seen many examples of individuals who outshone others because they had strong project management and resource management skills. From work-life balance perspective – the balance between devoting time to work and stopping to smell the roses along the journey – I learned to plan my time intentionally, mindfully and smartly.

In this chapter, I will look at non-productive and time-wasting activities we do at work, ideas to reduce these activities and a strategy to prioritize so we can focus on getting work done more effectively and efficiently.

Time-Wasters

According to a Harris Poll and CareerBuilder survey report on American workers (Economy, 2015), the top 10 time-wasters are:

1. Cell phone/texting
2. Gossip
3. Internet
4. Social media
5. Snack or smoke breaks
6. Noisy co-workers
7. Meetings
8. Email
9. Co-workers dropping by
10. Co-workers putting calls on speaker phone

I modified the above list from my observations and ranked them as follows:

1. Cell phone/texting/social media.

2. Gossip/socializing. This includes hallway mingles and long lunches.

3. Internet browsing on non-work activities.

4. Excessive number of meetings, including team meetings, project meetings, company/organization meetings, one-on-one meetings, emergency meetings, etc.

5. Email (reading and responding). This includes personal and work email.

6. Taking extra coffee/smoke breaks throughout the day.

7. Interruptions. This includes people coming by and interrupting you at your desk.

8. Commute time. This depends on where you live and how far you are from work. In many locations where traffic is terrible with no convenient public transportation, this can impact your time significantly.

While these findings were specific to American workers, I submit that they are not too different in your specific country. In addition to the above time-wasters, unexpected events, which may be out of your control, can consume a significant amount of your time. For example, your manager comes to you with an urgent request or you get called into a meeting to clear up the confusion from a previous meeting. Furthermore, when you get sick and have to take time out of work, your work is not getting done and the longer you're out, the further behind you get.

According to *The Telegraph*, half of all workers waste up to two hours a day (Huth, 2015). I would say that's a low estimate. But even two hours is a huge amount of time that could have been used to get more work done. Imagine if you could cut that time in half and use that time to get your work done and be able to leave earlier, how much more productive your life would be.

How to Reduce Unproductive Activities and Manage Time More Efficiently

It's unrealistic to eliminate all "non-work" activities. Moreover, it can be beneficial to our well-being and productivity to spend some time on those "time-wasting" activities. Taking a coffee break or a short walk helps us clear our mind. We cannot go through the whole day without touching base with our friends or responding to our family. Hallway chats are a good way to build relationships with our co-workers. The idea here is to not spend excessive amount of time on these activities but to keep them in moderation.

Here are the best practices to help you reduce time-wasters and be more productive:

- Reserve two continuous hours every workday to work on your highest priorities. If possible, choose the time when you do your best work – early morning, for example. Block this time on your work calendar to prevent people from scheduling meetings with you during that time. Otherwise, your calendar is an invitation for people to schedule you. Of course, there are times when you won't be able to keep this time for yourself, but be disciplined and try to stick to this practice as best you can.

- When you get an unexpected request from your manager, determine if you are the best person for this request. It tends to be by default that managers automatically come to the person they trust and depend on to get the job done. Refer to the "How to say no smartly" chapter to help you with this situation. One benefit of the two-hour block is that you have "extra" time to work on your manager's request in case you didn't have to use all of that time.

- Apply discipline to determine which meetings you need to attend versus the optional ones. Usually, we have many more meetings at work than necessary. Whenever there is an issue, someone will call a meeting instead of trying to see if it can be addressed offline by a few key people associated with the issue. And if there are meetings where you and a team member are invited and the purpose of the meeting is information-sharing, determine if you and your colleague can take turns attending. To help you decide whether you need to attend a meeting, ask yourself what the impact to you would be if you skipped it. Moreover, many meetings are run inefficiently, running longer than scheduled; worse still, multiple meetings are held to go over the same topic. While this sometimes is necessary, it's frequently a result of poor meeting management.

- If you and your team are preparing for an important presentation to company executives, you probably need to review your work with your manager and others before meeting the executives; this exercise can be time-consuming. While it's a good idea to have your manager's support before you present, there are ways for you to manage this task more efficiently. Refer to the "How to organize and develop presentation content" chapter for tips on developing effective presentation content.

- Unless you need to work at your desk, find a guest workstation or an empty conference room where you can hide and do your work. Since a majority of interruptions are not important, this reduces the potential disruptions from people coming to your desk unexpectedly. If an urgent matter comes up and you're not at your desk, people will either email you, call you on your cell phone or text you.

- Taking coffee breaks or walks is a good way to clear your mind, but be disciplined about the number of times a day you do this. Sometimes people come by your desk and invite you to take a coffee break; you can factor this into your daily number of breaks. Also limit the amount of time you spend on coffee breaks and be disciplined about it. However, we're not robots so we will need to be somewhat flexible with the times when we want to take more or longer breaks with our colleagues, but they should not be frequent occurrences.

- Moreover, resist spending time on the internet for personal use. If you need to, by all means. But before you start, ask yourself if you need to do it right now and what would be the impact if you did it later in your personal time. The risk of internet browsing is that once you start, you can move from one site to another or from one topic to another and lose track of time. Similarly with social media, unless you cannot wait, make a habit of using it during your break or lunch hour. Again, ask yourself the same question: what would happen if you waited to do it later in your personal time. In terms of texting, we do use it as a regular form of communication since it is quick and we can do it pretty much at anytime and anywhere. For non-work-related texting, limit yourself to when you take coffee breaks or your lunch hour. Let your friends or family members know you may take some time to reply to them.

- Emails are a notorious time-waster and they come in all forms – junk email, information-only email, personal email, work email that you need to reply to, etc. There could be hundreds of email arriving at your inbox daily. Use filter tools to filter out as many spam emails as possible. If you're unorganized with email, it can cost you a lot of time when you need to find a specific email urgently but have no idea where it is. One way to combat this is to organize your email folders in ways that work for you and help you locate email quickly. You can organize your email by main topics and have sub-folders for topics within the main topic folder. For example, you may have different "job" folders (folders containing materials you need for your work), one for each functional area you work with, and folders for external company partners you interact with. You may want to have a dedicated folder for email messages between your boss and you. This will help you quickly find a particular message and a good way to indirectly organize your boss.

- Moreover, prioritize your email by working on important/urgent emails first and leave non-urgent or unimportant ones for later. Lastly, make a habit of cleaning up your inbox on a regular basis. Having hundreds or thousands of emails in your inbox is a recipe for trouble when you need to find a specific email.

- Similar to email, organizing your computer folders will help you reduce time trying to look for forgotten files. I have seen disorganized employees who put all their working files on the desktop screen regardless of the document type, and later on spent precious time trying to locate a file among a forest of files. This laziness wastes valuable time. A few minutes of setting up a folder structure would have saved them a great deal of time later on.

- Getting sick is something we don't really have control over. Unfortunately, when we get sick, we're out of commission and may quickly fall behind on our work. Our work doesn't go away when we're sick and will pile up waiting for us when we come back. However, what we can do is to keep ourselves healthy and fit as much as we can. When we're unfit and stressed out, we are more vulnerable to getting sick. Fitness experts and doctors agree that a 30-minute workout done three times a week is good for our body and mind and helps us be more productive. If you're away from work and falling behind due to illness, you may want to ask your boss for an extension or to assign your work to someone else if the deadline is important.

- Working at home from time to time helps reduce the commute time significantly, especially if you live far from your workplace. Even working at home during morning rush hours can save you a lot of time. Many companies allow work flexibility such as working at home some of the time. Check with your company and your manager to see if this option is available to you. At one point, I lived an hour away from work with no convenient public transportation and it took at least two hours of commute time each day. That was a huge amount of mostly unproductive time. However, I was able to work at home two days a week, which reduced my unproductive commute hours significantly.

How to Prioritize

We are inundated with many work activities and projects, from small to big tasks, from unimportant to urgent and important. We can get overwhelmed trying to figure out how to prioritize our work and deciding which things to tackle first. While there are many complex tools, high-tech applications and devices to help us prioritize, I believe simple tools and methods are often more effective. Below are a few practical methods to consider in prioritizing your work.

1. **Important versus Urgent** – popularly known as the Eisenhower Box (Brandall, 2016). Important tasks are defined as:

    ▷ People or projects are affected if the task is not completed.
    ▷ Other tasks depend on completion of this task.
    ▷ The task contributes significant value.

    Urgent tasks are defined as:

    ▷ The task required to be completed is overdue or soon to be.
    ▷ The task demands immediate response and action.
    ▷ The consequences of not doing the task will be felt quickly.

You put your tasks in one of these boxes. If you have multiple tasks in the box, you prioritize the tasks within that box based on business needs (for example, does your manager's request have higher priority than your own task?)

Urgent and Important **Do it now**	Important but Not Urgent **Decide when to do it**
Urgent but Not Important **Delegate it**	Not important and Not Urgent **Skip it**

2. **Four category boxes** – a similar concept to the above method (Brandall, 2016).

Things you want to do and need to do **Do it now**	Things you want to do but do not need to do **Decide when to do it**
Things you don't want to do but need to do **Delegate it**	Things you do not want to do and do not need to do **Skip it**

3. **My modified method** – a variation of the first method that I use is as follows. I carry a work notebook where I take notes from meetings and write down information or things I learn throughout the day. I reserve

a number of pages near the end of the notebook for me to list all the "To Do" tasks. Then I write the priority code and deadline for each task. For example:

▷ The task: Complete business metric report for Quarter 3
▷ Priority level: 2 (important but not urgent)
▷ Due date: July 10 (3 weeks from today's date)

On the notebook page, I write: "#2. Complete business metric report for Q3. July 10." I cross off each item from the list when I complete it or if I don't need to do it anymore. The advantage of this is I can keep a running list and add or cross off tasks as appropriate. It also allows me to keep a history of all the tasks and it gives me a sense of satisfaction when I cross a task off the list when completed. While there are a multitude of e-planners or calendars on phones or computers to keep track of this information digitally, I find that writing things down also helps me remember them. Instead of using a notebook, you can do the same thing using an Excel spreadsheet that allows you to sort on the priority code or timeline as you want.

In Asia, time management and prioritization are important management skills and are seen as an important factor in separating top-tier performers. Even as companies are flattening their organization structure, they are still selective with the higher levels. If you have a desire to move up the chain and be part of the management team at some point, the sooner you develop this skillset and get ahead of others early in your career, the higher your chances of breaking out from the crowd. Time management is also an extension of efficiently using your resources. Perception of being average in this area could delay potential advancements.

A few more suggestions to consider:

- Develop impatience on wasting time, especially those "fragmented slots" while waiting, on public transport or coffee time. Use those times for learning and thinking. Sum up those fragmented 10 minutes to be greater than the sum of all. I would purposefully block out time slots in my schedule to pack up the day's "add-on" agenda. It would discipline me to be more conscious on time management throughout the day and focus my time for those "add on" topics. Focusing on a topic for a continuous 30 minutes is much more effective than revisiting the subject in between meetings or breaks.

- Leverage the tools you have to manage your time. Outlook, Dynamics, Dingtalk or a simple To-do list are good handy tools.

- Practise eliminating and summarizing to focus on core value-add. That will help separate objectives and means-to-an-end and to focus our time on what matters. I often witnessed meetings and discussions going too long and with no concrete resolutions, especially in large meetings and with emotions running high. In those situations, I would ask to confirm the objectives of the meeting. I would then summarize what was agreed and eliminate what was not helping the objectives. That usually would refocus everyone's attention back to the meeting's objectives.

- Generate ideas while exercising. I found this to be very useful and productive. If it's not in your routine, please try. I have many of my marketing creative ideas and business breakthrough concepts from my runs or swimming laps.

I'm confident that if you follow the suggestions in this chapter, you will be able to get more done at work and reduce the work you need to take home and, as a result, have more personal time to do what you like.

CHAPTER 29

How to Deal with Changes at Work

It's a given that the only thing constant in the workplace is change. It was kind of a running joke in my company that we could expect a major re-org every year. During my career spanning over 25 years, I have worked in 12 different organizations in five companies. I worked under 12 managers and experienced numerous company organizational changes. I can tell you my companies were not the exception; most of the people I talked to and interviewed also confirmed this. It's highly unlikely you will have the same manager or work in the same organization, same company in your entire career. Some changes will be the result of your decisions while other changes will be out of your control. Company organizational changes can be unnerving and introduce uncertainties. Many people don't handle changes well and take a long time to adjust. However, if you're able to deal with changes effectively and adjust to the transition quickly, you will be able to not only maintain but also enhance your standing in the company. In this chapter I will discuss possible changes at work and how to deal with them while maintaining your relevance in the organization.

While it's a given that changes in the workplace will happen during your career, the first crucial rule is to recognize what you can control and what you cannot. In Stephen Covey's book, *The 7 Habits of Highly Effective People*, he talks about the circle of concern and the circle of influence (Covey, 2002). Many of us focus on the concerns and react to things we can't control, rather than focus on areas we can influence and proactively work on. Covey

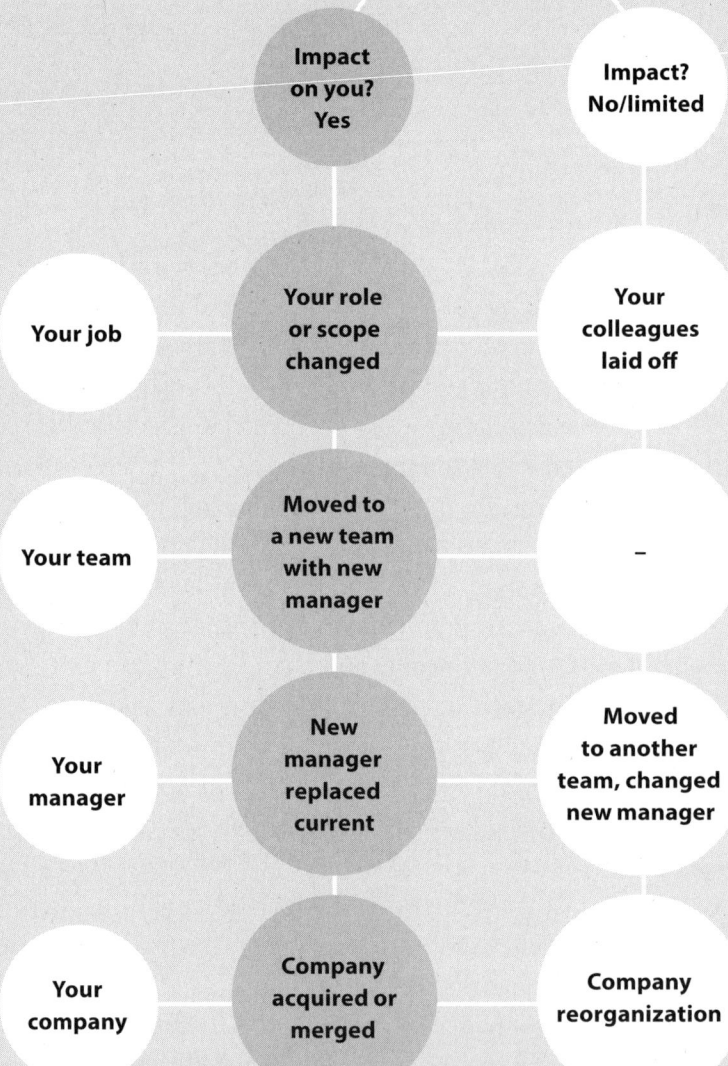

encourages us to focus our energy and proactively work on things we have influence over, thereby expanding our circle of influence. For example, your manager decides to leave the company and you end up having a new manager. Instead of focusing on your concerns and fear about the new manager, you should focus your positive energy on what you can influence in this new situation, such as helping the new manager get up to speed quickly with the new team.

Regardless of any organizational change in your workplace, the key is to first focus your time and energy on the changes that you have some control or influence over. Secondly, do your best to behave and act professionally – stay calm, keep things in perspective, focus on your work and avoid getting emotional or distracted. Just the fact of recognizing you don't have control over a particular company change will help you avoid taking it personally and keeping you sane. Thirdly, make sure your own "house" is in order – meaning your annual plan is up to date with clear job responsibilities, specific goals, results you have achieved to date as well as expected deliverables for the remainder of the year. If you have not updated the plan, work on it as soon as possible because it's an important document to demonstrate your role in the organization.

Here are several common company changes and ways to handle them.

- **Company changes/reorganizations**. Your team/department is moved to another organization under a new executive. An example of this move: currently you are a pricing analyst on the pricing team in the Product Management organization. With the company reorganization, the team is moved to the Finance organization headed by a Vice President of Finance. In this company organizational change, we will cover two scenarios: one where you still work for the same manager and one where you have a new one.

    ▷ **You still have the same manager**. In this scenario, your manager's initial objectives are: (1) to establish her and her team's credibility by educating the new executive about her and her team's role and value to the company; and (2) establish a good rapport and working relationship with the new executive. At this point your manager should treat this transaction as a new beginning with her boss and to find out as much as she can on how to work with the new executive effectively. With your knowledge of your manager's style, strengths and weaknesses, you should take this opportunity to offer her help during this transition. Meet with your manager as soon as possible and ask her for specific tasks you can help. Keep in mind this change is new to your manager as well and she may be feeling a lot of stress and pressure to establish her place in the new organization. For example, if your manager is disorganized and needs to prepare certain materials quickly for a meeting with her boss, she would welcome your help. Taking this initiative would further enhance your value to your manager.

▹ **You have a new manager.** In this scenario, the new organization's executive has chosen a new manager for your team. It's logical to assume the new manager already has a working relationship with her boss and may not know much about her new team's role and value to the company. Your objectives here are to educate your new manager about your and the team's role and value to the company as well as establish a good rapport and credibility with her. If the new manager has not already done so, seek a meeting with her. When you have the meeting, use the time to update her on the role and value the team offers. Review with her your annual plan and give your thoughts on business challenges and priorities. Although you're a member of the team, taking this initiative to discuss the team with her shows your leadership and your broad knowledge of not only your job but the overall picture of the team. In addition, ask your manager for any specific requests she may have that you can assist in this transition. Finally, take the opportunity to find out how to work with her going forward.

If your new manager comes from outside the company, she probably knows little about the company's business, organizational dynamics and about you and the team. There is a lot for this manager to get up to speed on; she may focus initially on syncing up with her boss, trying to understand the company business and as a result, may not put as much energy toward her team. Here, you have a great opportunity to make yourself valuable by proactively bringing her up to speed and sharing your insight on the team, the company and its challenges.

A friend of mine, Katie, recently went through this experience. Due to reorganization in the company, the Vice President of her group and his direct report were forced out (or "retired to spend more time with family") and Katie was worried about whether she would be next in line. The new VP, who came from a different industry, had little experience with the new company's business and industry. Katie seized the opportunity to work closely with the new VP. She helped bring her up to speed on the inner workings of the company business and she created presentation materials for the VP's important meeting with the company's executive staff. The VP was impressed with Katie's skills and deep knowledge about the company and its business. By taking this proactive approach, Katie established her credibility and positioned herself as a valuable asset to the VP.

Whether your manager is new to the company or not, after she has had time to digest the team information and meet her boss, you should ask to review your annual plan with her to see if it should be updated given the recent organizational change. New managers tend to want to add their own footprint to their organization and tend to make changes to their team and the team's charter. Your manager will appreciate your taking the initiative in helping her put her stamp on the team and succeed in the new role. By establishing your credibility and value, you stand a good chance to keep your job, or better yet, get a chance to be assigned to a more important role on the team. Lastly, you should proactively plan for the next step in your career; it's best to take control of your career and not put your fate in somebody else's hand or wait to see what happens next. By proactively exploring your options and planning your career, you're in control and have the confidence to drive your career.

- **You have a new manager replacing the previous one**. There's no change in company organizational structure. For situations where your new manager comes from outside the company or from another team, the discussion above applies here as well. The exception to the above situations is that this is less complicated since the organization structure remains the same. If you have been in this organization for any extended time, you should have a good understanding of the company's business, organization dynamics and priorities. As a result, you are in a great position to help the new manager get up to speed and to influence her on the team's priorities and needs.

If the new manager is one of your peers who was promoted, it may present a bit of an awkward situation and resentment among the team members, especially if you and other members feel the promotion was not warranted. However, once the decision is made, you have no control whether that person is your manager or not. While it may be difficult, you need to do your best to be professional and not let your personal feelings influence your behaviour. If you find this promotion completely unacceptable, you have a choice to explore different job options. If you choose to stay in your current position, at least for the time being, you must try your best to have a good professional relationship with the new manager and help her be successful in her new job. Keep in mind the new rookie manager is probably feeling a bit insecure as well and would appreciate your professionalism and best effort in working with her, although some new managers in this situation react to their insecurity by being more hands-on. As difficult as it may be, maintaining your professionalism by focusing on your work will gain the respect of your new manager and people in the company. Lastly, never burn bridges. It's a small world and things tend to have a way to come back to you.

- **You move to another team and have a new manager.** In this situation, you should already have some familiarity with the new manager, whether you wanted to move to that team or were assigned to it, and that should make establishing a rapport with the new manager easier. However, you should proceed as you would in other new management situations and work with the new manager to find out how best to work with her. In addition, since you're joining a new team, use the initial time to get to know the team – how they work together, their concerns, how they work with other teams and how you can best work with them. The best practices described in "How to start your job on the right foot" chapter apply here as well.

- **Your colleagues get laid off but you are not affected**. While this situation doesn't impact your employment status with the company, it will likely have an effect on you. In the short term, you may feel sad and sympathetic for your friends, disappointed or upset at the company's decision even while you feel relieved you still have your job. It can also be a difficult time for your manager. I have had to give the bad news to employees who were impacted and it was one of the least favourite parts of being a manager. I experienced a mix of emotions – sadness to lose an employee/friend, guilt of affecting someone's livelihood, failure that I wasn't able to keep this employee. One of the things you can do during this time is to be as low-maintenance to your manager as possible. In the near to medium term, the layoff may have a real impact on the manager and the team's workload, particularly if no replacement resource is available to cover the gap left by the laid-off employees. If this happens, the manager needs to prioritize and figure out how to cover the workload gap. This is where you can help your manager and yourself. Help your manager prioritize the workload, and at the same time, influence her to allow you to take on more value-add work and take some of the less important work off your plate.

- **Another team gets a new manager**. While this may seem to have little or no impact on you or your team, it actually can. Much of your work involves other teams and when a team inherits a new manager, that manager may change her team's priorities and the way they work with you and your team members. As a result, it would be good for your manager to hear from the new manager about any change in priorities and how both teams can best work together. Don't assume that things will continue to work as usual. Remember, new managers tend to want to put their own signature on the new team they inherit. So talk to your manager to find out if your manager has met or plans to meet with the new manager. If not, explain to your manager the importance of syncing up with the new manager to avoid future miscommunications or disconnects which can derail the project both teams have been working together on. You can say: "Have you had a chance to meet with the new manager? This project is important to both teams and it would be helpful to us to get her thoughts so we can be on the same page." Your manager understands that potential project mistakes would not reflect well on her and the new manager and would appreciate your taking the initiative.

- **Your company gets acquired or your company acquires another company.** This can be a nervous time for employees in both companies, especially if there are overlapping functions, product lines and services. This raises the likelihood of the company cutting cost and laying off people. As the companies begin the integration process and if your team is potentially at risk, your manager would likely be involved. The best you can do here is to control your own "house". Make sure your annual plan is up to date and your manager is clear about your role, responsibilities and contributions. Make sure you stay in contact and maintain a good relationship with your network contacts. They can help you explore opportunities. Refer to "How to build, maintain and grow your network" chapter for details.

    When my company merged with a competitor, it was clear there were overlapping products lines. Our business unit (BU) had similar products. Once my company announced that our BU products would be replaced by the other company's products, we all knew we'd be soon out of a job. Since I had maintained a good relationship with my network contacts, I was able to meet with several of them to explore job openings and opportunities in their organizations. Through these contacts I was able to land a position I liked.

Work changes are stressful and at times affect you subconsciously. Don't underestimate the impact and be aware if your temperament changes abnormally. Don't bring stress from work home as it is very unfair and damaging to family health. Check it at the door. Recognizing the stress early and talking with your family would greatly help you and improve your state of mind. If possible, get ahead of the change by volunteering to join the transition project team. This gives you advance notice of impending changes. I was involved in a few re-organizations and in Programme Management Office (PMO) to plan out the organizational changes. From my experience, it's much better to be involved early and plan forward. It allows more time to adjust to a new world.

Take a proactive approach to personal change management. Adjusting your mindset to the big picture quickly enables you to think through organization directions and plan out your next steps. Companies are not able to plan for each employee. Also, Asian markets tend to be at the downstream design process of the worldwide planning cycle. While you may not know what's coming, preparing yourself to accept potential changes will enable you to use your energy and time to plan the best path forward.

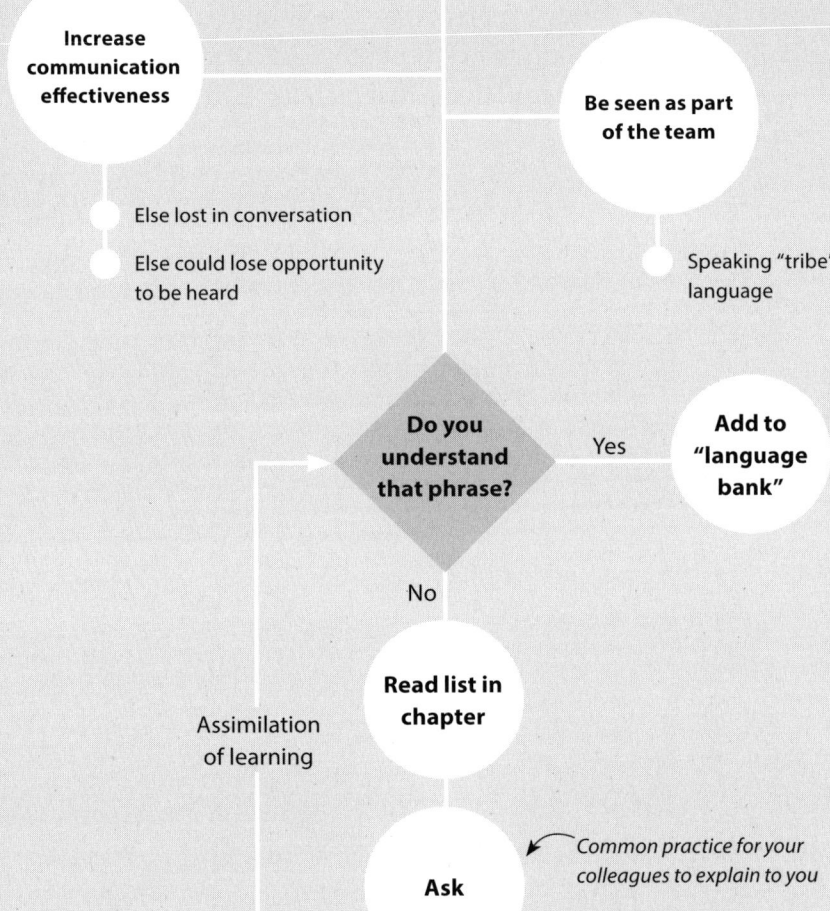

How to Understand and Use Business Idioms

You may have heard of the expression "When in Rome, do as the Romans do". Whether you work for a multinational company with headquarters in the United States or for a local/national company who works frequently with other companies, customers, partners, suppliers and others in the US or other Western companies, you should apply that motto in your daily work life interacting with your co-workers, managers/executives, customers, partners, etc. Business culture is a way of business operations and it defines how employees at different levels communicate and act with one another and with others outside the company. Understanding American or Western business culture, knowing how to conduct yourself and how to use business idioms is essential to your success. This chapter will show you how.

American Business Culture

America is a big country with more than 300 million people in 50 states. As a result, regions can differ from other regions on the culture and even one company can have some cultural differences from other companies. However, there are common themes, and while this may seem simplistic, I believe two phrases define American business culture:

1. "Results/Goal-Oriented"
2. "Time Is Money"

These two themes explain how Americans conduct business at work and how they interact and work with one another to get things done.

1. **Results/Goal-Oriented.** When employees start out on a new project, their focus is on achieving the project's goal. Forming personal bonds with team members is not a top priority. Now, if in the course of working and achieving results, they develop close bond with certain team members, that's wonderful. But they don't go into a business transaction with the focus of forming a strong bond with their counter parts. As a result, they tend to take individual initiatives and heroic acts. Americans also have a more favourable view on aggressiveness (or some would prefer to call it assertiveness). I'm not making judgment one way or the other, just pointing out certain unique characteristics of American business culture.

2. **Time Is Money.** With respect to time, being on time is expected, especially if there's a business meeting with clients or partner companies. Americans strive to get things done with just the right amount of time needed, with no unnecessary wasted time. They sacrifice other things in order to spend time working. My European counterparts commented on American professionals' strange practice of eating lunch at their desk. There are even "working lunch" meetings, unheard of in a lot of countries. But as much as Americans hate wasting time, here is a paradox: they sit through endless number of meetings. Sometime there's a meeting to talk about what was decided in a previous meeting. You know what one of the most common complaints from Americans is? Yes, too many meetings at work. I remember the times where I sat through meetings all day and ended up doing work in the evening at home. Oftentimes I think people attend meetings because they're afraid they may miss something important if they don't go.

Now that we have covered the two phrases defining American business culture, let's look at some key characteristics to give us deeper insight to the culture, and more importantly, prepare us to thrive in this business culture.

American Business Culture Characteristics

- **Yes means yes.** By and large, Americans are direct and speak their mind, especially in business environments. If they don't agree with you or have a different viewpoint, they speak up and voice their opinions. This is particularly important on matters requiring decisions or active discussions that may impact them. If someone disagrees but doesn't speak up, it is taken as agreeing or at least, not opposing. This can be quite a surprise and a bit of a shock for someone from a different culture where avoiding conflicts and avoiding embarrassing others in public is a good social practice.

  I had my first lesson when I initially worked with my co-worker in Japan. As a team lead, I needed to have the team members agree with the project assignments and so I assigned certain tasks to my Japanese co-worker. Being immersed in American business culture, I took his silence as acceptance since I assumed he would've spoken up if he didn't like what I proposed. A couple of weeks later when we had our team meeting to go over the project's status, he didn't show any progress. When I emailed him afterward, he replied that he didn't agree to take on the assignments. An element of Japanese culture is being polite and a desire to please people. Saying no is uncomfortable. So instead of objecting, my colleague remained silent. From that incident on, I learned to confirm or clarify with him to avoid any misunderstanding.

  One note of clarification: as I mentioned above, not all regions in US are the same in terms of culture. In regions/areas where there's a lot of diversity, with people from different backgrounds and cultures working together, the American culture has somewhat evolved and taken on a balanced blend of traditional American business culture and other cultures. For example, people are still direct but in a more diplomatic and friendly way. However, this requires you to be able to be more aware, to clarify and read between the lines to understand what they really mean. In my experience, I find it most effective in the workplace to employ a direct approach – a way of being direct while showing your understanding and without offending the other person. This is the approach I try to demonstrate throughout this book.

- **Greeting characteristics.** In general, Americans are personable, friendly and expressive. While some other cultures discourage making eye contact or shaking hands, as it's seen as disrespectful, American business culture is just the opposite, where making eye contact, looking someone in the eye while talking, handshaking and smiling are widely practised. Another characteristic is informality. Americans refer to each other by their first name in conversations in casual and even business settings. They don't often use titles, even with their superiors, unless it's appropriate and needed for the occasion.

  Upon meeting someone for the first time or being introduced, Americans proactively look at the other person's face, smile, say hi and their name, and extend their hand to shake the other person's hand. And if there's time, they then engage in small talk as a way to break the ice and build a rapport. If this social greeting practice is unfamiliar or uncomfortable to you, realize that it is normal practice in America, not disrespectful, but an excellent way to start a business relationship and get off on the right foot. Practise it with people you are comfortable with and it'll be more natural to you after a short time.

  One more note: "How are you?" is a very common phrase Americans use to greet one another. However, it is not an invitation to divulge our medical history (especially with someone new). A simple "Fine, thank you, and you?" is sufficient.

- **American business language: Idioms.** One important element of business culture is the way people use business language to communicate or express themselves – known as business idioms. They often are "shortcut" communication phrases people use so they don't have to spend more time explaining what they mean. Understanding the commonly used business idioms and knowing how to use them yourself will enable you to communicate more effectively with different audiences and impress them with your business language skills.

  Imagine a scenario where you're in a meeting and people are using a lot of business idioms unfamiliar to you. You would be lost in the conversation and not able to contribute meaningfully. And you also lose an opportunity to be heard and recognized by other people in the meeting.

Communication is required to be an effective team player. Learning business idioms is like learning a local language and it is a most effective way to be accepted as a member of the team.

In the following pages, I describe the common business idioms in American business environments and provide examples on how they are used. There may be other idioms not included here, or new ones created in the future. Don't worry. Many people, even people who have lived and worked in US for many years, don't know or understand all the idioms. When you hear a business idiom you don't understand, ask that person to explain it to you. This is a common practice and they will be happy to oblige.

Table 2
Common Business Idioms
(Trafford, 2019)

Idiom	Meaning	Example
24 by 7	24 hours a day, 7 days a week.	"I'm working 24 by 7 these days."
A chip on your shoulder	Someone holding a negative feeling such as feeling disrespected or resentment of being overlooked.	"Sometimes he behaves in the meeting like he has a chip on his shoulder."
A tough break	Something unfortunate or unlucky happens.	"It was a tough break for our manager when her best employee left the company."
Ahead of the curve	To be more advanced than other people or companies.	"We're #1 in our market because we're doing our best to stay ahead of the curve."
Ahead of the pack	To be better or more successful than the competition.	"If we want to stay ahead of the pack, we're going to have to continue to innovate."

Idiom	Meaning	Example
ASAP	"As soon as possible."	"I need to leave the meeting now. My manager wants to see me ASAP."
At stake or a lot riding on the line	A significant outcome or result is at risk.	"There's a lot at stake with this project."
At the end of the day	What you consider is the most important or relevant thing about a situation.	"At the end of the day, I'm the one being held accountable for my decision."
Back to the drawing board or back to square one	To start something over and go back to the beginning.	"The product demo didn't work. We have to go back to square one."
Ballpark number or figure	A rough estimate or forecast.	"My ballpark figure for sales this month is 5,000 units."
Beat a dead horse	Discussing or talking about the same issue over and over.	"Haven't we beaten this dead horse enough?"
Behind someone's back	To do something to someone or relating to someone without that person's knowledge and in secret way.	"You went behind my back to talk to my manager without telling me."
Behind the scenes	Something or event that happens in secret or not in front of the public or people.	"The marketing event went smoothly because the team did a lot of work behind the scenes."
Behind the 8-ball	A difficult position from which it is unlikely one can escape.	"I don't know how I can get this project completed on schedule and under budget. I'm really behind the eight-ball."
Between a rock and a hard place	A situation where one is faced with two equally difficult alternatives.	"You're between a rock and a hard place. I don't envy your decision."

How to Understand and Use Business Idioms

Idiom	Meaning	Example
Big picture	Looking at a higher, strategic goal or outcome instead of the details.	"Although you are busy with a lot of the details, don't lose sight of the big picture of this project."
Bottom line	Summary or conclusion of a discussion or an issue.	"The bottom line is we can't afford to pay for this marketing event."
By the book	To do things according to company policy, rules or procedure.	"He doesn't want to take any risk so he does things by the book."
Catch someone off guard	To surprise someone by doing something that they were not expecting.	"I was caught off guard when my manager asked me to travel on a business trip for him."
Cave (or cave in)	To agree to something that you or someone did not want to accept previously.	"The salesperson finally caves in to the customer's demand."
Come up short	To try to achieve something but fail to get the desired result.	"The promotion was supposed to generate 10% increase in sales, but we came up short."
Cop out	Using an excuse to not do something.	"That's a cop out for not wanting to take on the action item."
Corner a market	To dominate a particular market.	"Microsoft has cornered the PC market with their Windows OS."
Cut corners	To take shortcuts and find an easier or cheaper way to do something.	"They cut corners in order to get their product to market sooner."
Cut one's losses	To stop doing something that is not meeting the end goal even though some amount of investment had been spent.	"Our marketing campaign was expensive and not showing results, so we had to cut our losses."
Cut-throat	Something that is very intense, aggressive, and merciless.	"The PC market is a cut-throat industry."

Idiom	Meaning	Example
Cut to the chase	Tell someone to get to what they really want to say and not ramble or beat around the bushes.	"I don't have a lot of time to listen, can you cut to the chase?"
Diamond in the rough	Something or someone that has great potential but will require a lot of work.	"He is a diamond in the rough. He's smart with many great ideas, but he doesn't know how to work with people."
Drop the ball	Someone or some persons failed to complete a task that they owned.	"We didn't complete the project on time because you dropped the ball."
Fall through the cracks	Something needed to be done but no one was aware or took initiative to do it.	"The computer needs to be fixed but no one did. It fell through the cracks."
Fifty-fifty	Something is divided equally – 50% for one person, 50% for the other, or something that has an equal chance to succeed or fail.	"We have a 50/50 chance of completing this project on schedule."
From the ground up	Starting or building a business, project, or something else from zero.	"Steve Jobs built Apple company from the ground up."
Game plan	A strategy or plan.	"What is your game plan to compete against your main competitor?"
Get back in/into the swing of things	To get used to doing something again after having a break from that activity.	"After a long layoff, I'm trying to get back into the swing of things."
Get the ball rolling	To start or resume something such as a project.	"Our project deadline is coming soon. We need to get the ball rolling now."
Get or be on a person's good side	If someone likes you, you are on their "good side".	"I have a new manager and I want to be on her good side."

How to Understand and Use Business Idioms

Idiom	Meaning	Example
Get a foot in the door	To take a low-level position with a company with the goal of eventually getting a better position.	"I like this company a lot so I just want to get my foot in the door first."
Give someone a pat on the back	To tell someone that they did a good job.	"The VP gave me a pat on the back for giving a good presentation to the customer."
Give the thumbs up (opposite is thumbs down)	To give approval or endorsement.	"We're excited because management gave our new proposal the thumbs up."
Go for broke	Willing to risk everything to achieve a desired result.	"I went for broke to win a big customer deal."
Go down the drain	When someone wastes or loses something.	"He spent a lot of money on an expensive computer that didn't work. All his money went down the drain."
Go the extra mile or the extra step	To do more than what was expected in a positive way.	"He went the extra mile to make sure the product demo would work perfectly."
Go through the roof	Results are increasingly exceeding expectations.	"Our sales are going through the roof."
Ground-breaking	Something is new and innovative.	"The iPhone was a ground-breaking piece of technology when it was launched.'
Six of one, half a dozen of the other	The alternatives are the same.	"You can choose to work on challenging project A or difficult project B. It's six of one, half a dozen of the other."
Hands are tied	A person who does not have control over a situation.	"I would love to help you out, but my hands are tied."

Idiom	Meaning	Example
Have work cut out	A person has a lot of work to do or a particularly difficult assignment or tight deadline.	"We have to finish our design in 2 months. We have our work cut out for us."
Hit the nail on the head	To do or say something 100% correctly.	"You hit the nail on the head. That's exactly correct."
Hold your horses	To slow down, to thoroughly think through a situation before making a decision or moving ahead.	"Hold your horses, I'm still trying to follow what you're saying."
In a bind	You're in a tough situation where any decision you make or action you choose has some undesirable results or trade-offs.	"I'm really in a bind. If I decide to help you with your project, I have to say no to my other important project."
In a nutshell	In a few words.	"In a nutshell, this book is about succeeding at work."
In the black (opposite is in the red)	If a company is "in the black", the company is making a profit.	"After losing money last quarter, our company finally is in the black this quarter."
In the driver's seat	To be in control.	"We've achieved 90% of sales target with 3 more months to go. We're in the driver's seat."
Jump the gun	Making a decision or statement too early or quickly before the right time	"Jim jumped the gun by accusing my software as not working when he hasn't even looked at his software yet."
Jump through hoops	Do everything possible to achieve a goal or please someone.	"I have to jump through hoops to get my proposal approved."
Keep me in the loop or keep me posted	Telling someone to continue to inform you of their status or progress of a situation.	"Keep me posted on your job interview."

How to Understand and Use Business Idioms

Idiom	Meaning	Example
Keep one's eye on the ball	To give something full attention and to not lose focus.	"To reduce the number of software bugs, we need to stay focused and keep our eye on the ball."
Get up to speed	To learn something new in a job or a project and to become knowledgeable.	"I joined the company one month ago and I'm getting up to speed."
Long shot	Something that has a very low probability of happening.	"Getting a promotion this time is a long shot for me, but I'm going for it anyway."
Lose ground (opposite: gain ground)	To lose some type of an advantage (market share, time to market) to a competitor.	"Our company gained ground on our competitors in market share this year."
More than one way to skin the cat	There are different ways or solutions to a problem.	"That's one solution to this problem, but I think there's more than one way to skin the cat."
No brainer	The decision is really obvious or really easy to make.	"Joining this company is a no brainer. They gave me more pay and better job position."
No strings attached	Something is given or offered without expecting anything in return.	"We offer our customers the use of our products for 6 months with no strings attached."
Not going to fly	An idea, proposal or solution that's not going to work or get approval.	"I don't think your idea is going to fly with our manager."
Off the top of one's head	Giving a response without thinking about it much or doing any research on the subject.	"I'm not sure how many customers we have, but off the top of my head, I'd say about 200."
On a roll	Continuing successes.	"We beat sales quota the last 3 quarters. We're on a roll."

Idiom	Meaning	Example
On the ball	To be alert, aware and get things done.	"My new team member is really on the ball. He's really doing a good job."
On the same page	Two or more people are in agreement. about something.	"Let's go over the contract terms to make sure we're on the same page."
On top of something	To be in control of a situation and aware of changes.	"I try to stay on top of the latest market changes in my industry."
On your toes	To be alert.	"Stay on your toes. Anything can happen in this uncertain market."
Out of the loop (opposite: in the loop)	To not know something that a select group of people knows.	"I felt like I was out of the loop after taking time off from work for the past couple of weeks."
Out on a limb	To make a statement, suggestion or assumption that is risky and bold.	"I'm going to go out on a limb and predict that we will finish our project under budget."
Play hardball	To be very aggressively competitive and to do anything possible to win or get what you want.	"He's a tough negotiator who plays hardball working on a deal."
Play it by ear	To wait and see what happens before moving on or taking the next step.	"Before we change our pricing, let's play it by ear and see what happens in the market."
Put all one's eggs in one basket	To put all your resources and trust and rely on only one thing to bring success.	"You should apply to many different companies instead of just one. Don't put all your eggs in one basket."
Put the cart before the horse	To do or think about things in the wrong order.	"They were trying to get management approval on a proposal before completing their business plan. They were putting the cart before the horse."

How to Understand and Use Business Idioms

Idiom	Meaning	Example
Raise the bar	To set the standards or expectations higher.	"We raised the bar in our industry with our latest product innovation."
Read between the lines	To understand something that isn't communicated directly, to understand what someone is implying or suggesting.	"In reading between the lines, I think our manager will approve this project."
Rock the boat	To cause problems or disrupt a situation.	"Not sure if I should ask to be transferred to another project. I don't want to rock the boat."
Round-the-clock	24 hours a day.	"I'm working round the clock today."
Run around in circles	To do the same thing over and over again without getting any results.	"We keep discussing the same issue in the last few meetings without making any progress. We're just running around in circles."
Same boat	If people are in the same situation, they are in the "same boat".	"A lot of people are worried about layoffs. Everyone's in the same boat."
See eye to eye	To agree with someone's view.	"We work well together. We see many things eye to eye."
See something through	To do something until it is finished.	"I want to see this project through before taking vacation."
Sever ties	To end a relationship.	"We had to sever ties with several of our suppliers due to bad materials."
Shoot something down	To "shoot something down" means to reject something, such as a proposal or idea.	"I try not to shoot down people's ideas during a brainstorming meeting. The goal is to generate ideas, not to judge them."
Shoot the breeze	Talk casually about non-work topic.	"We're just shooting the breeze waiting for the meeting to begin."

Idiom	Meaning	Example
Sky's the limit	There is no limit to what can be achieved.	"With this untapped market, sky's the limit on how much sales we can get."
Slam dunk or hit it out of the park	Very certain about a successful outcome.	"I think you hit it out of the park in your customer presentation today."
Smooth/clear sailing	A situation where success is achieved without difficulties.	"Once we fixed the major product glitch, it was smooth sailing to get product to market."
Stab someone in the back	When someone betrays another person's trust to pursue or advance their own personal agenda or position.	"He helped her get the job here. How could she stab him in the back by getting him fired?"
Start off on the right foot (opposite is "start off on the wrong foot")	To start something in a positive way.	"I want to start off on the right foot when I start my job with this company."
State of the art	Something that is modern and technologically advanced.	"We have a state-of-the-art research facility."
Take the bull by the horns	To take charge, especially on a difficult situation.	"Our project was going in different directions, so I had to step in and take the bull by the horns."
Talk someone into something (opposite is "talk someone out of)	To convince someone to do something.	"I was apprehensive to take on a new project I didn't know much about, but my manager talked me into it."
The elephant in the room	An obvious problem or controversial issue that no one wants to talk about.	"We all know our manager is the problem to getting things done, but no one wants to talk about this elephant in the room."

How to Understand and Use Business Idioms

Idiom	Meaning	Example
Think outside the box	To think of creative, unconventional solutions instead of common ones.	"With social media, we had to think out of the box on ways to promote our products."
Throw in the towel	To quit.	"After repeatedly being unable to sell my ideas to my manager, I threw in the towel."
Touch base	To make contact with someone.	"I'll touch base with you later today after I get out of my next meeting."
Twist someone's arm	To persuade or convince someone to do something that they don't want to do.	"I had to twist his arm a few times to get him to agree to our proposal."
Up in the air	Something is undecided.	"With the new management team, things are up in the air."
Uphill battle	Something that is difficult to achieve because of obstacles and difficulties.	"Trying to convince his customer to leave our competitor and join us will be an uphill battle."
Upper hand	Someone has an advantage over someone else.	"Our main supplier has a key product we need that we can't get from someone else. They have the upper hand in pricing negotiations."
Water under the bridge	Past history which is being forgotten, forgiven, or no longer to be emphasized.	"We had a work problem in our last company, but that's water under the bridge now that we've joined a different company."
Win-win situation (opposite is "lose-lose")	A "win-win situation" is a situation where everyone involved gains something.	"We negotiated a contract that both parties are happy with. It was a win-win."
Word of mouth	People hear about something through informal conversation with friends, family members, acquaintances, etc.	"One of the best advertisements is through good word of mouth."

Idiom	Meaning	Example
Writing on the wall	Evidence and clues that something (usually negative) is going to happen.	"He's going to get fired. The writing is on the wall."
Yes man	A "yes man" is someone who always agrees with their superiors.	"The marketing manager just wants to hire yes men."

CHAPTER 31

How to Handle Workplace Politics Smartly

Workplace or office "politics" means the use of influence, power and social networking within an organization to achieve goals or changes that benefit the organization or the individuals within it. Many of us view it as a dirty word, even immoral. We view the people engaging in work politics as selfish, dishonest people who play dirty tricks, backstab, suck up to the right people and do whatever they need to do to get what they want, regardless of what damage they cause. We don't want to get anywhere near these people. If you are one of the people who view politics this way, I would like to present a different view, one based on my professional experience and that of many people I've worked with.

Politics exists in any company and organization. Politics is about human interactions and relationships, and as long as there are people interacting and working together, politics is a part of life. It's not the office or buildings that create political behaviour, it's people. While many of us associate political skills or behaviour as undesirable, it's up to us to practise good politics or bad politics. For sure we have seen undeserved people who got promoted by using their political skills, by scheming their way and by sucking up to the bosses. However, from my professional experience and talking to many executives, high-performing and successful employees are skilful politicians who practise good politics with the right intention – striving to achieve win-win outcomes, influencing people in a positive way and thinking "team first".

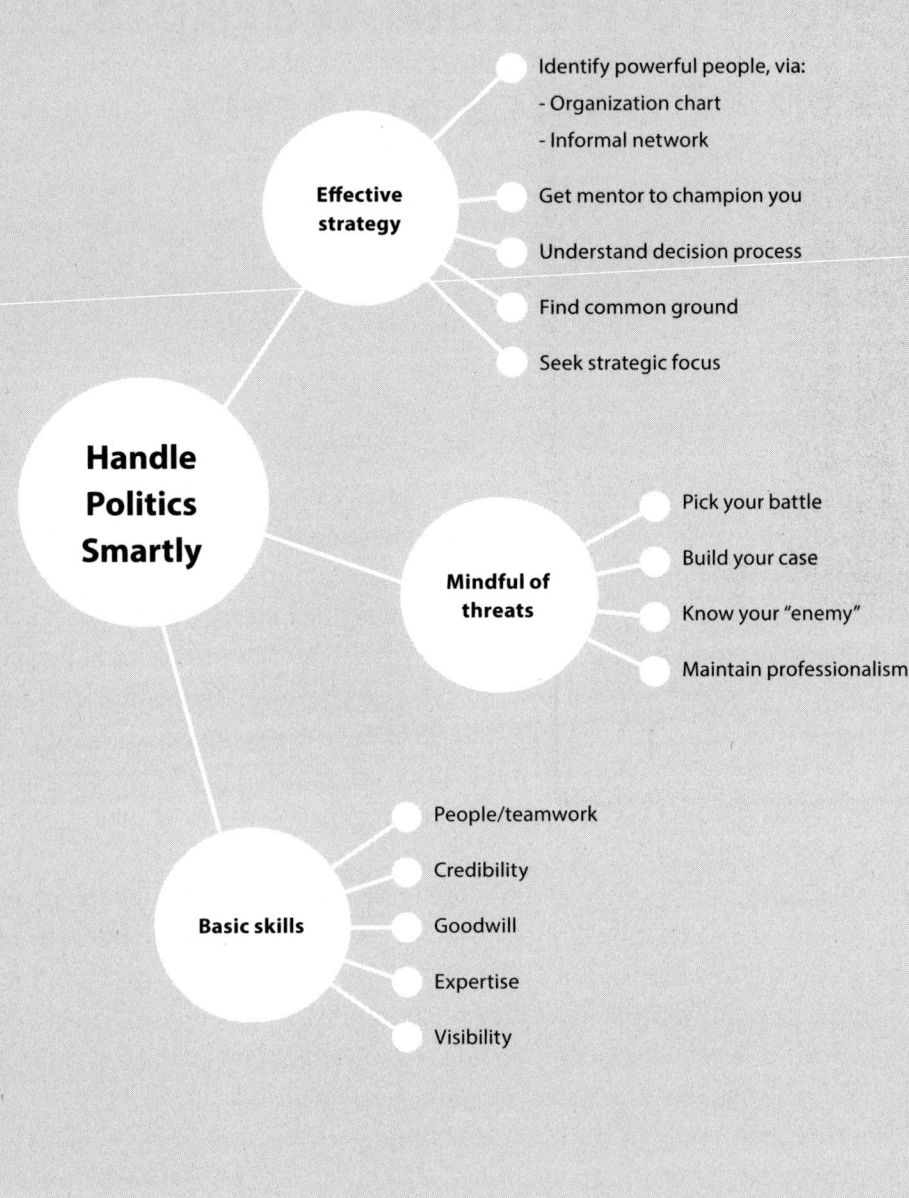

People who achieve some success through practising bad politics by backstabbing, spreading false rumours, bullying with "me first" attitude eventually will be exposed and they won't be able to sustain their success in the long term. Be confident that you can definitely participate in workplace politics without compromising your value or integrity. Especially in American business and corporate environments, having good political skill is crucial to your being able to get your work done, and to achieve great results and success throughout your career. This skill is a must in business culture all over the world. It took me a long time to realize a mindset change is essential to look at smart politics as a necessary tool. My direct manager Jos once told me that I'm politically savvy. I was surprised, did not like it and definitely didn't read that positively. But he clarified that I'm politically aware but just not very participative. I like to reiterate the point that good politics is part of your survival tool kit.

In this chapter, I'll describe what skills and qualities are required to be good at workplace politics, and I'll show effective strategies to "play" office politics.

Required Skills and Criteria to Be Effective at Workplace Politics

I have explained in detail many of the following skills throughout this book. I strongly encourage you to review the relevant chapters from time to time, and to continue to improve these skills. It's highly unlikely that you can succeed at workplace politics without them.

- **People/teamwork skills.** As I mentioned earlier in this chapter, politics is about human interaction and relationships. While you don't have to be best friends, you must be able to work well with people. These fundamentals include communicating, collaborating and negotiating skills (conflict resolution included). Having patience and really listening to people is a key part of being a good communicator. All good communicators are good listeners. Your colleagues will appreciate you when you go out of your way to help them when they need it. This will also earn you a lot of goodwill that will come in handy when you need it later. Being able to resolve issues and conflict in a professional manner without getting personal will endear you to them and earn their respect. I cannot emphasize this skillset enough.

- **Credibility.** Building credibility is something you earn over time. Credibility is earned by meeting our commitments, delivering excellent results on time, being dependable, and helping out when needed. This applies to everyone you work with, including your team members, colleagues, managers and executives. You need to do this continuously. Keep in mind that while it takes continuous track records to build credibility, you can lose credibility quickly. So remember to continue maintaining and building your credibility and not slipping up on your commitments.

- **Trust and loyalty.** You can earn trust and loyalty by being a good team player, by putting the team ahead of yourself and by showing genuine care for your co-workers. People will more likely give you the benefit of the doubt because they believe you are honest and you put the interest of the team ahead of your own. Respect what people say and genuinely seek to understand instead of being condescending and talking down to them. People in turn will reciprocate their respect to you and their trust in you. When you speak up, people will listen, take your words at face value and not have to wonder if you have any hidden agenda.

- **Goodwill credit.** You can accrue goodwill credit that you can use when you need help getting your idea through the corporate political process in the future. You can achieve this by helping your boss and other people succeed and making them look good. I once had a manager who said my most important responsibility is to help him succeed. If your boss is respected and has credibility with their peers and bosses, they can be your strong advocate in helping you sell your ideas. And by helping other people succeed, they know you put the team's success first and would be more than willing to support and carry your idea forward. I covered this in detail in the chapters on "How to stand out at work" and "How to manage up".

- **Expertise in a key area**. Being viewed as an expert in a key area expands your sphere of influence. You are seen as a "go to" person. Important people in the company and executives rely on you for your opinions and recommendations. A person could be an expert in a new and emerging technology, a master presenter or a business analyst guru while someone else could be recognized as a creative marketing expert. When I was in Product Operations, we had a person who was responsible for Business Analytics and Metrics. She was the person our manager and other executives went to when they needed a thorough analysis on a business problem, or company reports to prepare them for upcoming meetings with industry analysts. Everyone knew her as the go-to person in the business analytics area. Having "power" or "influence" is a key element to succeed in playing office politics.

- **Visibility**. If people don't know you, you will have a very difficult time persuading people in the company to buy into your idea. If you are recognized and are viewed positively by important people in the workplace – your manager, other managers, executives, influencers, key decision-makers, etc. – they are much more likely to meet with you and listen to your ideas and opinions. Getting an opportunity to meet with them to sell your idea is half the battle. You must seek out opportunities to get visibility with key people in the company.

Effective Strategies for Workplace Politics

Now, let's look at practical strategies to navigate workplace politics (Mindtools, 2019).

- **Identify powerful people**. Since politics is about people using their influence and connections to achieve their goal, knowing who the powerful people are is obviously one critical element to your success in workplace politics. From my experience, it is important for you to read the big picture. Go where the ball is heading. If you can see what you boss or higher management wants or where they are going, you should align towards that intent and be part of the actions. That helps you to be part of the strategic focus or key initiative.

▷ Study the organization chart. Begin at the top with the CEO and the Executive staff. Obviously the buck stops with the CEO. However, CEOs don't normally make every decision. It's not possible even if they wanted to since they need to focus on the strategy and direction for the company, and they would rather focus their limited time on the most important and strategic decisions.

While most important decisions are discussed and made at CEO/Executive staff meetings, one or more executives are responsible for driving the details in the meetings. For other decisions, certain executives decide or have their own management staff drive the decisions. In addition to the CEO/Executive staff organization chart, look for the organization chart of each of the executives on the CEO's staff. It shows you what department they lead and gives you an idea of the type of decisions they are driving. Moreover, you'll see the executive's management staff and that will give you more breakdowns of their department and respective reporting management staff. Depending on the size of the company, the number of management layers can vary, from very flat one or two management layers to six or more. In the most recent company I was at, there were seven layers – from the individual contributors to the CEO.

Refer to the figure that follows for an example of an organization chart of a Fortune 500 company. The CEO organization chart should be on the company's website. The other organization charts (for example, WW Marketing Exec/Staff chart, or the middle management chart for the Product Marketing group) can be found on their respective internal company websites. If not, contact their administrative assistants for the most recently updated charts. Since management turnovers are not unusual, make sure you keep up-to-date organization charts.

▷ In addition to the decision-makers you can identify fairly easily on organization charts, key influential players and gate-keepers are just

**Figure 1
Sample Organization Chart**

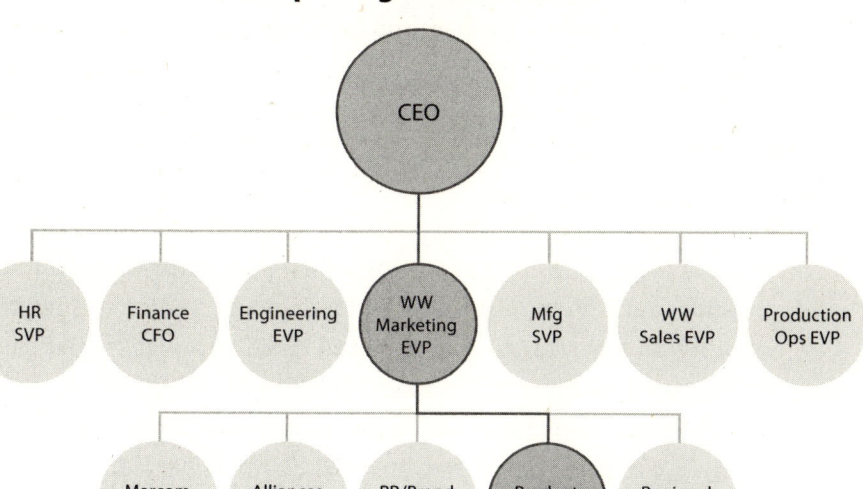

as important for you to acquaint yourself with. These people may not have executive titles nor can they be identified by their titles. Executives and decision-makers oftentimes value their opinions and rely on them for relevant information to help them make decisions. They are sometimes view as the right-hand people of the executives. Executive Chief of Staff and Executive Administrative Assistants oftentimes are key gatekeepers. They control access to executives, set and manage executive agendas, and determine the information flow to them. While they may not be involved with the content of the decision, they are no less important in determining your effectiveness and success in navigating workplace politics. I was Chief of Staff for a Senior VP in the Product Operations organization of a Fortune

500 company for a year. I set up his meeting agendas, determined for the most part the issues to be discussed, reviewed people's requests to meet with him one-on-one, and decided what information to provide him. So you can see that while I wasn't making decisions, I had a great deal of influence at managing workplace politics in his business unit.

▷ Find informal networks. These networks are not shown on the organization charts. They comprise employees who share some common ground – such as team members on a company initiative, members working on key strategic plans, members of company social clubs, participating members of company sporting events or company-wide events. These people tend to share some interests, knowledge or passion in a particular area; they meet regularly or periodically, sometimes outside of work hours, including lunch breaks or after-work social hours. Since company management and executives are aware of many of these networks, they pay attention to them, give them a lot of visibility, and lean on them for insight and viewpoints. As a result, these networks can have significant influence on the decision-makers.

▷ Find out about these networks, pick one or more that are of interest and benefit to you and find ways to join them. Talking to your co-workers, managers and mentor is a good way to identify these informal networks. Company newsletters or communications oftentimes include news and updates about these groups and their activities as well as invitations for people to join them. Pay attention in meetings or presentations to see who has visibility and credibility with executives. Through these tactics, you'll be able to identify not only these networks, but also who the leaders are. It's always easier to join these networks if they already know about you and have a good impression of you. So it'll benefit you to continue to build credibility and trust in your workplace. Refer to the "How to earn trust" and "How to stand out and promote yourself" chapters for more information.

- **Get a mentor who can be your champion**. A mentor can do wonders for you. A well-respected and connected mentor has a lot of insights you can tap into that you can't get easily. They know the key decision-makers, influencers, important informal networks, and they know how to get things done effectively. Not only are they fantastic resources for you to test your ideas and seek advice, but they can also help you sell your ideas and get buy-in from key decision-makers and influencers. While I didn't think much of it early in my career, I became convinced and appreciated having a mentor. When I first met with my mentor, I had very little idea of organizational politics and how to work with different people to get work done. Over a long period of time having regular one-on-one meetings with him, sitting in executive meetings he participated in, meeting key people he introduced me to and whose networks he helped me join, I truly understood and appreciated how to play workplace politics and I am truly grateful to him to this day. To identify potential mentor, observe in executive meetings, watch speakers at company wide meetings or presentations, ask your manager and talk to your colleagues. Ideally, your mentor should be at least at your manager's level or even above and also someone who is well liked, well respected and valued by people in the company. Once you know who you would like to have for a mentor, ask your manager to help you or if that mentor knows you and has a good impression of you, ask them yourself.

- **Understand the decision-making process**. A key element of understanding the decision-making process is knowing who the ultimate decision-makers are so you have good insights on how to develop your game plan. Depending on the size of the company, different types of decisions may be made by different people. In a medium/large company, decision-making is delegated to the appropriate people. For example, a decision of allocating resources to an engineering project may be made by the Head of Engineering or an Engineering Department manager, while a decision on whether to cut an important project is decided by the CEO/Executive. A decision on going ahead with a marketing event may be made by the Marketing PR (Public Relations) manager, while a decision to form a key strategic marketing alliance with another company is decided by the Marketing Executive. More narrow and specific decisions may be made by middle or lower-level managers or even team leaders, such as whether to do additional testing or what equipment to use for a customer demo event. At small companies, most decisions – whether big or small – may be decided by the CEO and a couple of executives.

Understanding how decisions are made is another important element. Are they made by consensus with a group of people or by one leader with input and recommendation from the working group and others? Are the decisions top-down or decided collaboratively? If you are a group leader working on a project and the decisions are made by consensus, you know you need to get buy-in from all the key participants. If the decision is ultimately yours with input from others, you can structure your meetings and discussion accordingly. Similarly, if you or your team needs approval on a proposal and the decision is made collaboratively by a group of managers, including your boss and their peers, then you know you need to get buy-in from all those participating managers. Obviously, the more consensus the decision-making process needs, the more challenging it will be, and this is where you'll earn your pay with your political skills.

So how do you go about understanding the decision-making process. You'll be able to develop a good insight by talking to your manager, your colleagues, picking your mentor's brain, asking to sit in to observe key decision-making meetings at all levels – CEO meetings, department head meetings, team meetings and project review meetings. When I left a company to join another company as a Pricing Strategist, I learned from my previous experience. I requested my manager (and he agreed) to take me to his meeting with the Executive Staff. He introduced me to them and described to them my role. After sitting in the back of the room and observing several sessions, I gained a good insight on the inter-workings of the group – whom did people listen to, who asked the right questions, who was the master at working the room, who was seen as the leader/decision-maker. I also learned about the decision-making process – it was very much collaborative and discussions could be lengthy with many differing points of view. I also did the same with other lower-level meetings.

- **Find common ground**. Common ground helps people gravitate towards each other and gives them a rallying point to work together. Find out what people are interested in, what they are passionate about, what their goals are, and similarities you have with them. In order to get people to gravitate toward you and to be excited working together, you first must establish your worthiness to them and to the company. You can accomplish this by exhibiting the skills and qualities I described in the first section of this chapter. Once people experience and see this first-hand, they will trust you and you will have gone a long way to be effective at managing workplace politics.

  With the example I mentioned above when I joined a company as a Pricing Strategist, I learned from sitting in meetings and talking to different people that the Senior Executive VP of Strategic Planning, who was widely respected, has a serious passion for pricing. During any meeting where pricing was discussed, she would perk up and engage even more than normal in the discussion. Recognizing this, I asked for a one-on-one meeting with her where we discussed in-depth about the company's pricing challenges and I got a great insight into her thinking. After the meeting, she asked me to set up monthly meetings with her to go over and discuss all things pricing. You can imagine my excitement about this opportunity to get such an important person to be an advocate for me. So keep your ears and eyes open and look for common ground.

- **Pick your battle and build your case**. Part of knowing how to play politics in the workplace is knowing when to fold, when to go for it and how to go for it.

  - ▷ Pick your battle. Throughout your career, you'll have many opportunities to take on, to lead and to shepherd projects through the organization. Not all opportunities are equally important or strategic, and while some opportunities are attractive to you, they may not be to your manager or company executives. It's important to show strong conviction, but realize that some opportunities you think are important and beneficial to your company, your manager and/or other managers may not share the same belief.

Although your idea maybe a great idea, it may not be a priority for the company. The first rule is to ensure the idea you want to pursue is aligned with key decision-makers. When working in product management for a mid-size company in the early 2000s, I had a colleague, David, who believed strongly the company must develop a blade storage server soon. Without convincing data, he nevertheless persistently pushed his case to the VP of Product Management and even after the VP made it clear that while the idea had potential, the market was not ready for this technology and the company had other more urgent priorities to pursue, David would not let it go. He became obsessed with his idea and grew increasingly frustrated, causing a lot of tension between him and the VP and between him and the engineering team. Out of frustration, he quit the company and did not leave on good terms. While one can argue for the validity of his idea, David did not make sure that his idea aligned with the key decision-makers' priorities, let his ego get in the way and did not pick his battle. I think it would have been better for David to put his idea on hold, work on another opportunity that aligned with the company's priorities and continue to gather research and go back to his idea at a better time in the future.

▷ Build your case with strong supporting data, credible intuition and stay with your conviction. Many executives, especially today, are driven by data and analytics. To be successful in getting buy-in for your ideas, you must prove your ideas have merit and facts. "Flying by the seat of your pants" or "swinging from the hip" proposals will likely not see the light of day. With the increasingly intense competition and the need to continue growing in sales and profit, companies must be selective in picking which opportunities to pursue. While intuition based on experience is important in considering potential ideas, it's not sufficient for decision-makers. Combining intuition and analytics and showing your conviction will give you the best chance of getting their approval.

When I managed a team of senior professionals at Hewlett-Packard, I hired a consultant, Robert, to research on a potential server opportunity. After extensive research, Robert was convinced that the company needed to develop a server technology to allow data centre customers to rack many servers in a tight space. I scheduled a review meeting for him to present his case to the General Manager's executive staff. At this meeting, he presented a compelling case on the need to develop this technology due to financial implications and competitive threats, and to bring it to market soon. However, two key executives did not agree with his recommendation. They were conservative and did not want to take the risk of spending millions of dollars on this prospect, even though the potential financial returns would be significant. After a lot of going-around-the-circle discussion, the executives still did not want to make a decision. Robert stood firm in his conviction, saying: "I'm not saying we need to do this for my own satisfaction. You hired me to do this work so you can reject my recommendation and I'll go on to the next project, but I strongly believe we must do this for the reasons I've discussed." Everyone was a bit stunned hearing this, but I think they were impressed with his conviction and that he was making his case for the right reason. That he was willing to put his job on the line showed his strong conviction. The difference between Robert and David from the earlier example is that while both had strong conviction, Robert showed he was willing to walk away as much as he didn't want to, and David stuck to his idea to the bitter end.

> ▷ Get frequent feedback and address issues right away. With the Robert example above, one thing I would have done differently would be to have Robert meet individually with the executive staff to learn about their concerns so he would be better prepared to address them in the meeting.

- **Seek out opponents and strive to understand them**. Most of us have a tendency to stay away from and ignore people who oppose us, oppose our ideas and who just want to shoot down our ideas. However, this would be the wrong action to take. You probably have heard the saying "Keep your friends close and your enemies closer." You want to not only know who they are but also why they oppose you or your ideas so you can take counter or preventive actions. Moreover, they may have legitimate reasons or concerns about your idea and if you know why, you can find ways to address them and come up with a win-win solution.

When faced with this situation, you should meet with them with an open mind. You can establish an open dialogue by telling them about your objective, letting them know that you would like to hear from them and get their feedback, and committing to them that you would address their concerns. The key word here is "listen". No need to get defensive; stay with the subject matter and don't get personal. If they get personal and attack you personally, do not let them. Let them know that you want to focus on the business issue and want to get their feedback, not personal insults or comments that are irrelevant to the idea. Ask for specific feedback and examples, not general comments. That should reset them to focusing their comments on the issue. If that doesn't work, thank them for their time and let them know you're always open to their input. At least this way you know whom you can work with and whom you can't. Refer to the chapters "How to deal with difficult co-workers" and "How to communicate effectively" for more suggestions.

- **Maintain professionalism**. I've heard often throughout my career that "So-and-so is such a professional." People view these professionals with respect. These people focus on building relationships, working with people to solve problems, thinking out of the box to find creative and win-win solutions. They focus on the business issues, not personal issues. They seem calm, maintain their poise under difficult situations and don't get ruffled. Moreover, they tend to be optimists – glass-half-full people who don't waste their time with rumours. When things are not going their way or when they are facing setbacks, they don't whine or complain. Instead, they focus on not just bringing problems to management, but bringing potential solutions as well.

    Of course, we are all humans with a full range of emotions. However, knowing how to express and control ourselves is important to play the political game. We have seen many real politicians who lost their elections because of one outburst. I have seen co-workers who lost their cool and started lashing out at their managers and other managers in meetings. They later regretted it but the damage was already done. Their outbursts painted them as immature people who don't have what it takes to function well under pressure. These people ended up receiving poor performance reviews and eventually leaving the company. If they did not learn from their experience when they moved on to another company, I think they'll likely repeat the same mistakes and face similar consequences.

If there's one advice I have it is this: The way to keep your cool and stay under control is to not take what people say or criticize personally. Focus on the business issue and even when other people get personal, you stay laser-focused on the issue and push them to get back on track with the issue. Refer to the chapters on "How to handle conflicts and difficult situations", "How to deal with difficult co-workers" and "How to communicate effectively" for more information.

CHAPTER 32

How to Engage in Small Talk Naturally

In today's social media world, face-to-face conversation skills are being diminished and not used as much. But make no mistake, being able to conduct conversation is as an important part as ever of our work and career success. While texting and chatting online has a convenient role in our daily life, it is not a common method of communication at a social outing or work event where people meet and conduct small talk with one another. Take an example: when you attend a business meeting with your co-workers or customers and before everyone begins serious discussion about the meeting topic, people engage in casual small talk to break the ice, to put people at ease and to get comfortable with one another. It sets the mood for a productive meeting. If while people are engaging in small talk you're sitting or standing alone by yourself and not part of the small talk, you would feel left out and somewhat awkward. It would make you less a part of the meeting when the discussion begins.

So what is small talk? It is a short, friendly conversation about a common topic. Small talk can take place among friends, co-workers, between executives and employees or strangers. It takes place in all kinds of situations: business meetings, interviewing for a job, making a presentation to customers, company business social outings, industry conferences and seminars, etc. It is an important people skill. The ability to make small talk in business settings is important because it allows people to be friendly at work without

Engage in Small Talk Naturally

Preparation
- Be well-informed and prepared
- Be proactive
- Remember and address people by name

Approach
- Really listen
- Identify common ground
- Engage with positive energy
- Body language
- Begin with ice-breaker
- Discuss safe/fun general-interest topics

Exit
- End conversation thoughtfully
- Set up follow-up discussion if needed

Avoid
- Religion and politics
- Offensive jokes
- Personal wealth
- Embarrassing family issues

getting too personal. It also helps us build and expand our networks and helps us do our job more effectively.

If English is not your native language, you may feel uncomfortable talking to people in business settings or related social events. But even many native English-speaking people have the same apprehension. Many or most of us are apprehensive about these settings and are not comfortable going into a place where we don't know the people there and don't really want to spend time talking to them. However, remember that it is an important skill and will benefit you and your career. Moreover, it's not hard to learn and doesn't take long to be able to do it well.

No matter if you are an introvert or extrovert, you need to prepare this necessary business skill in social etiquette. You should not equate business small talk to unpleasant tasks but think of them as relationship-building and information-collection events. For international engagement, there are some customs to be aware off, especially what not to do. You should also learn some interesting things about the people you're meeting and use that knowledge to show that you care and have genuine interest in them. It is easier than you imagine. For example, I was visiting Korea on business during the World Cup soccer tournament. Everyone in Korea was into it. So, I researched on the Korean team's performance, colour of uniform, tiger crest and the Red Devils fans. The next moment I was watching the game with the Korean business team and customers, drinking soju. I was definitely part of the team.

In this chapter, I'll discuss the strategies as well as specific ways for you to master and conduct small talk like a pro (Napier-Fitzpatrick).

- **Focus on the other person**. Having a curiosity and interest to learn about people will naturally help you put your focus on the other person when you talk to them. People are much more engaged and drawn to you when they sense that you genuinely want to get to know them. If you feel self-conscious talking about yourself, focusing on the other person will make you more comfortable and less self-conscious. Let me share with you a little secret: most people like to talk about themselves – it makes them feel good and important. It's a great way to establish a good connection and build rapport. I shared an example of this earlier in the book. Chloe, a friend of mine, told me about a dinner meeting with a client. Through the entire dinner, she made a conscious effort to focus her attention on her client. She asked a few open-ended questions and spent the rest of the time listening. When they said goodbye after the dinner, her client thanked her for an enjoyable evening and commended her for being a great conversationalist, even though for most of the dinner, Chloe just sat back and listened. We'll go over some techniques for engaging in small talk later, but I hope you can see that it's easy to make friends, to leave a great impression by focusing your attention on the person you're talking to.

- **Really listen**. Sometimes we listen but we may not hear what other people are saying. The highest compliment you can pay to another person when talking to them is to really listen to them, to make a real effort to understand what they're saying. Through listening, you show your focus is on them and that you are fully engaged and genuinely interested in them. One excellent way to show your listening ability is by asking open-ended questions, listening to their comments and asking additional questions and/or offering your own comments. Starting your question with "how/why/what" encourages them to explain and give more details, which in turn allows you to ask relevant follow-up questions. Although this is a two-way conversation, the fact is you just need to ask a few questions and the other person will do most of the talking, willingly. You'll be popular and make easy friends this way. You may wonder if people would be "turned off" if they think you're asking too many questions. While this is something you'll need to keep in mind, my experience is that we tend not to ask enough questions. So the risk here is low.

- **Identify common ground.** This can be a common topic that both you and the other person are interested in, a hobby you both share, a common issue you both are dealing with, an event that you both had recently attended or are interested in going, etc. Once you find common ground, whether with a co-worker, your boss/executive, business customer, or someone you haven't met before, you'll be able to communicate easily and naturally. At a recent social function with my co-workers and their respective spouses and significant others, my wife, Ann, was seated next to a co-worker's wife, Julie. Although my wife and Julie had never met, I noticed my wife and Julie were engaged in a lively conversation and they seemed to focus on one another. During a break, I told Ann that she and Julie seemed to have really connected. She shared that after exchanging hellos and polite pleasantries, they discovered a lot of common ground. Their kids had grown up and were soon to go to college, and they were interested in some meaningful hobbies they could do part-time. Ann shared with Julie a business hobby she has started and they were talking about what potential business hobbies Julie had the skills for and might be interested in exploring. They decided to hook up in the future to continue their discussion.

- **Be well-informed and prepared**. Stay up to date with world, work and local current events and news through watching or listening to TV/radio shows, reading newspapers, magazines and online sites. This helps you prepared to engage in small talk about a potential wide range of topics and gives you the flexibility to talk to more people, depending on their topic of interest. I spend a little bit of time everyday to learn about the latest news and what's going on in the world, at my company, in my city, not only to keep me up to date but also because I'm genuinely interested in knowing. In America, sport is a big interest, from team sports such as football, baseball and basketball to individual sports including tennis and golf. Travel and entertainment are also popular interests, including popular destinations, music, concerts, movies and theatre plays. Investing a little bit of your time keeping up to date in these areas will boost your confidence and make you comfortable engaging in small talk.

- **Be proactive**. Don't wait for people to come to you to say hello and talk to you. This makes you look apprehensive and not confident. If you are a bit shy or introverted and don't feel comfortable being there, know that there are likely many other people who feel the same way. So think of this as a chance to push yourself beyond your comfort zone. You are prepared, you know how to engage in small talk and convince yourself that this is a chance to show your small talk skills. So take the initiative and initiate the contact. Be the first to say hi and introduce yourself. If you had met someone before but don't remember their name, introduce yourself again and try to remember their name. I find saying their name in the course of your conversation makes it more personal and makes the other person feel good that you remember their name. This shows your confidence as well as your interest in meeting them. They'll come away with a good impression of you.

- **Engage people with your positive energy and body language.** Friendly eye contact and a warm smile show your interest to meet and talk. Maintain eye contact when listening and talking to them. Open your arms and use friendly hand gestures. All these are great ways to show your energy and enthusiasm of being there and mingling with people. Of course, remember to be genuine and don't overdo it. Things to avoid include looking at your watch or checking your phone too much while engaging in small talk. Or worse, texting your friends while talking to someone. This happens more often than not and shows a lack of courtesy and respect for the other person. I have seen too frequently at business meetings, company functions or social outings where people are constantly focusing on their phone with texting or engaging in online conversations while in the company of others. This does not create a good impression and it's best to be aware of and avoid this habit.

- **Begin the greeting with an icebreaker.** An icebreaker is a general statement or question to open a way to meet new people and also helps to jump-start conversations. For example, giving a compliment, asking about the event details, the location, how the person is associated with the event, even about the weather, are good ways to start a conversation. If the other person is from your company, ask what department they're in and what they do. If both of you are from the same department, ask about some news or event both of you have heard or attended recently. For example, "What do you think about the marketing training event last week?" or "Tell me about the technology networking conference last month" are good icebreakers after saying hi and introducing yourself. Remember to use open-ended questions to get people to talk more.

- **Discuss general-interest subjects.** When you have an opportunity to engage in small talk, remember to find a good, fun and non-controversial topic. This shows you are an approachable and friendly person to talk to. Some of the more common topics you can use for small talk include sports, music/movies/books, travel, hobbies, food/restaurants, jobs/occupations, technology, money/finance (housing cost, investments, etc.) and family-related topics (children, education, etc.). These topics are safe, not too controversial and mostly about sharing information and experience. And even if someone offered different views on a topic, people wouldn't get offended or strongly object. For example, when I talk to my co-workers about movies we've seen recently, we comment on what movies we saw and what we liked or didn't like about it. Even if we feel differently about the ending of the movie, that's okay and doesn't cause any issue between us. In business settings, even discussing a general topic can lead to unexpected opportunities. This was how I got my start in teaching at a well-known university. At one particular social function, I met and started a conversation with a friend of a co-worker's about the state of education in the US and the lack of professors with professional experience. I then told him that that's why I was interested in teaching in the future. It turned out that he was teaching at a university. A few months later, he contacted me and introduced me to the Dean of the Business School and I got my first teaching gig.

  However, one word of caution when talking about family/personal matter: depending on how well you know the other person, use your judgment on how much personal information to share or how deep you want to ask about their family or personal situation. This may not be appropriate in business settings.

  Here are some phrases you can use to start small talk and keep it going:

  ▷ Have you seen/heard…?
  ▷ What did you think of…?
  ▷ How did you find out…?
  ▷ Have you ever been to…?
  ▷ What is your favourite/least favourite…?

▷ Who is your favourite/least favourite…?
▷ What is your experience with…?
▷ What do you recommend on…?

- **Exit thoughtfully.** In many business situations, it may be important to make contact with many people in the place. The challenge occurs when you have limited time for small talk and need to find a good way to end the conversation and move on. Find an appropriate point in the conversation to make an exit, such as when the other person has just finished a thought or concluded a story. You can say: "It was great meeting and talking with you. I look forward to meeting you again in the future." If there's a business opportunity or matter you want to discuss, ask for their business card or tentatively schedule a time you'll contact them.

Small Talk Mistakes to Avoid

When you make small talk, try to avoid topics that are personally sensitive, or may upset the other person. Some topics to avoid include:

- **Religion and politics.** These topics can be very personal, emotional and controversial if people disagree.

- **Family/relationship status.** It's okay to ask about someone's family, but only if you already know them and have a good idea they're okay talking about it. The general rule is to avoid painful or embarrassing family issues, such as divorce, death and marital/children issues.

- **Money/wealth.** Telling other people how much money you make or asking them how much money they make is inappropriate and should be avoided. This is especially sensitive in American culture.

- **Offensive jokes.** Avoid telling offensive jokes that involve racism, sexism, violence, and other inappropriate workplace topics.

Hopefully I have impressed on you the important role small talk has in determining your effectiveness and success at work. By being able to learn the art of small talk, you'll be able to gain more confidence, expand your people network and obtain useful insight and information. And finally, I hope you are convinced that it's not hard to develop ability to conduct and engage in small talk by learning the practical strategies and practising proven small talk techniques.

References

Brandall, B. (2016, June 7). *How to Prioritize Tasks and Do Only the Work That Matters.* Retrieved October 29, 2017, from https://www.process.st/how-to-prioritize-tasks/

Covey, S. (1989). *The Seven Habits of Highly Effective People.* New York, New York, USA: Simon and Schuster.

Economy, P. (2015). *The Top 10 Ways Your Employees Waste Time at Work.* Retrieved July 1, 2019, from https://www.inc.com/peter-economy/top-10-time-wasters-at-work.html

Health and Style. (2015, August 2). *Ultimate strength and cardio workout: Stair Climbing.* Retrieved July 27, 2017, from www.Healthandstyle.com

Huth, S. (2015, June 20). *Employees Waste 759 Hours Each Year Due to Workplace Distractions.* Retrieved October 21, 2017, from www.telegraph.co.uk/finance/jobs/11691728/Employees-waste-759-hours-each-year-due-to-workplace-istractions.html

Mindtools. (2019, July 1). *7 Ways to Use Office Politics Positively.* Retrieved July 1, 2019, from https://www.mindtools.com/

Napier-Fitzpatrick. (n.d.). *Small Talk.* Retrieved July 1, 2019, from The Etiquette School of New York: https://etiquette-ny.com/

Neal, M.H. (1993). *Negotiating Rationally.* New York, New York, USA: The Free Press.

PayScale. (2016, May 17). *Workforce-Skills-Preparedness Report.* Retrieved October 29, 2017, from http://www.payscale.com/about/press-release.

Strutner, S. (2016, August 16). *Sitting All Day Is Even More Dangerous Than We Thought.* Retrieved July 28, 2017, from Huffington Post: www.huffingtonpost.com

Tolle, E. (1992). *The Power of Now.* Vancouver: Namaste Publishing.

Trafford, P. (2019, February 8). *Common Business Idioms.* Retrieved July 1, 2019, from https://www.businessenglishresources.com/learn-english-for-business/

Yate, M. (2012). Knock 'em Dead Job Interview. In M. Yate, *Knock 'em Dead Job Interview* (p. 256). Adams Media.

About the Authors

Dennis Mark

Dennis has more than 30 years of experience in the Information Technology industry and has held various senior leadership positions in regional strategic business units, sales & marketing functions, and executive mentoring programme in Asia-Pacific. He built his reputation on strong engagement amongst stakeholders in developing human capital, business management processes and operation cadence. He also believes in leading change ahead of the curve to seize time and space for strategic impact and business results.

Prior to his consultancy career, Dennis served as Vice President and General Manager of Solutions & Services practice for HP Inc Asia Pacific, where he led the regional Headquarters with diverse multi-country teams of employees, and the sales and market developments of the B2B and B2C segments. With talent development as a key strategic pillar, Dennis served as executive coach and teaching faculty in the Talent Development Programme for the pool of Managing Directors and Executives. He focuses his mentoring in areas of leadership development, organization building, career planning, change management and crisis management. In his international consulting capacity, Dennis provides business subject matter expertise supporting organizational development, critical research and business decisions.

As part of his community service, Dennis is currently serving as a Singapore Red Cross Council board member. He also volunteers as Deputy

Director of Red Cross Youth, leading the Human Capital Development and Safety/Operations. With interests in education and lifelong learning, Dennis developed academic modules championing humanitarian interest within Red Cross Youth and is currently the Lead Adjunct Lecturer in Singapore Polytechnic's Humanitarian Response Studies. He also actively participates in the National Level Disaster Management/Crisis Management activities as Trainer & Field Officer for local and overseas deployment.

Dennis holds an Engineering (Honours) degree from the National University of Singapore and an Executive Diploma in Board Directorship from Singapore Management University–Singapore Institute of Directors. He also attained Executive Development certification, General Management, by Stanford University–National University of Singapore.

In his ongoing pursuit of exploring boundaries, Dennis enjoys a healthy lifestyle and challenges himself in triathlon, endurance races, mountain climbing and yoga to achieve a balance of mind and body.

Michael Dam

Michael has extensive experience and knowledge on addressing business challenges and working with people from different industries and cultures. In his 25-year professional career, he served in several different disciplines, including Engineering, Product Management, Business/Strategy Planning, Strategic Pricing, Demand Forecasting and Business Analytics. During his years working for major multinational companies, he held various management positions, from first-line manager to Senior Director, and worked closely with many high-level management executives, including serving as Chief of Staff to a Senior Vice-President at NetApp, a Fortune 500 company.

To fulfil a life-long passion for teaching, Michael teaches college business classes as an Adjunct Lecturer at Santa Clara University. For the last several years, he has been volunteering his time conducting career talk events at universities as well as teaching career workshops to help college students develop job skills and prepare for their professional career after graduation. He continues to provide individual consultation and coaching to career professionals.

As an entrepreneur, he co-founded and has been managing a successful real estate company since 2007. He obtained a California Real Estate Sales Agent License and followed up with a California Real Estate Broker License in 2014. His educational achievements include a Bachelor of Science in Electrical Engineering (BSEE) and a Master of Business Administration (MBA). He was selected by Hewlett-Packard and participated in the prestigious Accelerated Executive Leadership Program at Stanford University.